INTERNATIONAL HANDBOOK ON
OLD-AGE INSURANCE

Greenwood Press
NEW YORK • WESTPORT, CONNECTICUT • LONDON

Library of Congress Cataloging-in-Publication Data

International handbook on old-age insurance / edited by Martin B.
  Tracy and Fred C. Pampel.
      p.   cm.
   Includes bibliographical references and index.
   ISBN 0–313–26137–7 (alk. paper)
    1. Old age pensions—Handbooks, manuals, etc.   2. Social security—
Handbooks, manuals, etc.   I. Pampel, Fred C.
   HD7105.3.I67   1991
   368.4'3—dc20   91–9252

British Library Cataloguing in Publication Data is available.

Library of Congress Catalog Card Number: 91–9252
ISBN: 0–313–26137–7

First published in 1991

Greenwood Press, 88 Post Road West, Westport, CT 06881
An imprint of Greenwood Publishing Group, Inc.

Printed in the United States of America

The paper used in this book complies with the
Permanent Paper Standard issued by the National
Information Standards Organization (Z39.48–1984).

10 9 8 7 6 5 4 3 2 1

Contents

Contents

Tables and Figures

TABLES

FIGURES

Preface

This international handbook analyzes the economic, social, and cultural impact of aging populations on government social insurance policies. It examines how governments, nongovernment organizations, communities, and families in different societies respond to changes in traditional income and social service support systems for the elderly.

One particularly interesting measure of public program response to rapidly expanding older populations that will be a major feature of policy formation in the 1990s and in the future is the approach to old-age pensions under social insurance, social assistance, and provident fund systems. Social insurance is clearly the preferred method of meeting the income needs of the elderly, but an amalgam of historical and current social and economic conditions is forcing many nations to evaluate the viability and sustainability of their social insurance programs from new perspectives. This has led to exploration into a variety of innovations in old-age pension program development involving revised benefit formulas, raised retirement ages, increased income testing, and greater reliance on private occupational supplemental provisions.

This handbook offers a view of the profuse and varied approaches to social insurance programs in twenty nations with different economic, political, and cultural situations, especially with regard to income maintenance programs for the elderly. It provides the reader with descriptions of existing program provisions and offers a better understanding of the factors behind them.

Introduction

Comprehensive information on how income protection for the elderly is provided in a variety of socially and economically diverse societies is not readily available to persons interested in developments in social insurance, especially old-age pension schemes. This is unfortunate given the growing awareness of the policy and program implications of aging populations in almost every nation in the world. As populations age, information on how other nations are coping with increased demands from the elderly and their families becomes especially important. A sizable number of descriptive studies of foreign systems and compilations of basic program features are available in scattered journals and texts. There is, however, a shortage in analyses of not only the fundamental provisions but also of the main factors that shape and mold public old-age insurance programs in industrial and economically developing nations.

To varying degrees, all societies are being confronted by the economic, social, and cultural effects of two trends: the aging of populations and changing family and community support structures. The policy responses of governments to these trends have been quite varied. Old-age social insurance or pension systems have been and remain the preferred strategy of meeting income needs for the elderly. Still, within the general framework of social insurance, nations have explored vastly different benefit formulas, income-testing requirements, and mixes of public benefits with private occupational provisions. Indeed, recent fiscal and economic problems have produced innovations in pension funding and provisions that have furthered worldwide diversity. All too often, however, policymakers, service providers, and researchers are unfamiliar with the international diversity of policies.

This handbook is designed to help fill the void in analytical material through the contributions of experts in old-age insurance programs in twenty countries.

The countries chosen represent wide geographic, political, social, and economic spectrums. The choices were also prescribed by the willingness of indigenous specialists to participate in the study and by the availability of information. While far from a complete or representative sample of all nations throughout the world, the nations studied here do reflect both the diversity and similarity in approaches to old-age insurance that have emerged in the last several decades. As is the case with most texts with a large number of country studies, the authors of the chapters have had to confine their analysis to the most salient aspects of policies, programs, and provisions in order to meet space restrictions. Still, compared to brief listings in reference books such as *Social Security Programs Throughout the World*, this handbook offers a more in-depth analytical view of the main features of old-age insurance policies, programs, and provisions.

ANALYTICAL FRAMEWORK

Each chapter describes the basic features of income programs for the elderly and the major current issues affecting policy decisions in a given country. With the exception of the chapters on Sweden and the United Kingdom, whose complementary programs are included in the analysis because they are integrally tied to the old-age program, discussion is focused on old-age income systems. The format of each country study is designed to provide as much uniform descriptive and analytical content as possible given the considerable variance in programs and policies among the nations under examination. While the outline provides a framework for analysis, the diversity of experiences and conditions of old-age insurance systems, as well as the frequent unavailability of relevant information, results in considerable variation in content among the chapters. As would be expected, this is particularly true of the chapters on economically developing societies.

The chapters follow a general outline comprised of seven basic parts: (1) historical development; (2) principal program characteristics; (3) funding mechanisms; (4) programs for special populations; (5) current policy issues; (6) supplemental provisions; and (7) a synopsis of the most salient program features.

The first part of the outline is intended to delineate the historical context of old-age insurance policy and the social, political, and economic factors that have been most influential in shaping policy. While the factors vary among nations, changing demographic conditions, work patterns, and women's labor force participation are common to most. The review of historical dimensions also includes observations on the most pertinent legislative developments.

The second feature of the study framework is a description of fundamental program features. This conveys information on what benefits are covered, the conditions required to qualify for benefits payment (years of employment and contributions, earnings, retirement ages), and various facets of the benefit level, including benefit formula, minimum and maximum benefit amounts, and procedures for adjusting benefits to inflation.

The means by which old-age pensions are funded constitutes the third area of analysis. Information on the method of funding and the amount of employer, employee, and public contributions to the old-age insurance system is provided. The relative scope of contributions is also examined, where possible, in terms of proportion of Gross National Product (GNP) or some other standardized measure.

The fourth element in the framework addresses provisions for targeted populations under special programs. In addition to a national public old-age insurance scheme, most nations have separate systems of income protection for civil servants and military personnel. Discussions include a description of systems of income protection for indigent elderly persons who do not qualify for benefits under the basic scheme. This includes old-age supplements, lump-sum payments, and income-tested benefits. Also covered in this section of the outline are programs for work sectors that are independent of the basic public program in Third World nations, such as agricultural workers, plantation employees, and domestics. Where appropriate, the provident fund and saving systems found in several former British colonies are examined.

The fifth aspect of the outline is an analysis of the major current policy issues confronting each country. These issues range from demographic changes that create pressures for government old-age insurance program expansion to foreign debt conditions that lead to pressures for program contraction.

The sixth feature consists of a discussion of supplemental provisions to the basic program of old-age insurance. This includes information on such provisions as occupational pension systems, mandatory savings plans, optional savings plans, severance pay, and benefits that are paid on the basis of need.

Each study concludes with an overview of the most significant aspects of the material presented.

PRINCIPAL FORCES SHAPING POLICY

The major forces that have shaped old-age insurance policy and that are likely to be influential in future program developments emerge from the separate studies. For the purpose of general discussion, although at risk of oversimplification, it is useful to separate these forces into those that prevail in industrial nations and those that dominate in economically developing countries. There is, of course, some overlap, especially when considering programs in Latin America, which appear most prone to aspire to emulate their European counterparts.

Industrial Societies

Two principal forces have shaped old-age insurance policy in industrial nations in recent years. The first is the goal of social solidarity that, briefly stated in the context of social insurance, obligates the state to protect all citizens against the contingencies of lost income, including old age. An integral part of income protection has been to provide both a basic income floor to all elderly individuals and an opportunity to supplement minimum benefits through covered employment.

This doctrine is put into practice through two basic methods. One approach is a provision for flat-rate (universal) benefits that are payable to all persons at a specified age regardless of income level or prior work status. Of the study countries, old-age income systems in Canada and Sweden use this strategy (Table 1). The more prevalent tactic is to give a minimum benefit amount to elderly persons whose income, means, or assets are below a specified level. Among the industrial nations included in this text, this approach is indicative of systems in Australia, France, the Federal Republic of Germany, Switzerland, and the United States.

The other major force found in most of the industrial countries is that of demographic change—the increase in the proportion of elderly persons who are retired and receiving an old-age pension. This is a predominant policy issue in all industrial nations because, over the long term, the ratio of retirees to workers who contribute taxes to finance the system is rising. It is expected to become an even greater problem in the early part of the next century when post-World War II children reach retirement age. Part of the problem stems from the practice of most European systems, which allow for early retirement so that more work opportunities will become available to unemployed younger people and so that workers can elect to retire at a time best suited to meet their individual needs. In light of this trend, many nations are reviewing their entitlement policies. Two of the study countries, the Federal Republic of Germany and the United States, have taken action to address this issue by raising the age of first entitlement in the next century when the population of children born after World War II will reach retirement age.

There is clearly a concern over the tendency for workers to leave the labor force at increasingly earlier ages under a variety of early retirement options. While some chapters allude to the negative social consequences of this pattern as it affects an individual's quality of life, most of the concern is expressed over increasing program expenditures that result from efforts to maintain generous benefits. At the same time there are fewer workers making payroll contributions.

In all the industrial study nations, concern over the cost of benefits has generated close monitoring and examination of the capacity of public old-age insurance schemes to be the main strategy of income maintenance. This has led to explorations of alternate sources of income support, especially occupational pensions (which have been formally institutionalized in France and Switzerland and have become a significant policy feature in Australia and the United Kingdom). Private pensions also cover a substantial portion of workers in other nations such as the Federal Republic of Germany, Sweden, and the United States. Switzerland is of special interest because occupational pensions have been mandatory there since 1985 and are a pivotal feature in the public retirement income scheme.

Table 1
Select Characteristics of Old-Age Pension Systems

Country	SI	UP	MP	PF	% 65+ 1988-1990	Age of First Award (women)
Australia	x				11.1	65 (60)
Canada	x	x			11.4	65
Chile			x			65 (60)
China*					5.5	60 (55)
Costa Rica	x				4.1	57 (55)
France	x		x		13.8	60
FRG	x				15.5	63
GDR	x					65 (60)
Ghana				x		55 (50)
India				x	3.4	55
Indonesia				x	2.8	55
Israel	x				8.9	65 (60)
Ivory Coast	x	x				55
Mexico	x				4.1	65
Sweden	x	x			17.7	65
Switzerland	x		x		14.8	65 (62)
Tanzania				x		55
Turkey	x				4.3	55 (50)**
UK	x				15.1	65
US	x				12.2	65

SI = Social insurance (financed by payroll contributions).
UP = Universal pension (payable to all).
MP = Mandatory private (occupational) pensions.
PF = Provident Fund (lump sum benefit).
* China is classified as an employment-related system.
** Age 60 (men) and 65 (women) after January 1, 1990.

Sources: M. Maguire. (1987). Making provision for ageing
           populations. The OECD Observer, October-
           November, N. 148, pp. 4-9.

           K. G. Kinsella. (1988). Aging in the Third
           World. Center for International Research, Bureau
           of the Census. CIR Staff Paper No. 35.
           Washington, D.C.

           U.S. Department of Health and Human Services.
           (1990). Social Security Administration. Office
           of International Policy. Social Security
           Programs Throughout the World - 1989. Research
           Report No. 62. Washington, D.C.: Government
           Printing Office.

The chapters on industrial nations focus on such recurring themes as demographic conditions, program costs, and early retirement. Although these chapters reflect collective concerns and shared approaches, there is conspicuous variation in what the authors identify as the most pressing issues regarding the old-age income systems of their nations.

For example, the age of first entitlement to an old-age pension award is unquestionably an area of policy consideration in all industrial nations, but is particularly highlighted in the chapters on Australia, the Federal Republic of Germany, and Switzerland. Similarly, program expenditures are a major issue everywhere, but are specifically targeted in the analysis of Australia, Canada, France, and Sweden. The adequacy of benefit levels is noted as cause for concern in Australia, Israel, and the United Kingdom.

Problems related to high taxes required to support old-age pension systems are stressed in the chapters on Canada and Sweden. Women's coverage and benefit adequacy are referred to as special issues in the German Democratic Republic, the Federal Republic of Germany, Israel, and Switzerland. The advantages and disadvantages of universal income protection as opposed to selective (income-tested) benefits, including the viability of privatization of programs, are given special coverage in the chapters on Australia, the German Democratic Republic, and the United Kingdom. Pension program administrative costs are mentioned as a distinctive problem in Switzerland while inflation and immigration are presented as major difficulties for Israel.

Economic instability is discussed as a prominent factor that has influenced pension systems in the German Democratic Republic and Israel. Relatively slow economic development combined with high inflation has had a negative impact on pension programs in both of these nations.

Less Economically Developed Nations

The chapters on the less economically developed nations depict, of course, a quite different set of conditions that have molded income programs for the elderly. Colonialism has been a predominant factor in pension program development, with the impact of colonial rule varying according to the colonizer. Old-age programs in the former British colonies, for example, are still distinguished by systems of compulsory savings plans that provide a lump-sum benefit at retirement under provident fund schemes. The provident fund systems of Ghana, India, and Tanzania indicate the influence of the British colonial system as explained in the respective chapters, especially the analysis of the system in India. There are efforts underway in such nations as Ghana to convert to a social insurance scheme as a means of protecting benefits from reduced value due to inflation.

Pension schemes in former French colonies, on the other hand, are more likely to be based on social insurance principles of comprehensive coverage and periodic, long-term benefit payments after retirement. As noted in the chapter on the former French colony of the Ivory Coast, however, old-age pensions have not been widely extended beyond civil servants and urban industrial workers as resources have tended to be concentrated on family allowances and workers' compensation programs.

A condition characteristic of the economically developing countries discussed in the text is the consequence of the shift from an agricultural to an industrial economy. This economic transference, accompanied by an increase in urban industrial workers, created a need for protection against the loss of income. The preferred system of protecting elderly employees from the loss of income due to old age has typically been some form of social insurance. Viable pension systems under social insurance, however, have been limited to a small proportion of the working population due to many reasons, including low levels of economic development, problems of administration, geographic isolation, and external debts. The chapter on India provides a good illustration of the pension quandary faced by many Third World nations.

The chapter on Turkey offers an example of a nation that has made substantial inroads in providing social insurance coverage for a significant proportion of its population. Yet this country is still struggling to fully implement its programs for rural agricultural workers against the risk of low income in old age.

Although coverage of workers under public old-age pension schemes in economically developing nations is typically confined to employees in large industries, civil servants, and military personnel, it is customary for most governments to be actively engaged in efforts to expand pension systems modeled after those of industrialized nations. One reason for this has to do with the various international labor conventions to which most countries subscribe. It is also a result of technical assistance on pension program development that is rendered by international bodies such as the International Labour Office. The influence of the International Social Security Association and the United States Social Security Administration has also been instrumental in inducing Third World nations to work toward income systems comparable to those of industrial nations.

A factor that shapes income policy for the elderly in Latin American nations such as Costa Rica and Mexico that is analogous to programs in European nations is the national commitment to universal pensions under the ideology of solidarity. As the authors of the chapters on Costa Rica and Mexico note, however, this constitutional pledge remains a goal rather than a reality. The limited resources available in these nations have been allocated to the development of health care under social insurance, relying on families and communities to provide most of the income support. Thus, the public old-age pension system in Mexico is restricted to benefits for industrial workers in urban areas. (Cost Rica, however, has a relatively extensive coverage of workers for old-age pensions.)

The chapter on Chile shows how that nation deviates from the norm in Latin America. Its approach to income maintenance has, since 1981, been founded on principles of private initiative and employer responsibility. The government is relegated to a relatively minor role and there is little concern for social solidarity.

As noted above, there is now much discussion in industrial nations about the desirability of reducing the government burden of caring for the elderly by increasing community and individual responsibility for income security in old age. In economically developing countries the theme of family care of the elderly takes on ever more importance in policy considerations. The authors of the chapters on Third World nations point to the strong concern for maintaining the family as the primary source of financial and social support. In China, for instance, filial piety plays a very significant role in policy development. Family, community, and private charity are also noted as core sources of care in India. In China and Tanzania there is a determined government effort to reduce reliance on national support systems by enhancing local traditional systems of support, especially the community and family.

Although most elderly are not pensioners in Third World nations, and the elderly typically constitute less than 10 percent of the population, increased numbers of elderly are stretching the abilities of families to continue as the primary source of support. The problem is compounded by the shift to a wage economy that not only has disrupted traditional means of care but does not protect the vast majority of workers who are engaged in nonformal work, agricultural work, and employment in small-scale industries. The rural to urban migration of young people has also left a high proportion of elderly persons in agricultural production in rural areas whose daughters, the traditional care givers, have moved to the city. These developments have helped lead to renewed efforts to expand old-age pension coverage to agricultural workers in Ghana, India, Indonesia, Mexico, Tanzania, and Turkey. Although atypical for most economically developing nations, the combined effects of an aging population and early retirement leading to an unfavorable dependency ratio are cited as important contributing factors to Chile's 1981 social security reform that introduced a national system of private pension funds.

Economically developing nations are faced with a number of other pressing problems relative to old-age insurance. Perhaps the greatest of these is that of external debts and inflation, which are major factors in curtailing expenditures for income programs (as noted in the chapters on Chile, Costa Rica, and Mexico). Weak economies and low national per-capita income are also discussed as constraints to expanded pensions, as in the Ivory Coast. Of course, funding programs in nations with few fiscal resources and great adversities presents a constant challenge as noted in the discussion of India and Tanzania. Another important issue is the role of the private sector and individual in meeting basic income needs in old age as opposed to government income protection programs. The system of privatization in Chile is providing a natural experiment with this approach.

The chapters in this text represent a wide spectrum of ideological approaches to old-age pension programs and an array of specific program strategies. The separate and collective information will provide at least an introduction to how and why foreign pension systems function and the issues that confront their future development. We hope that this knowledge will stimulate interest in learning more about these and other foreign systems through further research.

1

Australia

Allan Borowski

The income security arrangements for the elderly in Australia are quite different from those found in other industrialized nations. In fact, they are so different that some observers have even regarded them as "deviant" (Kaim-Caudle, 1973).

The system of state support for retirement income in Australia has two major elements: (1) the age pension, and (2) tax concessions to encourage the provision of future retirement income needs through employer-sponsored pension plans. These plans are referred to as "occupational superannuation schemes" and represent the market's contribution to the provision of retirement income.

AUSTRALIA'S "SOCIAL SECURITY" SYSTEM

Australia maintains an extensive public system of income support for people with insufficient income. The age pension is one element of this system. Indeed, the design features of the age pension are similar to those of the provisions that comprise Australia's public system of income security referred to as the "social security system."

The pensions, benefits, and allowances that comprise Australia's social security system have developed in an incremental and piecemeal manner. Nevertheless, the various provisions respond to most of the circumstances that result in insufficient income, including, for example, unemployment (the unemployment benefit), disability (the invalid pension), and reduced opportunities for labor force participation by a sole parent who must care for dependent children (the supporting parents benefit).

Australia's social security system is guided by a number of key principles. These include:

1. community responsibility for the income support of those unable or not expected to derive sufficient income from labor force participation or their own savings
2. the receipt of income support as a right by those who are categorically eligible (including satisfying a means test on income alone in the case of benefits and on income and assets in the case of pensions)
3. the transfer of income through vulnerable periods of the lifecycle and poverty alleviation through the redistribution of income (the reduction of income inequality)
4. the preservation of such socially valued incentives as work and savings. (Cass, 1986)

Australia's social security system, then, is essentially one that provides a guaranteed minimum income to various categories of "eligibles" on a selective basis.

THE AGE PENSION

In most industrialized nations public retirement income arrangements form the foundation upon which additional provision for private pensions and personal savings can be made to provide a three-tiered approach to providing a retirement income (Fuery et al., 1988). Often this public foundation is a contributory social insurance scheme that provides earnings-related benefits to retirees. In the case of Australia, however, the public foundation is a flat-rate, noncontributory provision entirely funded from general revenues—the age pension. Receipt of the age pension is conditional upon passing a means test comprised of an income test and an asset test. In view of the principles of the social security system and the design features of the age pension, it follows that the role of this provision is to provide a subsistence income *supplementary* to any provision for old age that the elderly may have made for themselves (Howe, 1980). The age pension is, then, essentially a mechanism to redistribute income in order to alleviate poverty among the elderly.

The age pension was one of the first income support provisions established in Australia and is an outgrowth of the Commonwealth Constitution of 1901, which authorized parliament to legislate with regard to age pensions. This the parliament did in 1908 after circumventing constitutional restrictions on its expenditure and opposition from the states (Foster, 1988). The actual payment of the age pension began in July 1909. This recognition of the need to provide income support for the destitute aged arose out of the economic depression that gripped Australia during the 1890s.

Although quite stringent eligibility criteria were applied when the age pension was first introduced, the next seven decades witnessed a steady and seemingly inexorable process of liberalization. Among the landmark years in this process were 1973 (when the means test for those aged 75 years and over was abolished) and 1975 (when the means test for those between 70 and 74 years of age was abolished). This process culminated in the abolition of the asset test component of the means test in 1976.

In the late 1970s the first of a number of steps was taken to restrict age pension eligibility. Thus, in 1978 pension benefit levels received by age pensioners who were *not* subject to the income-tested-only means test, that is, those aged 70 years and over, were frozen. Pensioners over 70, however, could apply for the normal income-tested pension. In 1983, the "frozen" pension payable to those aged 70 and over (and considerably eroded in value by inflation) again became subject to an income test. And, since March 21, 1985, age pension eligibility has, once again, imposed a means test made up of income *and* asset test components. All of these steps were fundamentally motivated by the government's desire to curtail its expenditure.

Main Features of the Age Pension

The age pension is indexed for inflation as measured by movements in the Consumer Price Index. Pensions are adjusted for inflation in June and December of each year. As of June 1988 the maximum amount payable to a single pensioner (the "standard-rate" pension) was $120.05 per week; that payable to a pensioner couple (the "married" rate) was $200.10 per week. To be eligible for the age pension, men must be 65 years of age or over and women 60 years of age or over. An equivalent pension, known as the "service pension," is payable to war veterans five years earlier—at age 60 for men and 55 for women. Further, a wife pension is payable to the wife of a pensioner who is not receiving an age pension in her own right. Applicants must be residing in Australia at the time of application and, generally, have continuously lived in Australia for a period of at least 10 years at any time. They must also satisfy the means test.

As noted above, the income test is made up of an income test and an asset test. Each test is applied separately to determine the pension entitlement. The actual pension payment is the lower of the pension benefit levels produced by the tests. Under the income test component of the means test a single applicant for the age pension can have an income up to $40 per week before the pension is reduced by 50 cents for each additional dollar of income (i.e., a 50 percent marginal tax—or benefit reduction—rate). Thus, the breakeven level of income (the level beyond which payment of a part, or "reduced," pension ceases) is $280.10 per week. Married couples, may receive a combined income of $70 per week before suffering a reduction in their age pension at the rate of 25 cents per dollar for each additional dollar of income. Thus, the breakeven level of income for pensioner couples is $470.20 per week.

Age pension receipt is also conditional upon satisfying an asset test. Asset disregard thresholds ("allowable asset" limits) under the 1985 asset test are indexed for inflation in June of each year. The asset test distinguishes not only between single pensioners and married couples but also between homeowners and nonhomeowners. Asset disregard levels are higher for nonhomeowners. This is because owner-occupied homes, irrespective of their value, are completely exempt from the asset test. Assets over specific amounts reduce the age pension by $2 per week for every $1,000 of assessable assets above the threshold levels. The breakeven levels under the assets test are $149,500, $213,500, and $291,500 for single homeowners, single nonhomeowners, and couple homeowners/couple nonhomeowners, respectively.

A special income test applies to persons aged 70 years and over. The amount of the pension received by single pensioners in this age group with an income of less than $177.20 per week is determined under the normal income test. Those with an income between $177.20 and $200 per week receive the "frozen-rate" pension of $51.45 per week, while those with an income between $200 and $302.90 per week receive the "frozen-rate" pension less 50 percent of the income over $200. In the case of married couples, the amount of the pension received for those with a combined income of less than $298.60 per week is determined under the normal income test. The "frozen-rate" pension of $85.80 per week is payable to couples over 70 years of age with a weekly income between $298.60 and $333.00. Finally, couples with a weekly income between $333.00 and $504.60 receive the "frozen-rate" pension less 50 percent of the income in excess of $333.

Additional Benefits Available to Age Pensioners

Age pensioners are entitled to additional forms of assistance, including tax rebates, rental assistance, and various fringe benefits.

Although age pensions are taxable, age pensioners enjoy a special tax rebate of $430 per year. This means that they may receive up to $6,892 per year in taxable income from all sources before being liable for any income tax.

Those age pensioners who rent housing in the private market are entitled to "rent assistance." For the single pensioner the assistance is half the weekly rent above $15 to a maximum of $15 per week. For a married couple, the rent assistance is $7.50 per week for each partner where their rent exceeds $45 per week.

Age pensioners are eligible for various concessions and fringe benefits, such as reduced fares for travel, reduced property taxes ("rates"), free pharmaceuticals, and reduced telephone charges. These fringe benefits have been valued at about $10 to $15 a week after tax (Dixon, 1988). Receipt of some of these concessions and benefits is also subject to a means test. This test, however, is a little more generous than that used to determine age pension benefit levels.

Cost and Coverage of the Age Pension

In fiscal year 1987–1988, $7 billion was spent in providing the age pension to 1.33 million older Australians. If Australia's 403,000 service pensioners are included, then almost 80 percent of the older population were receiving either an age or service pension at a total cost of about $9 billion (Economic Planning Advisory Council, 1988; Foster, 1988).

Although the rate of participation in the age pension program is quite high, it is important to note that in recent years there has been a decline in both the proportion and number of older Australians who receive it. This decline is largely due to the tightening of pension eligibility criteria in 1983 (reintroduction of an income test for pensioners over age 70) and 1985 (reintroduction of an asset test). While the cost of the age (and service) pension has continued to grow in nominal terms, the fall in pensioner numbers stemming from the tightening of the eligibility criteria has meant that total expenditure on the age and service pension programs has declined as a proportion of Gross Domestic Product— from 3.5 percent in 1982–1983 to 3.1 percent in 1986–1987 (Foster, 1988).

Contributions to Retirement Income

Although the age pension was intended to provide only a minimal level of income support, for many retirees it provides the only or main regular source of income. About three-quarters of all elderly pensioners receive the maximum pension, indicating that they have little or no other private income. The age pension, together with the service pension, provides about 60 percent of all retirement income (Foster, 1988).

To understand why elderly retirees rely so heavily on the age pension when Australia has numerous occupational superannuation schemes requires an understanding of Australia's employer-sponsored pension arrangements.

EMPLOYER-SPONSORED PENSIONS

Australia's occupational superannuation schemes are quite different from the employer-sponsored pension plan arrangement found in most industrialized countries in at least four respects: (1) the form in which benefits are paid; (2) the circumstances under which they are paid; (3) the role they play in contributing to retirement income; and (4) the tax arrangements under which the schemes operate. Before turning to these differences, however, we begin by considering the extent of coverage and the types of occupational superannuation schemes found in Australia.

Coverage

Employer-sponsored pension plans have a relatively lengthy history in Australia. The first formal occupational superannuation scheme was established in 1862 by the Bank of New South Wales. Developments in the private pension area, however, were limited and slow. The schemes that were introduced between the 1860s and the close of World War II were largely confined to white-collar civil servants and employees of financial organizations and large manufacturing concerns (Knox, 1983). Thus, they essentially served to provide a select group of salaried males with an independent retirement income (Gunasekera and Powlay, 1987).

Pension plan coverage expanded between the late 1940s and the early 1970s. By February 1974, however, only 32 percent of all employees were covered. During the late 1970s and continuing into the early 1980s, Australia experienced a particularly rapid expansion in coverage. Thus, by 1979, 42 percent of employees belonged to superannuation schemes (Hancock, 1983) and, by 1982, the coverage rate had climbed to 45 percent of all workers (Cumming and Whiteford, 1983).[1] By 1986 about 47 percent of workers (about 2.7 million) were members of superannuation schemes. Eighty-three percent were covered by schemes that were either arranged or provided by their current employer. The balance were covered by superannuation arranged through insurance companies (typically self-employed workers) or had superannuation entitlements preserved in a fund of a previous employer or a "rollover" fund (Gunasekera and Powlay, 1987).

The distribution of coverage in Australia is quite similar to that of other industrial countries. The incidence of coverage is highest among white-collar males between 45 and 59 years of age with above-average earnings who are employed full-time in the public sector and in industries that tend to be highly unionized.

Types of Superannuation Schemes

There are over 280,000 superannuation schemes in Australia. Traditionally, most superannuation schemes have been company-based. Recent years, however, have witnessed the emergence of industry-based (i.e., multiemployer) schemes. In large measure, the trend toward multiemployer schemes is the product of the heightened demand by the powerful Australian labor movement for either new or improved superannuation coverage.[2] The Commonwealth government, the labor movement, and the Conciliation and Arbitration Commission have an expressed preference for multiemployer schemes that are jointly controlled by labor and management.

Industry-based schemes are typical of the accumulated contribution (or money purchase) variety where retirement benefits are based on the accumulated contributions made on behalf of the employee and the investment earnings on those contributions. Industry-based schemes are also characterized by automatic membership, immediate vesting, portability, variable preservation conditions, the eligibility of part-time employees, and, because of their recency, modest benefit levels.

In general, the overwhelming majority of Australia's superannuation schemes are accumulated contribution schemes. In 1982–1983, however, 82 percent of the members of superannuation schemes were covered under defined benefit schemes. Thus, the larger schemes tend to be of the defined benefit variety while the smaller ones (most schemes) tend to be of the accumulated contribution type (Gunasekera and Powlay, 1987).

The Form of Benefits and the Circumstances of Payment

Two features that distinguish Australia's occupational superannuation schemes from employer-sponsored pension plans found in other industrialized countries are the form in which benefits are paid and the circumstances under which they are paid.

The most common form of superannuation benefit in Australia is the lump-sum payment. The reason why benefits are paid as a lump sum rather than as a pension annuity has to do with the differential tax treatment of lump-sum benefits compared with benefits received as an ongoing pension. The superannuation benefits received by retired workers are subject to taxation. Until June 30, 1983, however, only 5 percent of a lump-sum payment was included in annual tax-assessable income and taxed at the individual's marginal rate (an effective rate of tax on the total lump sum of less than 3 percent). Retirement benefits received as a pension, however, were fully taxable. The tax-advantaged status of lump-sum payments compared to the corresponding pension served to "entrench" benefit payment in lump-sum form.

A second distinguishing feature of Australia's occupational superannuation arrangements is that benefits are often paid in circumstances other than retirement (or disability or death). Most superannuation schemes allow the payment of the lump-sum benefit at any time a worker changes jobs—irrespective of the reason for the job change. Clearly, most schemes do not require the preservation of benefit entitlements until retirement. According to Gruen (1985), about two-thirds of those receiving lump-sum payments are less than 55 years of age and account for between 25 and 35 percent of the amounts paid out in lump-sum form. Thus, occupational superannuation schemes, although ostensibly mechanisms for providing retirement income, often function as a job termination or severance pay device (Borowski et al., 1987).

Contribution to Retirement Income

Although the situation is slowly beginning to change, the absence of preservation requirements in most superannuation schemes suggests that those workers who have held a number of covered jobs during their working life and dissipated their "job termination" superannuation payments should expect a small retirement benefit. Indeed, the levels of occupational superannuation benefits received upon retirement have tended to be quite small. In 1982, for example, over half of those over 60 years of age who had received a lump-sum benefit after turning 50 received lump sums of less than $10,000 while over 70 percent received less than $20,000 (Department of Social Security, 1984). More recent data indicate an improvement in lump-sum benefit levels. Thus, the average size of the lump sums received between 1982 and 1986 by males who were between 60 and 64 years of age in 1986 was $54,000 (Foster, 1988). Despite this improvement, for most retirees superannuation offers inadequate protection against the risk of longevity in old age—a period of retirement that can span one, two, or more decades.

The small size of lump-sum retirement benefits means that an incentive exists for many superannuitants to dissipate their lump sums (e.g., through using them to clear a mortgage or other debts) with a view to establishing age pension eligibility. This is a pattern characteristic of many workers who use superannuation to finance retirement prior to age pension age. As a result, despite substantial tax concessions aimed at supporting self-provision for retirement through employer-sponsored schemes, the Australian government nevertheless finds itself supporting the retirement incomes of superannuitants through the age pension program. Indeed, superannuation is a relatively minor source of retirement income, providing less than 10 percent of the total (Foster, 1988).

Taxation and Occupational Superannuation

The tax treatment of occupational superannuation contributions and benefits is yet another distinguishing feature of Australia's employer-sponsored pension plans. As shown below, superannuation taxation arrangements have become quite complex over recent years as a result of some major legislative changes.

Contributions and Taxation

Most workers pay part of the cost of employer-sponsored pension plans. A 1982–1983 census of superannuation funds found that 94 percent of covered workers contributed to superannuation schemes (Gunasekera and Powlay, 1987). The basis of payment into superannuation funds is usually a fixed percentage of earnings.

Although employee contributions to employer-sponsored superannuation funds are the norm, contributing employees currently receive no tax concessions.[3] Although employee contributions enjoy no tax advantages, employer contributions are fully tax-deductible by the employer. Further, the superannuation fund contributions made by employers and the earnings of superannuation funds were, until June 30, 1988, completely tax-exempt. In 1986–1987 these tax concessions represented foregone federal revenue of $3.5 billion (Economic Planning Advisory Council, 1988).

Taxation of Benefits

Major changes in the tax treatment of superannuation benefits were introduced in 1984 and 1988. In 1984 substantially higher rates of tax on lump sums were introduced for superannuation entitlement accrued after July 1, 1983. The tax rates applying to lump-sum superannuation entitlements accrued after mid–1983 were a flat rate of 31.25 percent on lump-sum benefits taken before age 55, and a rate of 16.25 percent on the first $55,000 taken after age 55 with the balance taxed at 31.25 percent. At the same time, approved deposit funds (ADFs) and deferred annuities (DAs)—two financial vehicles designed to foster preservation—were also introduced. By "rolling over" (i.e., depositing within 90 days) lump sums into either an ADF or DA, the lump-sum tax liability could be legitimately deferred until withdrawal. The investment income was also tax-exempt until withdrawal, at which time it was deemed to form part of the lump sum. And withdrawals used to purchase an annuity (i.e., pension) were not subject to any lump-sum tax at all. Of course, the annuity was taxable at normal rates.

There were a number of reasons behind the introduction of higher superannuation taxes. Among these was the desire to at least partially redress the more generous tax treatment of lump sums relative to pensions with a view to encouraging the preservation of superannuation benefits and the purchase of annuities that would serve as a source of retirement income *throughout* retirement. The higher lump-sum taxes were also seen as a revenue measure designed to reduce the amount of government support for superannuation benefits taken in lump-sum form. Indeed, the changes in the tax treatment of superannuation announced in May 1988 were, in large measure, yet another attempt by the government to tighten superannuation tax concessions with a view to reducing the level of government support in the form of tax concessions in this area.

In response to growing concerns over the size and rapid growth of superannuation tax concessions, further changes in the tax treatment of superannuation were announced in May 1988.

First, a new 15 percent tax on the investment earnings of superannuation and rollover funds (ADFs, DAs) went into effect on July 1, 1988. The annual taxation of investment earnings represents a major departure from the previous practice of allowing fund earnings to accumulate without taxation and deferring the payment of tax until money was actually withdrawn from the funds. Funds also became liable for payment of capital gains tax on the real value of gains made after July 1, 988.

The changes also provided that the effects of the new 15 percent tax on investment earnings could be offset with tax credits from "franked" dividends received by the funds from their shareholdings in Australian companies. (A franked dividend is a dividend paid out of company profits on which full company tax has been paid. To avoid double taxation, the dividend is tax-free in the hands of the shareholder.) The extent of the offsetting effect of the 15 percent tax will be dependent upon the pattern of fund investment. Greater offsets demand "equity" investment in the volatile share market while low-risk "capital-guaranteed" funds will have little opportunity to offset the 15 percent tax.

Yet another change that went into effect on July 1, 1988, was the imposition of a 15 percent tax on employer contributions. The tax on employer contributions, however, is levied on the superannuation fund while the employer may continue to claim superannuation contributions as a tax deduction.

There was also provision for some offsetting of the tax on employer contributions. The tax on lump-sum benefits and withdrawals from rollover funds attributable to contributions made after mid–1983 were reduced. Thus, the first $60,000 (indexed annually to average weekly earnings from 1989–1990) is now exempt from tax if the lump sum is preserved until age 55. The portion of the lump sum in excess of $60,000 is taxable at a rate of 15 percent (plus the Medicare national health insurance levy). Where lump sums are taken prior to age 55, the tax rate applying to the post–1983 component will be phased down from 30 to 20 percent (plus the Medicare levy).

Some of the other changes involved the placing of stricter limits on the size of superannuation payouts with a view to encouraging more higher-income earners to take their superannuation in pension form; and increasing the limit on tax-deductible superannuation contributions for the self-employed and uncovered workers from $1,500 to $3,000.

The changes just described are expected to generate revenues to the government of $980 million in 1989–1990 and $1.4 billion in 1990–1991 (Keating, 1988).

MAJOR ISSUES

The above discussion on the age pension and occupation superannuation has served to underscore the unique nature of Australia's retirement income system. What Australia does have in common with other industrialized nations is the fact that in recent years, retirement income policy has assumed a very prominent position on the national political agenda. The most recent expression of this prominence is the release of two major reports (Foster, 1988; Commonwealth of Australia, 1988) that examine the major issues currently confronting Australia's retirement income system. These issues include, for example: (1) the propensity for early retirement; (2) the age of age pension entitlement; (3) the interaction between the tax system and income test component of the means test; (4) the adequacy of superannuation arrangements in terms of coverage, vesting preservation, and the like; (5) the adequacy of benefit levels; (6) the basis of allocating the age pension; and (7) the interaction of the age pension and occupational superannuation. The latter three issues are briefly discussed below.

Adequacy

One of the major criteria used to evaluate income security programs is that of adequacy. Both the age pension and occupational superannuation fare badly in terms of this criterion.

While age pension benefit levels are adjusted for inflation, benefit levels may also be adjusted by the federal government on an ad hoc basis. These ad hoc adjustments arise when the government determines, in light of its other expenditure priorities, that sufficient funds are available to direct toward greater expenditure on the age pension. Thus, benefit levels are not established in relation to an explicit criterion of minimal income adequacy. The oft-quoted "target" for the age pension is benefit levels that are equivalent to 25 percent of average weekly earnings (AWE). Indeed, current levels hover around this target. But it must be emphasized that 25 percent of AWE is very close to Australia's semiofficial "Henderson" poverty line and this measure is acknowledged as a very austere measure of minimal income adequacy.

Reference has been made to the fact that superannuation benefits offer insufficient protection against the risk of longevity in old age and that superannuation plays a relatively minor role in contributing to income during the retirement years. With a view to encouraging greater reliance on superannuation as a source of retirement income and less reliance on the age pension, the government has taken a number of steps besides the changes in the tax treatment of superannuation. Legislation passed in 1987 (the Occupational Superannuation Standards Act) specified minimal portability, vesting, reporting, and other standards for occupational superannuation schemes (Fairley, 1988). The new standards also seek to improve preservation so that workers will have accumulated a more substantial superannuation benefit that, ideally, will actually serve as a source of retirement income. The new standards require all vested superannuation entitlement arising out of agreements for new or additional employer contributions[4] to be preserved until retirement on or after 55 years of age.

A minimum preservation age of 55 may be too low, however, and fail to discourage the phenomenon described above—early retirement and dissipation of superannuation benefits in the years before reaching age pension age. As Gunasekera and Powlay (1987) point out,

the age 55 requirement recognizes the reality of the labor market. . . . The needs of individuals who require support in the event of being involuntarily retired prior to age pension age and who might otherwise be forced to rely upon . . . direct government payments have to be balanced against the objective of using superannuation to reduce age pension outlays. (p. 35)

Basis of Allocation

The basis of allocation of the age pension (i.e., whether it should be universal or selective) has been a source of long-standing debate in Australia. Indeed, the debate even preceded the introduction of the provision.

The 1908 federal legislation was modeled on the earlier New South Wales provision that, since 1900, had provided the elderly "deserving poor" with a pension of 10 shillings ($1) per week. The preamble to the New South Wales pension legislation made reference to the notion of the pension as a social right flowing from past labor force participation and contributions as a taxpayer (Markey, 1982). Logic would suggest that, as a social right, the age pension should have been allocated on a universal basis. Political realism and fiscal constraint, however, precluded the universal payment of the age pension and demanded a selective provision with eligibility determined on the basis of a means test.

Nevertheless, because of the electoral appeal of universalism, means test liberalization received bipartisan political support over the decades, a process that culminated in the abolition of the asset test component to the means test in 1976.

The views of the major political parties concerning the basis of allocating the age pension have now come full circle: the steps taken over the last decade to tighten the eligibility criteria and thereby contain costs and facilitate the targeting of the age pension on those in greatest need now enjoy bipartisan political support. Nevertheless, the voices in support of universalism have not been stifled. Pensioner lobby groups have strongly resisted all of the various efforts to tighten eligibility. Further, as recently as early December 1988, the Senate Standing Committee on Community Affairs issued a report on retirement incomes in which it recommended, as a long-term option, the introduction of a two-tiered age pension program. The first tier (the "basic" pension and equivalent to 20 percent of AWE) would be allocated on a universal basis while a second tier (up to an additional 10 percent of AWE) would be allocated selectively (subject to a means test) (Commonwealth of Australia, 1988).

The Integration of the Age Pension and Occupational Superannuation

The integration of the age pension and superannuation is the crucial long-term retirement issue (Foster, 1988). The dissipation, prior to age pension age, of superannuation benefits that have enjoyed costly tax concessions has had a negative impact upon the adequacy of retirement incomes, incentives to save, and the equitable distribution of taxpayer support.

The ideal solution to the poor integration of the age pension and superannuation is the payment of superannuation as an annuity during the retirement years, an annuity that is assessable by the tax system and under the age pension's income test. The entrenched preference for lump-sum payments in Australia, however, suggests that tax incentives, for example, will not suffice as a means of increasing the numbers of workers who opt for an annuity in retirement.

The "ideal" retirement income system to which Australia aspires is one in which superannuation is received as a pension and, thus, provides an income flow throughout the retirement years. The publicly funded age pension should serve as a "residual" provision for those with insufficient retirement income. It is unlikely that this ideal will be realized in the foreseeable future.

NOTES

1. The 1979 and 1982 coverage figures are not entirely comparable. The former exclude the self-employed while the latter, although including the self-employed, refer only to persons working twenty or more hours per week.

2. In recent years the Australian labor movement has pressed for new or improved superannuation coverage. Australia has a highly centralized system for dealing with

industrial disputation between management and labor and for establishing wages and working conditions through the Conciliation and Arbitration Commission. An important stimulus to the extension of superannuation coverage was provided by the National Wage Case decision in March 1987, a decision that accorded with the government's desire for improved coverage. In that decision, the Conciliation and Arbitration Commission agreed to make consent awards (i.e., judgments) concerning *employer* contributions to approved superannuation funds up to a maximum of an equivalent wage increase of 3 percent. This decision opened the way for trade unions to negotiate for improved or, in many cases, initial membership of superannuation schemes. While the National Wage Case decision should result in an extension of coverage, the level of coverage (a 3 percent wage equivalent) will nevertheless remain poor for many.

3. Income taxation in Australia was introduced under the 1915 Income Tax Assessment Act. Under this act, employee contributions (up to $100 per year) and employer contributions (unlimited) were tax-deductible. Fund investment income was fully tax-exempt. In general, these concessions remained largely unchanged until the mid–1970s. The tax deductibility of employee contributions up to a maximum (which was increased regularly, finally reaching $1,200 per year in 1967–1968) remained until 1975, when a "universal rebate" was introduced. Only employees with total concessional expenditures *in excess* of the prescribed amount received any taxation benefit. The universal rebate was removed July 1985. Thus, employee contributions now receive no taxation concessions (Knox, 1987).

4. See n. 2.

REFERENCES

Borowski, A., Schulz, H., and Whiteford, P. (1987). Providing adequate retirement income: What role occupational superannuation? *Australian Journal of Ageing*, 1, 3–13.

Cass, B. (1986). *The case for review of aspects of the Australian social security system.* Background/Discussion Paper No. 1. Woden, ACT: Social Security Review, Department of Social Security.

Commonwealth of Australia. (1988). *Income support for the retired and the aged: An agenda for reform.* Report of the Senate Standing Committee on Community Affairs. Canberra, ACT: Australian Government Publishing Service.

Cumming, M. A., and Whiteford, P. (1983, December). Retirement income and superannuation coverage in Australia. *Social Security Journal*, 59–65.

Department of Social Security. (1984). *The economic and social circumstances of the aged.* Research Paper No. 25. Canberra, ACT: Research and Statistics Branch, Development Division.

Dixon, D. (1988, May 2). Why it is so hard for pensioners to learn the income and assets test. *Age*, 25.

Economic Planning Advisory Council. (1988). *Economic effects of an aging population.* Council Paper No. 29. Canberra, ACT: Australian Government Publishing Service.

Fairley, A. E. J. (1988, March). The new superannuation regime—How the occupational standards work. *Law Institute Journal*, 146–151.

Foster, C. (1988). *Towards a national retirement income policy.* Issues Paper No. 6. Canberra, ACT: Social Security Review, Department of Social Security.

Fuery, M., Huta, P., Gauntlett, K., and Murray, A. (1988). *Occupational superannuation arrangements in overseas countries*. Background/Discussion Paper No. 25. Canberra, ACT: Social Security Review, Department of Social Security.

Gruen, F. H. (1985, September). Australian government policy on retirement incomes. *Economic Record*, 613–621.

Gunasekera, M., and Powlay, J. (1987). *Occupational superannuation arrangements in Australia*. Background/Discussion Paper No. 21. Woden, ACT: Social Security Review, Department of Social Security.

Hancock, K. (1983). Income security: The economics of retirement provision. In R. Mendelsohn (ed.), *Australian social welfare finance*, 143–161. Sydney: George Allen and Unwin.

Howe, A. L. (1980, Spring). Retirement and pensions: A survey of recent trends in Australia. *Aging and Work*, 89–102.

Kaim-Caudle, P. R. (1973). *Comparative social policy and social security: A ten country study*. London: Martin Robertson.

Keating, The Hon. P. J. (1988, May 25). "The May statement." *Australian Financial Review*, 1s–8s.

Knox, D. (1983). Employer-sponsored superannuation in Australia. *Current Affairs Bulletin*, 59, 4–13.

Knox, D. M. (1987). *Taxation support of superannuation in Australia: Its costs, equity and efficacy*. Research Study No. 7. Sydney: Australian Tax Research Foundation.

Markey, R. (1982). The ALP and the emergence of a national social policy, 1880–1910. In Richard Kennedy (ed.), *Australian welfare history: Critical essays*, 103–137. Melbourne: Macmillan.

2

Canada

Brigitte Kitchen

Canadians are protected against income loss brought on by life- and work-related contingencies by the four pillars of the Canadian welfare state. These pillars consist of three income maintenance programs and a national health insurance system. The income maintenance programs are workers' compensation, an employer-funded social insurance program for the protection of workers in the workplace under provincial jurisdiction; and two federal contributory earnings-related programs—unemployment insurance and the Canada/Quebec Pension Plan. Quebec operates its own pension plan, which is so similar to the general plan in levels of benefits and rates of contribution that the two are usually referred to as the Canada/Quebec Pension Plans (C/QPP). There is full portability between the two plans. The medical care insurance system seeks to ensure that necessary health services are available to all residents of Canada regardless of their financial circumstances.

In fiscal year 1984–1985 total federal/provincial social security spending amounted to $42.7 billion. The share of unemployment insurance spending and of the Canada/Quebec Pension Plan was 23.8 percent and 13.7 percent, respectively (Statistics Canada, 1988). Together these two social insurance programs make up about one-third of all social spending on income maintenance in Canada.

The design of the unemployment insurance program and the C/QPP favors persons with steady, well-paying jobs that qualify them for maximum benefit levels; unskilled workers, most of whom are women with intermittent work patterns and low earnings, find themselves at the lower end of the benefit scale. The work-related nature of the unemployment insurance program and the C/QPP is reflected in their benefit structure. Benefits replicate the inequality of the wage system, rooted in the neoclassical assumption that market forces price labor in accordance with the marginal value of output attributable to the last worker hired.

This has led some critics of social insurance schemes to conclude that the relations of wage labor and extended into benefits and can therefore be described as work-tested (Shragge and Maclean, 1983).

WORKER'S COMPENSATION

Among industrial nations Canada was a latecomer in the development of social welfare legislation. When the Great Depression hit about 25 percent of male Canadians found themselves out of work. The country was singularly unprepared to tackle the rising costs of direct relief for which people in need had to apply at their place of residence. In 1920 workmen's compensation (now workers' compensation) was the only compulsory social insurance program in place in all the provinces except Prince Edward Island. Women and children, if they were in the workforce or dependents of men, were also covered under the act (Guest, 1985). It provided income protection against the risks of work-related sickness, disability, or death as a right. The primary objectives of the program were not only to provide adequate income protection for injured workers, but to find a more cost-effective way to meet employers' financial liabilities toward their workers. In this sense, this earliest of Canadian social insurance schemes "served . . . to benefit employers by reducing the risk and cost of compensation" (Jennissen, 1981:69).

SOCIAL INSURANCE

The idea of social insurance achieved popularity in the Depression years of the 1930s in Canada but its application to the practical task of government was new to Canadian policy makers. A government-commissioned report, the Marsh Report on Social Security for Canada in 1943, outlined a wide range of social insurance programs aimed at protecting Canadians against the insecurities of working and family life. Marsh believed that it would be impossible for workers and their families to meet the financial burdens of life- and employment-related risks from their wages alone. He favored the pooling of individual risks by collective means through the participation and controlling influence of the state. The fact that social insurance would enlist the direct support of the classes most likely to benefit was its particular attraction for him (Marsh, 1975).

UNIVERSAL PENSIONS

Since 1951 Canada has provided all residents who reach age 65 with a universal old-age pension that is paid regardless of income or employment history. The benefit is financed entirely from general revenues. As of July 1989, the amount of this benefit paid to each pensioner was up to $330.43 a month. An income-tested supplement could raise the monthly amount to $707.47 for a single person and $1,147.20 for a couple (USDHHS, 1990). The universal benefit is considered to be the first tier of a two-tier system of benefits with the earnings-related benefit under the Canada/Quebec Pension Plan comprising the second tier.

The Canada/Quebec Pension Plan

The Canada Pension Plan was implemented in 1965 after a long struggle with the private insurance industry. Although the insurance industry could not prevent the pension plan from being enacted, it won some major concessions that significantly reduced the benefit levels so that Canadians have to supplement their public pension benefits with a private insurance plan (Armitage, 1975). The provinces strongly favored the C/QPP because they were allowed to borrow excess program funds at an interest rate far below the market rate based on the ratio of contributions from that province to total contributions. The provinces were thus provided access to a substantial pool of investment capital to finance economic development.

Contributions. The Canada/Quebec Pension Plan operates as a compulsory contributory earnings-related pension plan in all provinces. As noted, the province of Quebec has its own similar pension plan. The two plans are broadly parallel to allow for easy transfer and portability. They cover most Canadians in the workforce from the ages of 18 to 65. Contributions are 2.2 percent (effective January 1990) of pensionable earnings for employees matched by an equal contribution by employers. The self-employed pay a 4.4 percent contributory rate on their pensionable earnings. Since 1986 the level of minimum and maximum pensionable earnings has varied with changes in the average industrial wage index.

Because of the increasing longevity of Canadians and the consequent rise in the number of persons of pensionable age, the costs of the plans have risen and contributions have been increased to ensure that the plans remain self-funding. The federal and Quebec governments wanted to make sure that the outflow of benefits would not exceed revenue, and justified the increases in contributions as reinforcing social insurance principles. As of January 1, 1987, the annual contribution rate was increased by 0.2 percent for a period of five years and by 0.15 percent for the following 20 years. By the year 2011 the current contribution rate of 3.6 percent will have increased to 7.6 percent, with employees and employers continuing to match their share of contributions. Those in the age group between 65 and 69 who remain in the workforce can continue making contributions to the plan and thus increase their benefit entitlement. Once benefits are paid, contributions are discontinued (*Canada Year Book*, 1988).

The funding of C/QPP is regressive. The first $2,800 of earnings are exempt from contributions and maximum earnings on which contributions are collected are $28,900 for the tax year 1990. (One Canadian dollar equals about U.S. 84.0 cents.) Anyone earning this amount and above is required to pay a maximum of $574 into the C/QPP during the 1990–1991 tax year. Contributions are allowed as tax deductions whose value increases with rising marginal tax rates. To arrive at the real amount of contributions made by individuals, the tax savings from the deduction must be subtracted from the required contribution.

Benefits. The standard pensionable age is 65 but workers have the option of receiving an actuarially reduced pension as early as age 60. Benefits are reduced by 0.5 percent for each month prior to the age of 65. This measure is aimed at increasing job opportunities for younger workers. At the same time, workers are rewarded for deferring pension receipt after age 65 as benefit levels are increased by 0.5 percent for each month beyond that age. The maximum benefit level is $577.08 a month (1990), which is paid in addition to the universal pension (International Benefits Information Service, 1989). Benefits are automatically adjusted for changes in the Consumer Price Index. Adjustments are made on a quarterly basis for the universal pension and annually for the earnings-related benefit.

Benefits under C/QPP are roughly set at 25 percent of the current value of a contributor's average monthly pensionable earnings during the entire period in which that contributor could have paid into the program. Persons who contribute at less than the maximum level or only part of the contributory period qualify for considerably lower pension benefits. Women are particularly susceptible to receiving lower benefit amounts because they tend to have fewer years of contributions.

Since 1974 public benefits have been adjusted quarterly based on changes in the Consumer Price Index in order to maintain purchasing power and increase benefit amounts for those already receiving pensions on January 1 of each year. Private pension plans have not matched this provision of the public plan. Benefits are not paid automatically; recipients must apply in writing through their nearest district office. Roughly, the replacement rate of the benefit is about 25 percent of the current value of a contributor's lifetime average monthly earnings.

For the first 10 years of the operation of the plan, partial pensions had to be paid until the plan became fully funded in 1976. Thus, in 1966, it was necessary to introduce a guaranteed income supplement (GIS) to raise the income level of elderly Canadians who had no other income except that provided by the state. GIS was expected to be a transitional income measure that could be phased out as soon as the C/QPP were fully funded. This expectation, however, has not been realized and today GIS has become a permanent dimension of the Canadian pension system.

The GIS is an income-tested system that—as distinct from a needs test—is self-administered and does not require an extensive examination of personal assets and resources. It is more akin to an income tax return. Partial benefits are payable to pensioners with some income in addition to the old age security pension, but which is less than the guaranteed income level (Guest, 1985).

The current income replacement level of the C/QPP has been widely criticized as too low to provide Canada's retired population with an economically secure future. Suggestions to increase the replacement level to 50 percent of pensionable earnings have faltered so far against the resistance from the private insurance industry. The low earnings replacement rate of the plans has been defended on the grounds that C/QPP benefits are intended as a second-tier income level built upon universal old-age security benefits financed from general revenues. Furthermore, the state is to provide only a minimum income floor so that individuals would be encouraged through their own initiative to supplement their state pensions by private pensions and savings.

Survivor Benefits. The patriarchal assumption that husbands are responsible for the financial support of their wives found practical application in the survivor benefits (which until 1982 were only paid to women) (Kitchen, 1980). Widowers whose wives had contributed to the C/QPP could qualify for survivor benefits only if they were disabled or had been substantially dependent on their wives' income. Women and men have now achieved equality in relation to survivor benefits. Survivor benefits are made up of a flat-rate component of 37.5 percent and, according to the age of the survivor, a variable amount based on the imputed retirement pension of the deceased contributor. Age and family status of the surviving spouse affect benefit calculations. Widows or widowers aged 65 and over receive 60 percent of the insured's pension, up to a maximum of $333.75 a month. Benefits are adjusted automatically on an annual basis based on increases in the Consumer Price Index (USDHHS, 1990).

Widowed spouses under the age of 35 qualify only if they have dependent children or are disabled. The practice is to defer survivor entitlement until the surviving spouse reaches the age of 65 or becomes disabled. Since January 1987, persons receiving survivor benefits can continue to do so if they remarry (*Canada Year Book*, 1988).

The Drop-Out Clause. It was the intention of parliament in 1978 to give some recognition to mothers who had taken time out of the workforce to take care of children. Subsequent legislation allows mothers who resume paid work to drop the years of low or zero earnings from the calculations of benefits under C/QPP. This change required the agreement of two-thirds of the provinces with two-thirds of the population of Canada. The government of the province of Ontario (which has more than one-third of the total Canadian population) adamantly resisted the drop-out clause despite the fact that the clause had been implemented in the Quebec plan in 1979. When Ontario gave up its opposition women in English Canada were finally able to enjoy the same pension protection as women in French Canada.

Pension Splitting. In the case of marriage dissolution, women's domestic labor is given some recognition through the splitting of pension entitlement between the couple. The credits earned by one or both spouses are equally divided between them, regardless of who paid more into the plan. Thus, housewives who have never contributed to the plan as well as those who contributed only intermittently or whose earnings were limited, are able to share in the pension credits of their spouse built up over the years they lived together. Couples must have lived together for at least one year. Spouses aged 60 and over can request equal sharing of retirement pensions acquired during the marriage even when there is neither divorce nor separation (ISSA, 1989).

PRIVATE PENSION PLANS

About half of all employees in Canada are covered by private pension plans and about half of all pension plans are in Ontario (Pittman, 1990). Employer-sponsored pension plans are subject to federal regulations if the business is considered to be a federal undertaking, such as banking. If this is not the case, the pension comes under the jurisdiction of the province where the largest number of the firm's workers are employed.

Provincial regulations of private plans vary significantly. Some provisional features include membership after two years of service subject to a minimum earnings requirement; a normal retirement age of not later than age 65; an entitlement to early retirement; a two-year vesting period; death benefits; indexing of certain benefits; and pension splitting on the dissolution of marriage (Pittman, 1990).

Employers may also participate in a retirement savings plan under the registered retirement savings plan (RRSP), which may be administered by employers on a group basis. Funds can be withdrawn totally or partially at any time prior to age 71. These funds can be used to purchase a lifetime annuity or a registered retirement income fund that provides annual payments to age 90. Employers may also pay up to Can $2,000 per year of service and an additional Can $1,500 per year of service that the worker was not a member of a pension plan to an RRSP.

HEALTH INSURANCE

Canada does not have a single national health insurance plan. Nationwide universal coverage is achieved through a series of interlocking provincial and territorial plans. The Hospital Insurance and Diagnostic Services Act of 1957 and the Medical Care Act of 1968 were designed to provide Canadians with health care services at no direct cost to patients.

Saskatchewan was the first province to introduce public health care, but because of vehement opposition by the medical profession the system did not become fully operational until 1971. The acts of 1957 and 1968 were combined and amended by the Canada Health Act of 1984. Under this act, the federal government contributes about half (the actual contribution varies from province to province) of the program's funding. In order to receive a federal contribution, each province's health insurance system must: (1) cover the entire resident population; (2) have portable benefits; (3) comprehensively cover all medically necessary hospital, physician, and surgical/dental procedures; (4) provide reasonable access to insured services without out-of-pocket expenses in the form of deductible coinsurance or extra billing; and (5) be publicly administered on a nonprofit basis.

A related feature of particular importance for the elderly population is that the federal government matches per-capita expenditures for long-term care. This matching program helps to fund nursing home intermediate care services, adult residential care, home care, and ambulatory care (Leader et al., 1988).

Administrative/Key Features

Each province has administrative autonomy within the federally mandated minimum criteria. The system allows for local experimentation, diversity, and expansion of basic benefits that are reflective of local needs and priorities. The funding mechanism, provider payments, amount of expenditures for health care, and cost containment measures are all decided by provincial governments (Leader et al., 1988).

Some of the key features in various provinces include negotiated fee schedules, control of technology through budgeting processes, physician income caps, free prescription drugs for the aged, mandatory private automobile insurance for medical coverage, and streamlined billing practices.

Funding

The share of funding from the provinces is derived from general revenues except in Alberta, British Columbia, and Ontario, where monthly premiums are assessed. Manitoba and Quebec levy a payroll tax on employers and supplement costs from general revenues. In Ontario, the most populated province, children continuing their education are covered by their parents' contributions until the age of twenty-one. Full-time students receive free coverage. Low-income earners qualify for premium assistance calculated in accordance with their net income. Social assistance recipients are automatically covered by provincial health plans.

Physicians are paid on a fee-for-service basis, which accounts for about 95 percent of the costs of insured medical services. The 1984 act outlawed the billing of patients above the fee schedule of provincial plans, which had become the practice of about 17 percent of physicians across the country to augment their incomes. Extra billing was viewed as inhibiting low-income persons from seeking medical services and the federal government had been withholding contributions to provincial plans to force the provincial governments to protect universal coverage and equality of access.

Policy Issues

The most serious threats to Canada's public health care system are the rapidly rising costs of physicians' services, medication, and the use of expensive technology. Doctors' incomes are about four times the national income average, which is slightly higher than it was before the introduction of the public scheme (Finn, 1983). There is agreement that if the system is not to become financially crippled by the turn of the century some drastic steps will have to be taken. One way of finding additional funds that has been suggested is to add the imputed costs of medical services to personal taxable income. This proposal would avoid the emergence of a two-class medical services system, but wealthier people would have to pay a larger share of the costs of their personal treatment (Kent, 1988).

CONCLUSION

In the context of the welfare state in Canada social insurance has been used as a powerful device for the rationing of income needs among individuals through premiums and contributions. The Canadian programs illustrate the strength of social insurance as a method for the pooling of collective resources against income loss, yet they also demonstrate its weakness. Social insurance, writes John Morgan (1969: 88), "is really only a valid instrument of income maintenance in situations where the risks and benefits can be directly related to those regularly employed." But wage levels too are important in defining the social validity of social insurance programs. Without decent wage levels and without full employment, the income needs of the long-term unemployed, the retired, or the disabled cannot be met without imposing a heavy tax burden on the economically active part of the population or producing substantive government deficits. While real wages have been declining and full employment seems a distant goal in the present economic and political conditions (unemployment currently runs at 8.4 percent), the continued pressure for fiscal constraints by the corporate sector in Canada can only lead to further demands that social needs must be largely paid for by the future beneficiaries themselves.

The deduction of social insurance premiums from wages will reduce the take-home pay of those in the labor force even further. The Canadian welfare state in its present form is not meant to reform the economic system but to require workers by law to provide for themselves and their families so that they can withstand the vagaries of capitalism (Gilbert, 1966). The attraction of social insurance based on actuarial principles remains "to help workers help themselves" without requiring a redistribution of resources from the rich to the poor.

REFERENCES

Armitage, A. (1975). *Social welfare in Canada: Ideals and realities*. Toronto: McClelland and Stewart.
Finn, E. (1983). *Medicare*. Ottawa: Canadian Centre for Policy Alternatives.
Gilbert, B. (1966). *The evolution of national insurance in Great Britain: The origin of the welfare state*. London: B. T. Batsford.
Guest, D. (1985). *The emergence of social security in Canada*. 2d ed. Vancouver: University of Toronto Press.

International Benefits Information Service. (1989, December). *Canada*, 37. Briefing Service. Chicago: Charles D. Spencer.

International Social Security Association. (1989). Development and trends in social security 1987–1989. *International Social Security Review* 42(3), 247–349.

Jennissen, T. (1981). The development of the workmen's compensation act of Ontario, 1914. *Canadian Journal of Social Work Education*, 7(1), 55–71.

Kent, T. (1988, February 20). The making of medicare. *Toronto Star*, M11.

Kitchen, B. (1980). Women and the social security system in Canada. *Atlantis*, 5(2), 89–99.

Leader, S., Guildroy, J., Kennan, S., Lehrmann, E., and Skinner, E. (1988). *The Canadian health care system: A special report on Quebec and Ontario.* Washington, D.C.: American Association of Retired Persons.

Marsh, L. (1975). *Report on social security for Canada, 1943.* Toronto: University of Toronto Press.

Morgan, J. S. (1969). An emerging system of income maintenance: Canada in transition. In Shirley Jenkins (ed.), *Social security in international perspectives: Essays in honor of Eveline Burns*, 105–128. New York: Columbia University Press.

Pittman, P. W. (1990). Employee benefits and compensation in Canada. *Benefits & Compensation International*, 17(7), 2–7.

Shragge, E., and Maclean, M. (1983). Canadian pension policy: A critical analysis. *Canadian Social Work Review*, 83, 77–92.

Statistics Canada. (1988). *Canada Year Book.* Ottawa: Census and Statistics Office.

U.S. Department of Health and Human Services. (1990). *Social security programs throughout the world—1989.* Social Security Administration. Office of Research and Statistics. Office of International Policy. Research Report No. 62. Washington, D.C.: U.S. Government Printing Office.

3

Chile

Joseph L. Scarpaci and Ernesto Miranda-Radic

Few countries in the western hemisphere have enacted such radical social security policies in the twentieth century as Chile. Chile's early history of industrialization and unionization led to the spread of old-age pension programs among the general public as early as 1924. Old-age pensions spread in a steady, yet piecemeal fashion until the 1970s, at which time a neoliberal model of economic development was introduced by the military regime. State- and employer-supported old-age pensions prevailed until 1981, when workers were given the option of continuing in public and union pension programs, or selecting private pension-fund administrators (AFPs). The privatization of social security in the 1980s stemmed from the larger restructuring of public services under military rule (Scarpaci, 1988).

HISTORICAL DEVELOPMENT

Chile, like its Southern Cone neighbors Argentina, Uruguay, and southern Brazil, entered the global economy much earlier than the rest of Latin America. Endowed with strategic minerals such as copper (Chile), oil (Argentina), and coal (southern Brazil), metallurgical industries were well established by 1900. The burgeoning Latin American export economies fostered even greater ties with Europe as the region looked to the Continent for markets as well as political and social ideas (Hale, 1986).

Bismarck's experience in Prussia with employer-funded health care and retirement programs was not unnoticed in the Southern Cone. European immigrants, mainly from Spain, Italy, France, Eastern Europe, and the former Ottoman territories provided skilled and semiskilled labor during the late nineteenth and early twentieth centuries. These immigrants organized mutual-aid societies (*sociedades mutualistas*) to provide burial funds, sickness and life insurance, and old-age pensions. The state also took an active role in funding social programs as the ideas of liberalism took hold throughout Latin America, but especially in the Southern Cone. "The classic liberal doctrines based on the autonomous individuals gave way to theories construing the individual as an integral part of the social organism" (Hale, 1986: 369).

The liberal heritage in funding old-age pension programs was clearly evident in Chile. Although the colonial, civil-servant pension programs (*montepios*) continued throughout the nineteenth century, landmark social security legislation was passed between 1880 and 1930. Under the presidency of José Manuel Balmaceda (1886–1891), civil servants received retirement pensions financed by public funds. In 1911 the powerful railroad workers, responsible for moving commodities throughout Chile's nearly 3,000-mile-long territory along the edge of western South America, were successful in pressing for retirement pensions.

Progressive social and political changes abroad in the first part of this century influenced social security legislation in Chile. The 1917 Bolshevik Revolution established a labor code that incorporated the principle of total insurance. In that same year, the Mexican Revolution created the Constitution of Mexico, which was the first in Latin America to include declarations about social security and labor rights. The founding of the International Labor Organization in 1919 resulted in international conventions on matters of social security and labor. Carmelo Mesa-Lago (1978) has noted that all these issues came to the fore in Chile during the 1920 presidential race. For the first time, blue-collar workers (*obreros*) and middle-class employees (*empleados*) worked together to establish social security and labor programs under the Liberal Alliance Party of President Arturo Alessandri Palma (1920–1924). This led to the creation of the Ministry of Labor and Social Security, the legal recognition of unions, and the establishment of insurance for occupational accidents and old-age pensions, thereby ending the parliamentary system and opening a progressive era of social and welfare reform (de Shazo, 1983).

Social security and labor reforms continued throughout the next half-century, varying only by the impetus of distinctive pressure groups. In general, groups with the greatest economic and political power received the most generous benefits. During the 1930s and 1940s, blue-collar workers were supported by the Radical party (a centrist social democratic party) and won protection for occupational diseases, and pensions were granted to blue- and white-collar workers, journalists, merchant marines, and racetrack workers. In the two decades following the Second World War various administrations complemented social security in important ways and in programs that were lacking full coverage. The shift in electoral politics to the left in the 1960s and 1970s brought attendant increases in the number of pressure groups that pushed for more legislation.

Groups that benefited from the progressive political period included white-collar workers (health-maternity care), the self-employed, and small employers. Significantly, neither the Christian Democratic government of Eduardo Frei

Table 3.1
Rate of Contributions under Old Social Security System, 1980
(as a percentage of taxable income)

Pension Funds[1]	Pensions only			Pensions and health care		
	workers	employer	total	worker	employer	total
Servicio Seguro Social						
	7.25	15.7	22.95	7.25	25.95	33.2
Caja Empleados Particulares (EMPART)						
	10.16	14.75	24.91	12.33	28.71	41.04
Caja Nacional Empleados Publicos (CANEMPU)						
	1 1	4.75	15.75	18.5	1 4	32.5
Average[2]	7.7	13.33	21.1	9.02	23.51	32.54

[1] Pension funds considered to account for approximately 95% of all affiliates.
[2] Affiliate-weighted averages.

Sources: Hernan Cheyre. 1988. La prevision en Chile: Ayer y Hoy. Santiago: Centro de Estudios Publicos, pp. 33-34; Superintendencia de Seguridad Social, Boletines.

(1964–1970) nor the Popular Unity coalition of Salvador Allende (1970–1973) was able to unify the many social security programs. In short, social security programs were highly duplicative in the amount and types of coverage and varied greatly in the levels of benefits (Mesa-Lago, 1978).

The checkered provision of old-age pensions created a social security system with a major advantage that perhaps was outweighed by several weaknesses. The principal advantage from the perspective of organized labor was that, unlike a privatized system, employers contributed at least the same amount as workers, and usually more (Table 3.1). The traditional old-age pension funds (*cajas de prevision*) were predominantly public. By the early 1980s, public funds accounted for about 30 percent of all social security payments but had fallen to levels of a decade earlier (Table 3.2).

The disadvantages of the old system, not at all unique to Chile, were many. Although the three largest funds covered about 95 percent of all workers (mostly public employees and salaried and manual workers in private industry), there existed 32 pension funds (*cajas de prevision*) in the late 1970s (Cheyre, 1988; Myers, 1986). No central public agency was responsible for the overall planning and policy making of social security programs. These features made the old system regressive in several ways. For example, pensions for blue-collar workers were fixed at 70 percent of their last years of salary whereas white-collar workers (*empleados*) could, in some funds, receive up to 100 percent. Blue-collar workers received pension funds based on wages earned during the last five years of

Table 3.2
State Contributions to Social Security Funds, 1968–1980

Year	Millions of 1986 Pesos	Index: 1968 = 100
1968	42,465.4	100.0
1969	n.a.	-
1970	68,126.6	160.4
1971	110,810.8	260.9
1972	103,297.2	243.3
1973	60,172.8	141.7
1974	54,355.3	128.0
1975	58,432.7	137.6
1976	52,639.9	124.0
1977	72,063.3	169.7
1978	73,486.6	173.1
1979	77,852.9	183.3
1980	91,919.9	216.5

Note: Exchange rate in 1986 was 192.93 pesos per US dollar.

Source: Superintendencia de Seguridad Social, cited in Cheyre 1988, p. 67.

their working lives, but the first two years of wages were adjusted for inflation. in computing benefit levels.

Pensions for salaried workers were determined after salaries were adjusted at the second of the last five working years, but used an index other than the one used for calculating the benefit levels of blue-collar workers. Another inequity that plagued social security under civilian administrations was the varied but usually low age of retirement that, for some salaried workers, was after 35 years of service, regardless of age (Myers, 1986). Although most programs mandated retirement at age 65 for men and 60 for women, there were exceptions; journalists could retire at 55 and bankers at 50. In the military, retirement could occur through seniority.

Within certain factions of the armed forces, personnel were eligible for retirement as early as 28 years of age (Mesa-Lago, 1978). In most of the *cajas de pension* affiliates could draw from more than one old-age fund, which led to duplicative and unequal benefits. Finally, the system was perennially underfinanced as a result of generous benefits and a steadily aging population.

One of the greatest inequities of the old social security system was that for some workers it pegged benefit levels to current salaries and not to lifetime earnings or pensioners' salary levels just prior to retirement or disability. This disbursement mechanism, called *perseguidoras* (literally, the "chasers") applied exclusively to high-level public white-collar employees, including the military. Beneficiaries were guaranteed social security payments that were the same as the current salaries of those working in the same position as the pensioners. Criticisms of the *perseguidora* method were that it was confined to the public sector (and thus led to political appointments), was generous to a fault, and was

Table 3.3
Relationship between Actives and Passives, 1960–1980

Year	Ratio
1960	10.8
1965	5.9
1970	4.3
1975	3.2
1980	2.2

Source: Superintendencia de Seguridad Social. Cited in Cheyre, 1988, p. 169.

inequitable compared to the inflation-adjusted method of granting benefits to affiliates of other *cajas de pension*.

The 1973 coup d'etat that deposed democratically elected Salvador Allende brought with it a strong backlash against public services. The predominant ideology that guided the military was that the state was inefficient and should assume a subsidiary role to an unfettered market economy (ODEPLAN, 1983). The regime set out to shrink the size of the public sector such that within the first seven years of its tenure nearly 400 state agencies were privatized (Ffrench-Davis, 1983).

The problem of underfinancing the former social security system (*cajas de prevision*) came to the forefront after World War II. An aging population and early retirement ages led to a widening gap between the ratio of actives to passives in the system (Table 3.3). Responses to the problem were usually to increase payroll deductions among both blue- (*obrero*) and white-collar (*empleados*) workers as well as to raise state contributions derived from tax revenues.

The magnitude of the former social security system was evidenced by the 32 social security programs that operated in 1980, three of which covered 95 percent of all workers (Table 3.4). These programs, moreover, provided wide-ranging benefits given the ambiguous labor laws. As a result, high administrative costs plagued the system. Benefit levels were inequitable in that they were largely determined by the salary level of workers in the years just before retirement as opposed to the actual amounts of lifelong contributions. These inequities led not only to cross-subsidies among different social security plans, but made the system highly vulnerable to political manipulation.

THE NEW CHILEAN OLD-AGE PENSION FUNDS (AFPs)

With the old social security system as a backdrop, we can identify seven major objectives that the Social Security Reform (*Reforma Previsional*) of 1981 set out to achieve. A first objective aims to eliminate the inequities of the older system in a manner consistent with the economic and ideological principles of the military regime.

The principal feature of the new system is a set of standardized norms for all workers regardless of the new social security fund to which they belong. Particularly noteworthy is the creation of the individual annuity account (*cuenta de*

Table 3.4
Enrollment in Chilean Social Security Funds (*Cajas de Pension*), 1980

Fund	(A) Affiliates	(B) Pensioners	(A)/(B) Dependency Ratio	Disbursments US $mill.
Servicio de Seguro				
Social	1,394,300	508,808	2.74	$364.7
EMPART	430,000	98,264	4.38	116.8
(Caja Empleados Particulares)				
CANAEMPU				
(Caja Nacional de Empleados Publicos y Periodistas)				
(public employees)	264,195	103,602	2.55	236.9
(journalists)	15,763	15,337	1.03	18.5
Caja Bancarias de Pensiones(bankers)	15,820	4,272	3.70	11.1
TRIOMAR	29,101	8,763	3.39	13.4
(merchant marines)				
CAPREMER	24,805	7,230	3.83	17.6
(merchant marines)				
Railroad	9,919	42,177	0.25	81.1
Empleados Municipales[1]				
(Municipal Workers)	7,916	6,606	1.20	12.0
Obreros Municipales de la Republica				
(municipal workers)	12,684	7,572	1.70	6.2
Armed Forces and National Police	n.a.	87,901	n.a.	469.7
Other funds	42,248	15,793	2.68	308.6
TOTAL	2,226,931	1,047,325	2.13	1,476.6

[1]Includes the funds Caja de Empleados Municipales de la Republica.

Source: Boletin Seguridad Social: Estadisticas 1981 - 1982 - 1983. Santiago: Superintendencia de Seguridad Social, Departamento Actuarial, 1985, pp. 15-16 and 39-48.

capitalizacion individual) for each worker. These accounts are comprised of the monthly contributions by each worker and collectively form the pension fund of each particular social security program, the AFPs. The AFPs aim to maximize these funds by optimizing their risk-return profile. Pension funds remain active throughout the lifetime of workers and their dependents and are determined by national insurance standards. Benefits for disability and premature death are covered by insurance premiums paid by workers while the state guarantees minimum pensions. These minimum pensions are maintained by a state subsidy and are used when the pension funds of individuals are too small to guarantee minimum levels of benefits.

A second goal of the reforms seeks to end the majority of the cross-subsidies that characterized the pay-as-you-go method under the traditional *cajas de prevision* system. Cross-subsidies exist only for cases of survival insurance and disability (which do not differentiate by health status) or for minimum pensions. This practice provides beneficiaries and investors with accurate information about investments (*transparencia*) and sets benefit levels according to individual (versus group) contributions.

A third objective was to eliminate active voucher pay for retired persons (*pacto intergeneracional*). In essence, the aging of the population and increased life expectancy meant fewer active workers per pensioner. Thus the level of dependency of pensioners on workers increased markedly while the former lost much of their negotiating power. The active voucher pay for retired persons (*pacto intergeneracional*), therefore, worked against the interests of retired persons.

A fourth objective is to improve the efficiency of the social security system by establishing unified laws and norms. One such law is that each AFP remains a publicly-held firm with more than 100 shareholders. These shareholders cannot be contributors to the pension funds. Following the logic of neoclassical economic theory, the AFPs are expected to generate competition and maximize returns on investments so that workers receive the greatest possible pension. It is in this regard that the free-market ideology of the regime is most apparent: AFP investments in near-perfect competitive market conditions are expected to solve the problem of underfinancing at the lowest possible cost to the firm and the state.

A fifth goal is to implement the so-called Subsidiary Role of the State Principle (*Principio de Subsidiario del Estado*). This principle contends that the provision of social insurance of all forms, including social security, should be left to the private sector as much as possible. Unlike the state, the private sector would be motivated by the profit principle, which, in turn, would generate more efficient social security coverage through careful investments of pension funds. Moreover, the quality of coverage would be improved while the costs for workers would be reduced to a minimum. It is noteworthy that this principle allows sufficient economic space and market deregulation so that the private sector takes full advantage of optimum market conditions. Strict and efficient state guidelines for ensuring the fulfillment of AFP operations, coupled with astute private-sector administration, would allow for the attainment of optimal goals.

A sixth goal is to isolate the social security system from political manipulation. Workers under the new AFP system are all subject to the same obligations and legal guidelines. Cross-subsidies have been eliminated (except for survival insurance as noted above), mechanisms for providing direct subsidies based on tax revenues have been incorporated into the new system, and information about the yields and balances of pension funds as well as individual accounts are public information. These features serve as safeguards against preferential treatment or political manipulation. In essence, an individual pension account with the AFPs has become a fundamental part of the regime's concept of private property.

Perhaps the most significant goal of the reforms is to ensure that each worker's individual annuity fund remains a part of that worker's patrimony. The goal is to encourage workers to take responsibility for their own contributions to these social security funds during their working lives. As a result, there is much incentive for workers to place their payroll deductions in the AFPs and not to try to avoid social security deductions. Many contend that this feature of not avoiding payroll deductions was absent under the old social security system. Also workers would be expected to be the first ones to object to any sort of preferential treatment granted to groups of pension fund contributors in case subsidies are granted based on workers' pension funds. In brief, the regime has emphasized a new concept of private property that allows workers direct control over their contributions to the social security system. Worker control over individual retirement accounts is the fundamental pillar of the social security reforms enacted under military rule.

Affiliation and Payroll Deductions

Both the self-employed and those who work for others are allowed to affiliate with AFPs. In the case of those who work for others, however, affiliation is mandatory while the self-employed join an AFP only if they choose to do so. The incorporation of the self-employed into the social security system aims to increase the coverage of the labor force.[1] All workers are permitted to select an AFP of their choice and they may change from one AFP to another at any time.

Pension funds consist of mandatory payroll deductions that are 10 percent of taxable income (Table 3.5), this latter amount being limited to the value of UF (*Unidad de Fomento*) 60.[2] Workers can voluntarily extend this ceiling up to UF 120 and still remain exempt from being taxed on this amount. In January 1988 workers were allowed to set up a retirement savings account (*cuenta de ahorro voluntario*), which is similar to individual retirement accounts in the United States. These accounts also form part of each AFP pension fund, but are registered separately from the individual annuity accounts. These retirement savings accounts also enjoy tax-exempt status. Employers deduct amounts that workers wish to allocate to these savings accounts. Unlike the individual pension funds, workers can draw from these accounts up to four times a year. AFPs charge a

Table 3.5
Rate of Contributions under the AFP System, 1988

AFP	Trait	Fixed[1] Contribution (Monthly)	DIB[2] & AFP Revenue	Rate of Contribution Pension Fund[3]	Total[4]	Health	Total Social Security
Habitat	low rate	125	3.30%	10%	13.55%	7%	20.55%
Invierta	high rate	497	3.97%	10%	14.96%	7%	21.96%
Provida	largest	258	3.48%	10%	14.00%	7%	21.00%
AFP Average[5]		239	3.65%	10%	14.13%	7%	21.13%

1. Fixed commission per AFP affiliate.
2. Consists of an insurance premium (renegotiated by the AFP for its affiliates and affiliates' taxable income-variable revenue).
3. Mandated by law to form the individual funds.
4. Estimated for the average taxable income per affiliate.
5. Affiliate-weighted average.

Source: Superintendencia de AFP, Boletín Estadístico Mensual, 1988 and 1989. Santiago, Chile.

small commission for each withdrawal. Retired workers can add these savings as part of their retirement benefits.

Benefits

Three types of payment structures exist for social security payments made for old-age, disability, and survivor insurance: fixed lifetime income, temporary income, or temporary income with deferred lifetime income. Old-age pensions are granted when male workers reach 65 years of age and when women turn 60. Pension amounts are based on 70 percent of the inflation-adjusted average of all wages and salaries earned during the ten years before retirement. This formula assumes, of course, that workers have contributed sufficiently to the funds. Because the AFP system is less than ten years old, these payments are currently based on transfers from the old pension system (*cajas de prevision*), and are issued through transfer vouchers (*bonos de reconocimiento*) that workers must activate in order to bring their previous social security payments into the new AFP system. Current old-age pensions can also be based on the voluntary retirement savings accounts and state contributions (in cases of minimum pensions established by law).

Disability pensions are granted when workers lose at least two-thirds of the ability to perform their job. Essentially, the financial mechanisms of the disability pensions are the same as old-age pensions, but are financed by payroll deductions that are especially earmarked for disability insurance. Insurance complements the pension derived from regular retirement financing so that all sources of financing amount to 70 percent of the income level just prior to disability.

In the case of survivor insurance, the family members are the designated beneficiaries. Family members can receive benefits when the affiliated worker dies, becomes disabled, or retires. Survivor insurance is also funded by survival and disability insurance as well as regular retirement financing.

In each of the three types of pensions under the AFP system the worker (or his or her designated family beneficiary) is able to opt for one of three payment structures. One consists of a fixed lifetime income (*renta vitalicia*) disbursed by an insurance company. This lifetime income covers workers while they live as well as their designated beneficiaries (survivors) as long as they fulfill the stipulated requirements. The major advantage of the fixed lifetime income is that payments are constant and are adjusted for inflation.

A second type of pension is the temporary-income method (*retiro pactado*) in which the retired worker designates a fixed monthly payment until the time of death. Any remaining funds that have not been expended up until the time of death are distributed among the designated beneficiaries in the same way as the lifetime income (assuming there are sufficient funds in the worker's AFP account).

The third payment structure, temporary income with deferred lifetime income (*renta temporal con renta vitalicia diferida*), is a combination of the previous two methods. The chief feature of this method is that benefits are disbursed prior to the death of the pensioner. Temporary income benefits span a specified period of time determined by the pensioner. When this period expires, the pensioner signs up with an insurance company in the same way stipulated by the lifetime income disbursement method. Thus the advantage of both the temporary income with lifetime income and the agreed retirement disbursement methods is that they allow workers to schedule benefit levels according to anticipated short-term expenses that they will incur immediately following retirement.

Pension Funds

The pension funds of the AFPs are comprised of the individual social security accounts and voluntary savings accounts within each AFP. The administrator of each pension fund (i.e., the AFP itself), just like the case of mutual funds, is not the owner of these funds. Rather, the main purpose of the administrator is to invest the funds in order to maximize rates of return.

These rates of return of investments, the monthly charges for handling each account, and the quality of the service (punctuality of sending periodic account statements, courtesy of AFP workers, and perhaps the geographic accessibility to various AFP offices) are the only features of the AFPs that set each administrator apart.

The law has tacitly identified the nature of AFP investments in order to set limits on risk taking and speculation. Areas of investment are confined to:

• government securities
• time deposits issued by financial institutions
• securities guaranteed by financial institutions
• credit notes issued by financial institutions
• private and state corporation debentures
• other AFP pension fund shares
• stocks of public corporations that have been previously approved by a state agency that assesses risk (called the Comision Clasificadora de Riesgo, or the Risk Classification Commission)

The law also establishes a set of rules on diversifying risk. These rules are identified according to the type of investment and firm in which the funds are placed. At present, no more than 20 percent of the funds of an AFP can be invested as stocks in a limited number of public corporations. In addition to the incentives for investing adequately and taking the necessary precautions in investing these social security funds, the law also stipulates that the rate of return for any AFP pension fund cannot be less than two percentage points of the average profit level of all AFPs, or 50 percent less than this average, or the lesser amount of the two (Figure 3.1, section c). In instances where the rate of return of the funds administered by the AFPs is less than the amounts stipulated above (Figure 3.1, section d), the AFP covers the difference by a combination

Figure 3.1
Rate of Return for AFP Pension Funds

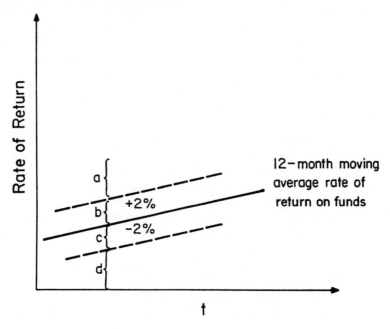

Section a: Surplus yield (average rate of return plus 2% points)
              constitutes a reserve of profit earnings.

Sections b and c: Yield within acceptable range; increase at value of
              the pension fund.

Section d: Deficit yield; individual pension fund yields less than is
              legally mandated acceptable return. Difference is
              covered by:
                        - reserve of profits (section a); if insufficient,
                        - AFP reserves are used. If still insufficient,
                        - State funds are tapped.

of two mechanisms: by a reserve of profit earnings accumulated in previous
periods by the particular AFP for all earnings above the average rate of return;
or by employing a reserve (*encaje*) in the amount of one percent of total funds
that each AFP is required to maintain by law. If these two methods are insufficient
(Figure 3.1, section d) the state is required to insure the difference.

Investment and Financing

AFPs are regulated by the *Superintendencia de Administradoras de Pensiones*,
a public agency belonging to the Ministry of Labor and Social Security (*Minis-*

Table 3.6
Annual Real Yield of the Pension Fund, 1981–1989 (deflated by the CPI)

AFP	Average Annual Yield	1988
	(6/81 - 1/89)	
Concordia	14.2	5.6
Cuprum	13.5	6.1
El Libertador	12.4	5.1
Habitat	13.1	4.7
Invierta	13.4	7.0
Magister	13.0	5.4
Planvital	13.2	5.5
Proteccion	a	6.0
Provida	13.5	4.6
Santa Maria	13.0	4.0
Summa	13.4	4.7
Union	14.7	5.4
Average	13.4	4.8

a. Activities since 1986 only.

Source: Banco Central de Chile, <u>Boletin Mensual</u> No. 734, April 1989, Santiago.

terio del Trabajo y Prevision Social). This agency has broad legal powers and may apply sanctions to all AFPs that violate the law. To date, nearly 90 percent of AFP investments are at least partially guaranteed by the government; about 40 percent is invested in purely public enterprises and 50 percent is invested in private financial institutions (stock brokers, savings and loans, banks). The remaining 10 percent is invested in stocks of public corporations whose level of risk has been assessed by the Risk Classification Commission. The average annual rate of return on AFP pension funds for the period 1981–1988 was 13.4 percent, but showed a steady decline such that it amounted to 4.8 percent in 1988 (Table 3.6).

Expected Benefit Levels

Benefit levels are expected to be higher under the AFP system than the old system for several reasons. First, the old system will eventually fade away because all workers entering the labor force since 1981 must enter an AFP of their choice. The *cajas de previsión* should disappear by the end of the first quarter of the twenty-first century. All pensions will then depend on funds accumulated by workers and not on a relatively decreasing stock of active workers' contributions.

Second, competition among the AFPs is expected to create greater net yields (returns of funds invested less administrative costs) of funds. Those AFPs that attain lower net yields are expected to lose market share, while those that invest the most profitably and operate at the lowest administrative costs should attract more affiliates.

Third, workers can open a voluntary savings account in addition to the individual annuity account administered by the AFP. Recall that these savings accounts are managed by the AFP and allow workers to make withdrawals up to four times a year.

Fourth, strict guidelines have been established as a backstop against risky investments and the use of workers' old-age pensions as venture capital. As an example, AFPs are not allowed to invest more than 5 percent of their funds into any single firm. These should reduce the size of the losses.

Fifth, there exists a minimum acceptable rate of return, related to the average rate of return for all AFPs. The logic here is that the variation in payments to workers who have had similar salary histories and who are affiliated with different AFPs should not be great. Ultimately, as discussed previously, the government must guarantee all investments (see Figure 3.1).

Finally, the potential under the new system for generating greater returns should translate into greater self-financed pensions for workers. Supporters of the AFP pension system argue that in the long run pension levels could approach 70 percent of workers' wages in the final years of their working life. Currently, retired workers receive the full pension corresponding to their individual annuity accounts. But widows receive about 60 percent of the pension; with one surviving child the amount rises to 65 percent and then increases 15 percent for each living child.

Because the new AFPs have been in operation only since 1981, a transfer voucher (*bono de reconocimiento*) exists to transfer contributions from the old system to the AFPs. It is paid to all workers who had at least 12 months of coverage under the old system during the last 60 months before the creation of AFPs in 1981. Transfers from the old system (state-financed) to the AFPs are adjusted according to the Consumer Price Index (CPI) of mid–1978 (when a new CPI was put into effect) and then subsequently earn 4 percent interest annually.

Coverage

As of December 1988 there were 13 AFPs that accounted for just over 3 million affiliates (Table 3.7). This covers about 25 percent of the total population and about 75 percent of the labor force. The great majority of these AFP affiliates transferred from the old *caja de previsión* system, and since 1981, all new entrants into the formal-sector labor force are required to join an AFP of their choice. Table 3.7 shows the average ratio of actives to affiliates, 0.731, which is rather low. In other words, about 30 percent of the workers do not consistently contribute to the system. Consequently, the chances of underfinancing the AFP pension system is very high. Legally, those workers are supported by state-guaranteed pensions that are drawn from tax revenues. Although no clear-cut explanation exists for this phenomenon, it may be attributable to the high proportion of self-employed workers, high unemployment rates, and changes in hiring practices over time. This latter trend refers to the increasingly favorable conditions that result from employing part-time workers.

Table 3.7
AFP Affiliates and Active/Affiliate Ratio, 1988

Pension Fund	Number of Affiliates	Ratio of Active/Affiliate
Concordia	97,843	0.601
Cuprum	39,843	0.758
El Libertador	77,132	0.592
Futuro	2,051	1.000
Habitat	498,738	0.775
Invierta	144,024	0.550
Magister	53,550	0.912
Plan Vital	87,192	0.587
Proteccion	18,959	0.996
Provida	901,476	0.737
Santa Maria	650,822	0.701
Summa	281,855	0.697
Union	330,124	0.610
Total:	3,183, 609	Average: 0.731

Note: The number of active contributors to the AFPs is much smaller than indicated by the data because the self-employed workers do not regularly contribute.

Sources: <u>Boletin Mensual Santiago</u>. Banco Central de Chile, April 1989, p. 1176 & <u>Boletin Estadistico Mensual</u>. Superintendencia AFP, December 1988.

The concentration of affiliates in the AFPs is fairly high: the two largest AFPs (Provida and Habitat) account for 50 percent of the market share and the four largest incorporate nearly 75 percent (Table 3.7). One explanation for this could be the economies of scale of AFP operations, which, over time, could increase and further concentrate market share.

Benefits of AFPs

AFPs have invested heavily in the past in public bonds and securities (Table 3.8). As of December 1988, these latter amounted to U.S. $1.12 million, which is roughly 25 percent of all pension funds. The government used these funds to finance current operation deficits, mostly associated with financing pensions of the old social security system. As Table 3.8 shows, this source of financing was increasingly used up until 1986 (in tandem with the economic downturn of the early 1980s), but has since sharply reduced its relevance. Critics argue that by reducing welfare benefits those funds were reallocated to finance pensions of the old social security system.

Reductions in securities' investments have accelerated the new infusion of capital in Chilean AFPs. Although it has not been proven, it is thought that the increase in the average share of the Santiago Stock Exchange is closely related to this trend. The methodological difficulties in tracing this relationship are many, however, and few studies have been able to corroborate this association. With the return to civilian rule in March 1990, it may be possible to further investigate

Table 3.8
Pension Fund Investments in Securities, 1981–1988 (in 1986 U.S. $ mill.)

	Holdings (each December)	Rate of Increase	Annual Flows
1981	47.5	--	47.1
1982	135.7	188.1	88.6
1983	420.5	209.9	284.8
1984	524.0	24.6	103.5
1985	728.7	39.1	204.7
1986	1,048.0	43.8	319.3
1987	1,141.9	9.0	93.9
1988	1,196.0	4.7	54.1

Source: Superintendencia de AFP, <u>Boletin Estadistico Nacional</u>, Santiago. Cited in Cheyre 1988, pp. 94 and 97.

the relationships among AFP investment, securities, and foreign debt. In 1988 the Chilean debt reached U.S. $1.2 billion, which translated into one of the highest per-capita debt levels in the region. Chile has been prompt in meeting payments of interest on its debt as evidenced by the high percentage (55%) of the nominal value that its foreign debt reaches on secondary markets; only the Colombian debt has a slightly higher value (CEPAL, 1988).

One economist (Cheyre, 1989) has argued that some portion of the AFPs should be invested outside of Chile as a means of diversifying systematic risk and increasing yields. Estimates revealed that if an average-salaried worker had joined an AFP in 1981, worked until age 65, and had one percent of the contributions invested in the United States at a fixed rate of return, the monthly pension would be roughly U.S. $44 greater than funds invested in Chile. Critics of this position claim that profit should not be the sole determinant of investment levels. Rather, investment in the national patrimony should take priority over investments outside Chile.

Policy Issues

The new private social security system in Chile has had a fairly successful track record in the short time it has been operative. It has provided greater accountability. The use of market criteria has generated greater yields than under the older system, and its economies of scale have produced generally lower operating costs. To be sure, however, its fiscal soundness remains to be tested with the return of a democratic regime in March 1990. Because the fundamental premises behind the creation of the private old-age pension funds were established in the absence of any parliamentary body, organized labor and the newly elected congress are likely to debate some key issues in the 1990s.

First, we may expect organized labor to demand greater employer contributions to AFPs. The 1980s were relatively prosperous for the business community in Chile, and labor may demand greater employer contributions to workers' welfare. A related question is whether workers will demand these increases in the form of pension contributions or (directly) as wage increases. This issue is related to the larger question of whether investments of social security funds should favor individual or collective interests.

A second issue involves AFP investment and the percentage of investments guaranteed by either the state or AFP agencies. At an ideological level the debate is likely to center on whether old-age pension funds should be invested at all and, if so, to what extent full guarantee of investment should be established by law. At an administrative level, there will likely be a review of firms and sectors of the economy that should be given priority for the receipt of AFP-invested funds. This discussion will hinge on ways of resolving the high per-capita debt problem that will afflict Chile in the years to come. Related to this issue is whether the investors (i.e., the able-bodied labor force) should incur the costs of marketing. Also, should such large sums of money be invested in sectors of the economy with questionable redistributive benefits such as profits for the corporate sector as opposed to investments in social welfare areas like housing, education, or health care?

Finally, workers who are presently dissatisfied with AFPs are unable to return to the old *caja de previsión* system of old-age retirement. As well, new workers must select an AFP when they enter the labor force. Thus, there may be some legal provision to allow beneficiaries to return to the old system. Workers with vested interests in the old system may pressure congress to mandate this option, although the assets of the *cajas* are very meager compared to the AFPs.

CONCLUSION

By creating private old-age pension funds the Chilean military government attempted to eliminate a number of irregularities in benefit levels and entitlements. AFPs have the additional advantage of providing huge amounts of capital that can be used for targeted areas of investment. The extent to which these funds are tied to the problem of financing the national debt and stimulating private sector-financed economic development is an empirical question that has not been examined in this chapter, although it seems evident that the relationship exists.

The private old-age pension funds in Chile have shifted the incentive of workers to increase contributions to their own individual funds. The legal structures currently guarantee fixed income levels based on worker contributions. In doing so, the problem of underfinancing that plagued the old *caja* system should not develop. As well, levels of benefits have been fairly standardized in both the public and private sectors. While the ten-year-old system has not begun to disburse large amounts of funds, the evidence to date suggests that a competitive investment climate will continue to emerge and that old-age pensions in the twenty-first century will count on unprecedented levels of private capital.

NOTES

1. In practice, this has not happened for two main reasons: high levels of unemployment between 1981 and 1987 and changes in hiring that have increased those workers classified as self-employed (including women). See Prentice, 1988.

2. The *Unidad de Fomento* is a standardized value used for keeping track of inflation. Mortgages, credit loans, and assessments of income levels often use UFs in order to translate rising costs into constant, deflated pesos. The UF is adjusted daily, is a standard reporting item in the financial and daily news, and serves as a sort of barometer of inflation. In July 1989 a single unit of the UF equaled $4,870 Chilean pesos, which has an official rate of about U.S. $2,508. Thus in the example in the text, all workers earning more than UF 60 (U.S. $1,169 monthly) would pay the same 10 percent rate of U.S. $117, or $29,250 Chilean pesos toward their social security fund.

REFERENCES

CEPAL (Comisión Economica para America Latana). (1988). *Notas sobre la economia y del desarrollo*, No. 470/471. Santiago: United Nations.

Cheyre, H. (1988). *La previsión en Chile: Ayer y Hoy*. Santiago: Centro de Estudios Publicos.

———. (1989, June 12). Talk presented on AFP financing in Chile. Santiago, Chile.

de Shazo, P. (1983). *Urban workers and labor unions in Chile: 1902–1927*. Madison: University of Wisconsin Press.

Ffrench-Davis, R. (1983). *El experimento monetarista en Chile*. Coleccion Estudios CIEPLAN, 9, 5–40.

Hale, C. (1986). Political and social ideas in Latin America, 1870–1930. In L. Bethell (ed.), *The Cambridge history of Latin America*, 367–643. Cambridge: Cambridge University Press.

Mesa-Lago, C. (1978). *Social security in Latin America: Pressure groups, stratification, and inequality*. Pittsburgh: University of Pittsburgh Press.

Miranda-Radic, E. (1988). *Administradoras de fondos de pensiones para trabajadores Empresa Nacional de Carbon S.A.* (mimeo).

Myers, R. (1986). *Privatización en Chile del sistema de seguridad social*. In S. Baeza (ed.), *Análisis de la Previsión en Chile*, 13–34. Santiago: Centro de Estudios Públicos.

ODEPLAN. (1983). *Informe anuario*. Santiago: Oficina de la Presidencia de la Republica, ODEPLAN.

Prentice, W. (1988). *Industrial promotion in Tierra del Fuego, Argentina: The feminization of labor and poverty in the electronics industry*. San Diego: Department of Political Science, University of California (mimeo).

Scarpaci, J. L. (1988). *Primary medical care in Chile: Accessibility under military rule*. Pittsburgh: University of Pittsburgh Press.

4

China

Lillian Liu

The People's Republic of China (PRC) was founded in 1949. At present, it is an economically less-developed country with one-fifth of the world's population. The over one billion people are unevenly distributed in a land area of 9.6 million square kilometers, only slightly larger than the United States. Because two-thirds of the land is mountainous or semidesert and only about one-tenth is cultivated, some 90 percent of the population live on one-sixth of the land, concentrated in the plains and deltas of the eastern part of the country.

Partly due to the great majority of the population engaged in agricultural pursuit and partly because of the government's deliberate policies in restricting the expansion of its urban sector up until 1984, more than 75 percent of the population was considered rural until that time. In 1984, the government expanded the urban sector by reclassifying formerly rural towns as cities (Banister, 1986). This move reduced the number of rural population in 1987 to less than 55 percent of the total. Still, almost 75 percent of the country's civilian labor force was engaged in agricultural pursuits (see Table 4.1).

Historically, the PRC government has committed itself to a high level of activities promoting the welfare of the population relative to the nation's economic development. The country's Gross National Product ranks among the lowest one-fourth in the world, while its life expectancy and infant mortality rate rank among the top 25 percent among over 100 nations (*World Bank Atlas*, 1987). During the last forty years, the PRC government's efforts in improving health care have increased life expectancy and reduced the death rate (Banister, 1987; Jamison, 1985).

China's population has more than doubled since 1949. The average life expectancy at birth increased from just about 40 years in the early 1950s to about 66 years by 1984. By the end of this century it is expected to reach 71 years

Table 4.1
Population and Labor Force in the People's Republic of China, 1952–1987, Select Years (in millions)

	1952	1965	1978	1985	1986	1987
Total Population	574.82	725.38	962.59	1050.44	1065.29	1080.73
Rural	503.19	594.93	790.14	665.98	624.26	577.11
(% of Total)	88%	82%	82%	63%	58%	53%
Urban	71.63	130.45	172.45	384.46	441.03	503.62
(% of Total)	13%	18%	18%	37%	41%	47%
Civilian Labor Force	207.29	286.7	401.52	498.73	512.82	527.83
(% of Total Population)	36%	40%	42%	48%	48%	49%
Rural	182.43	235.34	306.38	370.65	379.9	390
(% of Labor Force)	88%	82%	76%	74%	74%	74%
Urban	24.86	51.36	95.14	128.08	132.92	137.83
(% of Labor Force)	12%	18%	24%	26%	26%	26%

Note: In 1984 the Chinese government redefined "urban areas" to inclued the newly formed townships and the like. Residents in these townships are now part of the urban population, thus contributing to the rapid increase in urban population.

Source: Chinese Statistical Yearbook, 1988.

(Liangjin, 1990). The 1953 national census reported 4.5 million aged 60 and over. The number of persons in this age group reached 80 million in 1985, accounting for 8.2 percent of the population, and will attain 11 percent by the year 2000 (Liangjin, 1990; CASS, 1988).

China's welfare system is a combination of state and collective programs providing a network of income security, medical care, and social assistance. From the 1950s to 1978, the country's income security and welfare policies for its urban and rural populations evolved in tandem with its political and economic institutions.

The establishment of the People's Republic of China by the Chinese Communist party (CCP) in 1949 ushered in a new era during which the CCP-ruled government restructured the nation's economic system from a market-dominated economy to a centrally planned economy modeled after the system then extant in the Soviet Union. A great majority of private industries and commerce were incorporated into the government-controlled "state sector," whereby their production, profits, and losses became part of the state plans. A large state apparatus appeared as the government also took control of all scientific, educational, and cultural institutions.

Outside the state sector, private ownership was gradually phased out. Urban collectives for industry, commerce, and service were organized as transitional economic institutions before advancement into the state sector (Tang and Ma, 1985). In rural areas, the state took over land ownership, replacing private farming with collective production and accounting. Communes were set up in 1958 as administrative and economic entities of rural life and agricultural production.

Consequently, the majority of China's urban labor force had the protection of formal, established government-guaranteed income security, and enjoyed extensive in-kind and cash benefits with established rules and regulations applicable nationwide. The rural labor force, on the other hand, had primarily in-kind benefits provided by communes (see Table 4.2).

LEGISLATIVE HISTORY

Two sets of regulations provide income security for state-sector employees—the enterprise labor insurance and government/institution programs. They first appeared in the early 1950s and, although developed separately initially, later converged to adopt similar provisions. From 1958 to 1978, these two programs provided workers comparable benefits, and both had the total financial backing of the central government (Davis-Friedman, 1985). In the 1980s, however, these two programs began to develop along different paths as a result of economic reforms.

Because of likely divergent future developments for the two programs, and for purposes of comparing with social insurance systems in other countries, the labor insurance program for state-sector enterprise workers is considered in this chapter as the principal program for workers in industry and commerce, and the government/institution program is treated as the special scheme for civil servants.

Enterprise Labor Insurance (1949–1978)

In 1951, the government promulgated labor insurance regulations (LIR, Laodong Baoxian Tiaoli), thereby introducing China's first income security system for enterprise employees nationwide. The 1951 regulations (as amended in 1953) and the 1958 provisional (draft) regulations regarding the retirement of workers and staff, were the basic documents that governed income security programs for state-enterprise workers.

Participating enterprises initially included those in the state sector and those under joint state-private management, private ownership, or collective ownership. By 1956, about 94 percent of all the enterprises adopted the LIR (Wang et al., 1987). As privately owned enterprises were fast disappearing and a majority of enterprise workers became incorporated into the state sector, these

Table 4.2

Labor Insurance Coverage and Employment by Sector, 1978 and 1985

(in millions)

	1978			1985		
	Total Workers	Covered Workers	Percent Covered	Total Workers	Covered Workers	Percent Covered
URBAN LABOR FORCE						
	95.14	88.85	93%	128.08	112.68	88%
State Sector:	74.51	74.51/a	100%	89.90	89.90/a	100%
A. Labor Insurance						
State Enterprises:	59.55	59.55/a	100%	66.67	66.67/a	100%
B. Civil Service						
Gov't, Party, & other inst./b:	14.96	14.96/a	100%	23.22	23.22/a	100%
Collective Sector:	20.48	14.34/a	70%	33.24	22.78/a	69%
Private Sector:	.15	none		4.50	none	
Others/c	--	--		.44	none	
RURAL LABOR FORCE/d:	306.38	n.a.		370.65	n.a.	

a. Estimate based on total number of workers in both State and collective enterprises.
b. Includes government, party institutions and cultural, educational, scientific, and other institutions.
c. These include joint state/collective, state/private, joint foreign-PRC enterprises, etc.
d. Rural communes were established in 1958 and abolished in 1982-1985.

Sources: Chinese Statistical Yearbook, 1988.
Chinese Social Statistical Materials, 1987.

regulations covered workers in all state enterprises. These workers constituted almost 63 percent of China's total urban labor force in 1978.

The LIR provided cash benefits for old-age, survivor, and disability insurance (OASDI). The LIR also provided cash benefits for sickness and maternity, free medical care, and work injury. There were no provisions for unemployment because, in theory, the socialist economy predicated full employment. In 1986, however, the government promulgated its first unemployment insurance program to be implemented by local governments.

The OASDI programs were financed by individual enterprises. Employees did not contribute. According to the 1953 LIR, each enterprise submitted to the People's Bank an amount equal to 3 percent of its payroll as the labor insurance fund. Thirty percent of this monthly contribution was deposited in an account for the All-China Trade Unions to set up welfare facilities for the aged, disabled, and other labor insurance-related expenses. The remainder went to the enterprise's trade union account for benefit payments. Surpluses from the monthly expenditures at the enterprise level would be submitted to municipal, provincial, or ministerial administration (depending on enterprise affiliation) for resource pooling (Fujian Province Revolutionary Committee, 1973). The central government routinely subsidized program expenditures in case of shortfalls (Davis-Friedman, 1985).

Trade union organizations at the enterprise level administered the programs. Government labor insurance offices at all levels had the oversight of the financing and administration of labor insurance programs. They also processed appeals from workers over labor insurance disputes (Fujian Province Revolutionary Committee, 1973).

Political upheavals during the Cultural Revolution (1966–1976) caused de facto changes in the perception of "pensions" and in the funding and administration of labor insurance programs, even though LIR provisions remained untouched. Contemporary "radical" political factions regarded "pensions" as "capitalistic" and retirement as "antisocialist" behavior. The abolition of all trade union organizations brought an end to resource pooling via national and local trade union organizations. Moreover, the responsibility of administering labor insurance programs fell on enterprise employees themselves (Davis, 1988; Wang et al., 1987). These changes were to bring about unexpected problems in the 1980s under economic reform initiatives.

From 1978 to the Present

Since 1978, the PRC government has set out to modernize the country's economic and social institutions. Income security programs have been in a state of flux, interacting with the government's modernization initiatives. The LIR were amended in 1978 by "provisional procedures for retirement and disability" (Gongren Tuixiu Tuizhi de Zhanxin Banfa) to encourage retirement and to place youths in the workforce. These new provisions relaxed qualifying conditions, improved benefit levels, created a minimum pension, and added new categories of grants and subsidies.

In 1986 the government took the first step in setting up a different pension system for some newly hired state-sector employees. The "contract workers"— those employed by state enterprises for a specified term, without the promise of the customary "life tenure" accorded to regular employees—must contribute up to 3 percent of their wages to the funding of their pension program in order to be entitled to the same level of retirement benefits as regular workers.

MAIN PROGRAM FEATURES

The 1978 "provisional procedures for worker's retirement and disability" is the basic document for the current income security programs for old-age, survivor, and disability insurance (OASDI) (Ministry of Finance, 1979).

Coverage

These regulations cover all state-enterprise workers, except those hired in recent years as "contract workers." Due to the fragmented administration of these programs, there is no exact count of a national total of covered workers. Moreover, available statistics do not separate those covered under state-enterprise labor insurance from those under the collective enterprise programs. It is assumed here that all state-enterprise workers are entitled to the labor insurance program according to government regulations (see Table 4.2).

Qualifying Conditions

Retirement Age. Retirement age is 60 for men, 55 for women white-collar employees and 50 for women blue-collar workers. Workers in arduous and unhealthy employment can receive a pension up to five years earlier. Retirement ages for men and women have remained unchanged since 1951, even though life expectancy at birth has improved by more than 25 years in the interim.

Years of Employment. The 1978 amendments reduced the minimum years of service to qualify for the old-age benefit from 25 years of general service to 10 years of continuous service in the same enterprise. Prolonged work tenure, however, is credited with increased benefits.

Benefit Levels

Benefit Formula. The old-age benefit formula is earnings-related. It rewards prolonged service and participation in the communist cause before 1949 and/or outstanding service. Pensioners who meet the minimum of 10 years of continuous service receive a monthly benefit equal to 60 percent of the last month's standard wage. In addition, an earnings-related supplement is added to the basic monthly pension of workers who meet one of the following conditions: (1) an extra 10 to 15 percent of the preretirement wage for 15 or more years of continuous service; (2) an extra 20 to 30 percent for participation in the communist "revolutionary work" beginning before the outbreak of the civil war (1945–1949) or before the founding of the People's Republic in 1949; or (3) an extra 5 to 15 percent for those named as national model workers, labor heroes, or combat heroes. The combined basic and supplementary pensions cannot exceed the worker's preretirement monthly wage or cannot be lower than 30 yuan (about 23 percent of average monthly wage in 1987 for state-sector employees). The 1978 provisions stipulate that retirement is mandatory at the statutory retirement age, except for those who are deemed indispensable by the management.

Pensioners who choose to relocate also receive a lump-sum payment of 150 yuan for expenses and transportation costs, or receive a lump sum of 300 yuan plus transportation costs if they relocate from an urban to rural area.

A special provision for "lixiu" (i.e., lizhi tuixiu) offers regular pay to middle- and upper-grade Communist party and technical cadres while allowing them to "withdraw from work for recuperation." In addition, they are entitled to a special "subsistence grant," which could be as high as one to two months' earnings per year for those who participated in "revolutionary work" before 1945. Cadres on "lixiu" status retain all the privileges associated with their positions, and have the opportunity to decide the level of their "withdrawal from work" (Ministry of Finance, 1979; Davis, 1988; Wang et al., 1987). Some continue to be actively involved in their work.

Adjustment to Inflation. Benefits are not automatically adjusted for inflation, although the government has adopted ad hoc measures to alleviate rising prices in recent years. In November 1979 and May 1985, the government supplemented the pension payment by awarding pensioners "subsistence grants" of 5 yuan and later, 12 to 17 yuan a month, at the discretion of enterprise management (Wang et al., 1987).

All retired workers continue to qualify for free medical care as regular workers, including ambulatory and inpatient care, surgery, and ordinary medicines.

Other Benefits for Older Workers

Disability Benefits. A monthly, permanent, total disability pension (tuizhijin) is payable in the same amount as the retirement benefit if the worker has at least 10 years of continuous service and has reached age 50 (men) or 45 (women). The disability pension equals only 40 percent of the last month's wage (but not less than 25 yuan a month) if the worker does not meet the service and age requirements. Total disability is defined as the total loss of capacity to work. Disabled pensioners are entitled to a relocation grant, equal to their 2 months' wages.

Survivor Benefits. The surviving spouse and dependent children of an insured worker receive a lump-sum grant equal to the worker's six to 12 months' wages based on the number of dependents. Survivors of a pensioner receive a lump-sum grant equal to 24 to 50 percent of the old-age benefit of the deceased according to the number of dependents.

Administration of Programs

There is no central administration for these programs. At the national level, the Ministry of Labor establishes guidelines and has the responsibility of oversight and policy development. It does not, however, have the administrative mechanism or staff to enforce rules and regulations. Individual enterprises administer the programs according to established guidelines, presumably under the supervision and control of local government and Communist party cadres.

Some enterprises set up their own labor insurance committees (baoxian wei-yuanhui) to administer the programs. Committee members keep records, determine eligibility and benefit levels, distribute payments, and supervise the funding of the program and other activities relating to program operation (Wang et al., 1987). Many enterprises, however, administer the programs through their personnel and finance offices.

SPECIAL PROGRAMS

Civil Servants

The State Council has issued a series of regulations since 1950 to provide various programs for civil servants, including employees of government and political party organizations (primarily the CCP), and of cultural, educational, and scientific institutions.

Chronologically, these documents included the 1950 Provisional Regulations for Compensating Government and ''(Communist) Revolutionary'' Workers for Injuries and Death; the 1952 Instructions for Implementing Medical Care Programs for All Levels of Government Workers and Employees of Political Party Organizations and Affiliate Institutions; the 1952 Provisional Procedures for Awarding Cash Sickness Benefits (subsequently revised in 1954 and 1955); the 1955 Announcement Regarding Maternity Cash and Medical Benefits for Women Employees; and the 1955 provisional regulations for retirement and disability, respectively. Three years later, the above-mentioned 1958 Provisional (draft) Regulations for the Retirement of Workers and Staff, and a companion Draft Regulations for Disability of Workers and Staff brought the government/institution plans in line with those for state-enterprise workers (Wang et al., 1987).

In 1978, the "Temporary Procedures Providing for the Old, Weak and Disabled Cadres" (Guanyu Anzhi Lao Ro Bing Can Ganbu de Zhanxin Banfa) stipulated retirement (old-age and disability) and "lixiu" provisions for employees in party and government organizations, and scientific, educational, and cultural institutions. Retirement age, benefit formula, and cost of eligibility requirements are the same as those for state-enterprise workers. The 1985 cost-of-living adjustment was a uniform 17 yuan.

Individual agencies process the determination and payment of benefits. Local government offices of civil affairs administer benefit distribution to government institution pensioners who relocate away from their home agencies. Those who decide to relocate receive benefits from local government offices of civil affairs after the first year (Wang et al., 1987).

The Ministry of Personnel has the responsibility of policy development and oversight of these programs, although not necessarily the administrative where-withal to enforce uniformity in practice. Recent economic reform initiatives have not affected the civil service programs as they have the enterprise income security programs. Because party and government agencies are "nonprofit" organizations not held accountable for "losses" and "profits," they continue to have the full financial backing of the central government without any threat of shortfalls.

Workers in Urban Collectives

Large urban collectives could seek permission to adopt retirement programs for their employees (Wang et al., 1987). It is estimated that about two-thirds of all urban collective workers are covered by retirement programs (see Table 4.2).

There are no standard provisions for these programs. Generally speaking, they offer benefits lower than those provided by the state sector. For years 1978 through 1987, average per-capita income security expenditures in urban collectives were consistently (50–70 percent) lower than those in the state sector (CASS, 1988). Collective labor insurance programs generally depend on the enterprises' financial and administrative resources and do not have the backing of the People's Bank. They are financially less stable.

Rural Workers

Rural workers in China represent 74 percent of the labor force. There are no national income security programs to provide for their livelihood in old age. A great majority of these workers depend on their adult children or grandchildren for support as stipulated in the Marriage Law. Those who have no families to care for them and are destitute may be provided for by the so-called Five Guarantees—guarantees of food, shelter, clothing, medical care, and burial expenses—from local governments.

In recent years, some prosperous rural communities have established their own retirement programs for their older workers. Provisions for retirement age, qualifying conditions, and benefit formulas vary. Generally, retirement age is 65 for men, 60 for women. A majority of these villages set up a two-tiered system: the first tier provides a uniform flat-rate basic pension for all retirees in the village; a second tier provides supplementary pension, determined according to the number of years in service.

Stability of these programs depends on the economic prosperity and collective will of the communities concerned. In 1984, reportedly 660,000 rural aged received retirement pensions in 9,410 (or, about 1 percent of total) villages (Wang et al., 1987).

Funding Pensions

The retirement pension programs for employees of the state enterprises are entirely financed by employer contributions. Since the early 1980s, with the introduction of an "economic responsibility" system to make enterprises accountable for their own profits and losses, older enterprises with a large number of retired workers have been overburdened with retirement expenditures. Some enterprises no longer receive subsidies from the central government for their labor insurance shortfalls. Some have found that large retirement expenses cut into enterprises profits and, as such, serve as a disincentive for their employees to be productive.

To counteract these problems, an increasing number of local governments (at the county and municipal level) now organize compulsory resource pooling for state enterprises, except those affiliated with provincial governments and national ministries. Participating enterprises contribute an average of 18 percent of payroll to a pool, so that young industries can share the cost of those with a longer history and a higher proportion of retirees to workers.

Resource pooling came into practice in some cities and counties in Jiangsu, Guangdong, and Liaoning provinces in 1984. By late 1988, many enterprises in some 2,000 cities and counties (or 87 percent of these jurisdictions) had participated in resource pooling for labor insurance (Fu, 1987; Wei, 1988).

THE NATIONAL BUDGET

Since 1978, an increasingly large number of older workers have responded to liberalized terms for retirement, receiving old-age or disability benefits, or enjoying the "lixiu" status. Accompanying this trend is the escalating enterprise expenses on retirees. As the number of retired workers in the state sector (including civil servants) increased from 2.84 million in 1978 to 11.65 million in 1985, old-age pension and other related expenditures (e.g., transportation and subsistence grants to retired workers) grew rapidly from 1.6 billion yuan in 1978 to 11.9 billion yuan in 1985. The grand total of labor insurance for state-enterprise, civil service, and collective-enterprise retirees grew from 1.7 billion yuan to 15 billion yuan during the same period. The estimated cost to the national economy grew from about 0.5 to 1.8 percent of China's Gross National Product available for these years (see Table 4.3).

Table 4.3
Social Insurance Expenditures for Retired and Disabled Older Workers,
1978–1985 (in billions of yuan)

Years	GNP	State Sector	Coll. Sector	Total Exp.	%GNP
(1)	(2)	(3)	(4)	(3)+(4)	(5)/(2)
1978	348.2	1.6	.1	1.7	.49%
1980	433.6	4.3	.7	.5	1.15%
1981	462.9	5.3	.9	6.2	1.34%
1982	503.8	6.2	1.1	7.3	1.45%
1983	562.7	7.4	1.3	8.7	1.55%
1984	671.1	8.5	2.1	10.6	1.58%
1985	830.6	11.9	3.0	14.9	1.79%

Sources: <u>Chinese Statistical Yearbook, 1988.</u>
<u>New Milestones, New Accomplishments, 1987.</u>

POLICY ISSUES

Key policy issues in income security programs confronting PRC leaders are both immediate and long-term. In the state sector, immediate concerns focus on the administration and financing of old-age programs. At present, these programs are administered and financed at the enterprise level with nominal oversight from the Ministry of Labor. These programs, together with enterprise-based housing and other fringe benefits to employees, hinder labor mobility at a time when such movement could help expedite the country's economic development. Further, the rapid increases in the number of retired workers in recent years have proven to be burdensome, both administratively and financially, to older enterprises that have a large proportion of pensioners to employees. Some enterprises, with the mounting pressure of taking responsibility for their own profits and losses, have made ad hoc adjustments of program benefits without adhering to government regulations (Pei, 1986; Yu, 1986). The operation of resource pooling is carried out at the city and county levels; its success or failure depends largely on the resourcefulness of local officials and enterprise management.

The high cost of old-age benefits has become burdensome even to the national economy, as urban retirees are taking an impressive share of the country's GNP for their old-age support. It should be noted that, in 1985, 1.8 percent of GNP represented benefit expenditures for programs covering a mere 23 percent of the country's total labor force (albeit about 87 percent of its urban workers).

About 77 percent of the total workforce, the noninsured urban and rural workers, must rely on family support as old-age security. Of particular concern is the welfare of those uninsured seniors who have no surviving family members to care for them. The rural reform in the early 1980s abolished agricultural communes, which had, until then, set up welfare funds to provide the rural indigent with subsistence, that is, under the Five Guarantees program. Since then, some villages that have benefited from the reform and prospered economically have established retirement pensions for agricultural workers. The population covered by these schemes, however, remains very limited. Besides, these programs are subject to uncertainty in the economic well-being of respective agricultural communities.

In 1987, the Ministry of Civil Affairs drafted a proposal to remedy the lack of support for the indigent in most rural areas. It proposes that in the well-to-do regions, peasants will pay for their own old-age insurance policies; in developing regions, rural enterprises and the central government would subsidize peasants to set up savings cooperatives, welfare facilities, and the like. In ''hardship'' regions, the local and central government will shoulder the entire cost of social welfare. This 1987 proposal was subsequently approved by the State Council (Chow, 1988). At present, it remains a policy statement. Its actual implementation still depends very much on the resourcefulness of local administrators in collaboration with the central government.

In the long term, the rapidly aging population threatens to overload the current system and bring about adverse economic and social consequences. Improved health care and recent official birth control campaigns (limiting each young couple to having only one child) have contributed to a rapidly aging society that will rival challenges already faced by some industrialized nations in Europe today.

In the state sector, both enterprise management and the Ministry of Labor need to reconsider the feasibility of the highly decentralized administration and funding of the program as the proportion of older workers rises rapidly. The cost issue will be even more ominous in the twenty-first century if these programs continue to provide retirement benefits to older workers at 5 to 15 years before age 65.

Family support for the majority of the country's older population (who do not have formal pension benefits for their retirement years) will be less reliable in the future. Both the exodus of rural youth to urban areas and the government's family planning policy will have greatly curtailed family resources for old-age support (Banister, 1988).

CONCLUSION

In China, as in most other developing countries, a majority of urban workers (especially employees of state-owned enterprises) are provided with formal programs of old-age support, whereas rural workers are not.

The PRC government's historical commitment to ensure the economic wellbeing of its needy citizens has been overtaken by events in the wake of the country's modernization initiatives. These reform initiatives, while designed to further improve the welfare of the population, have simultaneously caused immediate and long-term problems that threaten the feasibility of current labor insurance programs of urban workers and of relying on family support as the primary resource for a majority of the country's aged.

First, China must determine how best to revise existing programs for state-sector workers, control the run-away costs of labor insurance, and improve resource pooling and coordinated administration. Second, China must devise income security schemes for both urban and rural workers who are not protected by any income security programs.

NOTE

The views expressed in this chapter are those of Ms. Liu and do not necessarily reflect those of the Social Security Administration or any other branch of the U.S. government.

REFERENCES

Banister, J. (1986). *Urban-rural population projections for China.* Washington, D.C.: U.S. Bureau of the Census.

———. (1987). *China's changing population.* Stanford, Calif.: Stanford University Press.

———. (1988). The aging of China's population. *Problems of Communism,* November–December, 62–77.

CASS. (1987). *China 1987 aged population over 60 years sampling survey data.* Computer tabulation (in Chinese). Beijing.

———. (1988). *Chinese statistical yearbook, 1988.* Beijing.

Chinese social statistics materials, 1987. (1987). Beijing.

Chow, N. W. S. (1988). *The administration and financing of social security in China.* Hong Kong: University of Hong Kong.

Davis, D. (1988). Unequal chances, unequal outcomes: Pension reform and urban inequality. *China Quarterly,* 114, 223–242.

Davis-Friedman, D. (1985). Chinese retirement: Policy and practice. *Current Perspectives on Aging and Life Cycle,* 1, 295–313.

Fu, H. (1987). Issues concerning resource pooling for financing retired workers' benefit expenditures (in Chinese). *Zhongguo Laodong Kexue,* 6, 9–11.

Fujian Province Revolutionary Committee (1973). *Selected documents on labor wages* (in Chinese). Fuzhou.

Jamison, D. T. (1985). China's health care system: Policies, organization, inputs, and finance. In S. B. Halstead, J. A. Walsh, and K. S. Warren (eds.), *Good health at low cost,* 21–32. New York, N.Y.: Rockefeller Foundation.

Liangjin, C. (1990). Social developmental mechanisms and social security functions. *International Sociology,* 5(1), 89–100.

Ministry of Finance. (1979). *Excerpts on the system of social, cultural, and educational administration and finance* (in Chinese). Beijing: Chinese Finance and Economics.

Pei, S. (1986). Considerations regarding the reform of the retirement pension system (in Chinese). *Jingji Yu GuanliYenjiu,* 5, 36–38.

Tang, J., and Ma, L. J. C. (1985). Evolution of urban collective enterprises in China. *China Quarterly,* 104(12), 614–640.

Wang, K., et al. (1987). *Wage, employee welfare, and social insurance in contemporary China* (in Chinese). Beijing: Zhongguo shehui kexue chubanshe.

Wei, X. (1988). Social security system in mainland China. Paper presented at the Seminar on Social Work Education in the Asian and Pacific Region, December 15–19, 1988. Beijing.

The World Bank Atlas. (1987). Washington, D.C.: World Bank.

Yu, C. (1986). Labor insurance reform in Sha City (in Chinese). *Jingji Tizhi Gaige*, 6, 59–60.

5

Costa Rica

Guido Miranda-Gutiérrez

Social reform in Costa Rica began after World War I and continued for more than twenty years. One of the most important reforms during this period involved the delivery of health and income programs under the aegis of three institutions: the Banco de Seguros (Insurance Bank), the Ministerio de Salud (Health Ministry), and the Caja Costarricense de Seguro Social ("La Caja") (Costa Rican Social Security System).

The role of the state as an active participant in the provision of social security programs increased following a political crisis in 1948, which changed government from a "liberal" democracy (established in 1871) to a "social" democracy. This event contributed to important changes in the distribution of social and economic benefits. Since that time the state has been constitutionally dedicated to the creation, supervision, promotion, and distribution of social benefits. Various autonomous institutions were created to provide an infrastructure that promoted government jurisdiction, including the nationalization of the banking system (which was placed under the control of the Central Bank).

In 1961, the Constitution was modified, obliging the state to protect all persons against the risks associated with illness, maternity, disability, old age, and death. The constitutional mandate was in part a response to international pressures to adopt a sound social security doctrine as defined by the International Labour Organization (Rosenberg, 1979).

From 1950 to 1960, the country experienced a four percent annual population growth rate—one of the highest in the world. The population of persons under 35 years of age tripled in this period due to higher birth rates accompanied by lower mortality rates.

Birth rates declined, however, from 45 per thousand in 1950 to 31 per thousand in 1986. By the 1970s, life expectancy at birth had been extended to 76 years

Table 5.1
Population Structure by Age Groups

		0-14	15-59	60+	TOTAL
1950	#	343,080	419,975	38,016	801,071
	%	42.8	52.4	4.8	100.0
1963	#	636,665	629,775	67,736	1,334,176
	%	47.8	47.2	5.0	100.0
1973	#	824,462	943,205	104,113	1,871,780
	%	44.1	50.3	5.6	100.0
1984	#	884,498	1,374,167	158,144	2,416,809
	%	36.5	57.0	6.5	100.0
2000	#	1,197,494	2,237,262	275,900	3,710,656
	%	32.3	60.3	7.4	100.0

Source: Latin American Demographic Center (LADC).

of age with projections for 77.2 in the year 2000 (Ministry of Health, 1989). By the year 2000, 7.4 percent of the population will be 60 years and older and comprise nearly 4 million elderly inhabitants (see Table 5.1).

The Costa Rican economy in the period 1962–1979 grew at an averaged annual rate of 6.0 percent, which is one of the highest growth rates in Latin America. A serious economic crisis occurred between 1979 and 1982 as a consequence of production problems, external factors, and a series of inadequate steps taken in economic policies. There was a 7.3 percent fall in real production from 1981 to 1982, accompanied by a worsening of fiscal problems, deterioration of the balance of payments, high inflation and unemployment rates, and growth of the external debt to $3.12 million. Currently, relative stability has been obtained and the socioeconomic situation has notably improved with production increases, reduction of inflation rates, and a real salary increase, along with a marked decrease in the unemployment rate.

SOCIAL SECURITY CASH BENEFITS AND HEALTH PROGRAMS

National social security laws provide protection against all risks, except unemployment, for employed persons. Health and maternity insurance coverage under social security has risen from about 5 percent of the labor force in 1947 to around 70 percent of the economically active population. There is also a social assistance program to provide health care and pensions to those in the lowest income sector. The income-tested assistance program is the Basic Amount Noncontributive Pension System. The noneconomically active population is also entitled to health benefits that are financed by the state. Cash benefits under the old-age, invalidity, and survivor insurance (OASI) system cover about 47 percent of employed and self-employed persons. Other pension systems that are financed by general revenues provide protection for an additional 20 percent of the population.

Old-Age, Invalidity, and Survivor Benefits

The OASI system includes all public employees and private workers. Coverage is concentrated among civil servants and industrial workers in urban areas, although the government is committed to extending coverage to agricultural sectors in rural areas. The self-employed are covered on a voluntary basis.

Old-age pensions are payable to men at age 57 and to women at age 55 with 408 months of contributions. Both men and women can receive a pension at age 65 with 120 months of contributions. Workers are encouraged to work beyond the minimum entitlement age by counting any one month of actual contributions as three months for work performed during the period between the minimum age and age 65. An invalidity benefit is payable to persons who have lost two-thirds of their earning capacity and have at least 36 months of covered employment.

Survivor benefits are paid to dependents of deceased workers who had a minimum of 24 months of coverage. The benefit amount is 70 percent of the insured's pension if age 55 and over; otherwise it is 60 percent. Full orphans under age 18 (age 22 if invalid and 25 if a student) receive 60 percent and half-orphans receive 30 percent of the insured's pension.

The benefit amount for both old-age and invalidity is 40 percent of the average of the highest 48 monthly salaries during the last five years of coverage. The benefit is increased by one-eighth of one percent of average earnings for each month of contribution and by 20 percent if the pensioner has a wife and one child or by 10 percent if there is either a wife or child. The maximum pension payable is 60,000 colones a month (1989) and the minimum is 7,000 colones a month (Board of Directors, 1989). (At the end of 1989 one colon equaled U.S. 1.3 cents.) Thirteen monthly pensions are paid in a year (USDHHS, 1990).

The monetary value of pensions is reviewed every year for possible adjustment. In 1987 the amount of pensions in payment was raised for older pensioners. Pensions awarded before 1961 were raised by 20 percent, those awarded between January 1961 and December 1970 were raised 12 percent, and those awarded between January 1971 and May 1987 were increased by 5 percent (Rys, 1990).

Since 1987 workers are also entitled to a lump-sum benefit when work is terminated because of death, invalidity, or retirement. The benefit is equal to the average wage during the last three months of contributions to the general scheme with a minimum of 10,000 colones and a maximum of 50,000 colones (Rys, 1990).

Noncontributory Benefits

As part of the Social Development and Family Assignation Law, the social security system administers a noncontributive pension system for a basic amount designed to offer protection to population sectors needing immediate economic assistance.

Health Care Coverage

The possibility of protecting agricultural workers for income and health risks was included with the creation of the 1941 law that established the social security system. Initially, this was limited to the extension of health and maternity protection to an important rural area of the Central Plateau.

Increased social insurance coverage at the national level developed slowly throughout the 1940s and 1950s. In 1944, only 4 percent of the population was covered under social security. By 1960 this had risen to 15 percent. In 1961, a constitutional reform was introduced that obligated the state social security system to provide total health and income coverage for every family.

In the years that followed this mandate, priority was given to meeting basic health care needs. Typical of many other Latin American nations, the social security infrastructure was viewed as the principal vehicle for extending health care. In 1973 all hospitals and their financing sources were transferred to the social security system under the Hospital Transfer Law, which established universal health and maternity coverage governed by an integrated health system. The hospitals and health centers under the Ministry of Health and the social protection boards were transferred to the social security system in accordance with the law.

Between 1974 and 1977 health insurance was made obligatory for all independent workers, including retired persons and their beneficiaries. These measures resulted in the extension of health coverage to approximately 89.5 percent of the population by the end of 1987. The extent of coverage is actually close to 100 percent, as the noninsured and indigent are also protected.

Article 2 of the 1973 law provided that the Caja de Seguro Social (social security system) "must also provide medical-hospital assistance to uninsured persons who are incapable of paying for services and . . . the state will provide the necessary funding."

An important complimentary feature was an executive decree in 1983 that ratified universal health and maternity insurance. This guarantees health services to those "insured by the state" in that services for health protection are received with no direct payment on the part of the individual.

This provision of health as a fundamental right has been an integral component in reducing mortality rates. Thirty-five percent of the decrease in the mortality rate between 1940 and 1980 was due to the control of malnutrition and infectious or parasitic diseases. Forty percent of the reduction is related to improvement in sanitary conditions, and 20 percent to the availability of new services and technological development.

While the country has obtained excellent basic health levels, there are some population sectors in which there is an incidence of pathologies that is considerably higher than that found in the general population. There are also some groups, especially in rural and marginal urban areas, which do not have adequate access to health services.

Newly Insured Groups

There is growing evidence of confidence in the social security system as reflected in the constant requests from independent labor organizations in different agricultural, industrial, handicraft, domestic, academic, intellectual, and clerical areas to receive social security benefits. By the end of 1987, there were 135 agreements with the government comprising a total of 39,000 beneficiaries. There are more than 103 agreements with cooperatives, unions, and farmer organizations with 33,009 beneficiaries. Of the total amount of agreements with labor, 76.3 percent are with farm organizations, protecting 83 percent of agricultural workers.

The state also has bilateral agreements to provide health and maternity insurance for workers outside the country. Agreements have been reached with various Central American countries defining the application of medical services in accordance with regulations established under these bilateral agreements.

Administration and Financing

The Costa Rica Social Insurance Fund is responsible for the financing and administration of provisions for old-age pensions, invalidity, survivor benefits, health care, cash sickness, and maternity benefits.

The system is financed through mandatory tripartite contributions from employers, employees, and the state. For old-age, invalidity, and death benefits insured workers contribute 2.5 percent of earnings, employers pay 4.75 percent of payroll, and the state provides 0.25 percent of total covered earnings. Self-employed workers pay 7.25 percent of income.

Health care, cash sickness, and maternity benefits are funded separately. Employees contribute 5.5 percent of earnings, employers 9.25 percent of payroll, and the state 0.75 percent of covered earnings. The self-employed pay from 5 to 12.5 percent of income, and pensioners pay 12.5 percent of pension.

In addition to tripartite contributions, there are other sources of income that are not within the social insurance framework, including medical assistance services sold to noninsured groups, professional risk beneficiaries, and professional illnesses covered by the National Insurance Institute (Table 5.2).

The system obtains additional income through the sale of medical care to retired persons, contributions from workers covered by independent systems,

Table 5.2
Additional Sources of Financing

	Employer	Employee	State	Total
Banco Popular y Desarrollo Comunal (Popular Community Development Bank)	0.50%	1.00%	–	1.50%
Asignaciones Familiare (Family Assignations)	5.00%	–	–	5.00%
Instituto Mixto de Ayuda Social (Mixed Social Assistance Inst.)	0.50%	–	–	0.50%
Instituto Nacional de Apredizaje (National Learning Institute)	2.00%	–	–	2.00%

and the payment the state makes for indigent workers (Law 5349). Historically, there has been a problem in the state meeting its payment obligations. This has contributed to a growing debt in the health and maternity benefit system, as well as old-age, invalidity, and death benefits. The state makes periodic payments that are, in effect, a "revolving credit."

In 1986, expenses for each government health sector were as follows: social security, 65.7 percent; Ministry of Health, 14.6 percent; the Aqueduct and Sewage System Institute, 12.4 percent; and the National Insurance Institute, 7.3 percent. Total spending on health was about 9 percent of the Gross National Product.

DIRECT MEDICAL CARE

The Social Insurance Fund provides medical care directly to patients through facilities that are owned and operated by the fund. Currently, the fund has 30 hospitals with 7,000 beds and is gradually extending jurisdiction as part of a policy to integrate health care delivery under social security.

The health and maternity insurance system is charged with the provision of health services through 30 hospitals and more than 215 external consultation clinics throughout the country. It also awards short-term cash benefits for temporary disability.

The Health Sector was created in 1974 under the National Planning Law giving authority to the president of the Republic, as well as to the minister of health, over the various institutions of the health sector, including the Ministry of Health, the Ministry of Planning and Economical Policy, the Ministry of the Presidency, the Costa Rican Social System (Health and Maternity), the Costa Rican Aqueduct and Sewage System Institute, the National Insurance Institute

(Professional Risk Department), and the University of Costa Rica (Health Investigation and Medical Science Area).

In agreement with an interinstitutional organization and its respective legal framework, the Health Sector is charged with offering health care to the entire population, improving the morbi-mortality indicators, preventing accelerated development of ailments common to developed countries, and obtaining harmonic functioning and coordination among respective institutions.

The objectives of the program are aimed at the creation of a national health system to guarantee the use of all resources through an efficient and effective administrative system. The purpose of this is to develop a health system that complies with the following basic principles:

1. Health is a human right.
2. The state is responsible for the health of the population and the minister of health is the governor of the Health Sector.
3. Beneficiary medical services must be integrated with an emphasis on primary health care.
4. Integration of the services is peremptory in relation to prevention, cure, and rehabilitation.
5. Ambulatory consultation is a priority in the system.
6. Promotion and prevention are of top priority.
7. Community participation complementing that of the state is the basis of adequate functioning.
8. Resources must be redistributed in accordance with priorities.

EXTERNAL DEBT

The economic crisis, especially the national debt, has affected the social security institution's finances appreciably. The most adverse effect has been on the health and maternity programs, particularly a marked deterioration of the quality of medical-hospital services in 1981–1982. At that time the authorities in charge made a series of decisions aimed at achieving financial stability for the system under the "Financial Stabilization Plan." On the one hand, this involved an attempt to obtain efficiency and optimum use of funds available. On the other hand, measures to increase funds were also considered.

In 1979, Costa Rica's external public debt was the equivalent of a little more than half of the yearly exports (60 percent). In 1980 and 1984 it represented 1.8 and 3 times the annual exports, respectively. It should be noted that the coefficient external debt/exportations has worsened in recent years in comparison to the rest of the nonpetroleum producing development countries.

In 1984, the total external public debt was U.S. $3,826 million, which was equivalent to 111 percent of the GNP in the same year. In 1980, it corresponded to 50 percent of the yearly product, in 1970, it represented less than 20 percent of the GNP.

Costa Rica, like the rest of Latin America, has been affected by an increase in interest rates. This phenomenon is partially due to the increase in the debt service payments. This may be deduced by examining the coefficient interest payment/exportations, which was 3.5 percent, 16.2 percent, and 24.0 percent in 1970, 1980, and 1984, respectively. This tendency was accentuated in 1982, when the percentage reached 35.5 percent.

SUMMARY

Costa Rica is historically and constitutionally committed to extending health and income protection to the entire population but the primary emphasis has been on expanding direct health care programs. Almost all the population now has access to primary health care while income protection is largely restricted to government employees and industrial workers in urban areas. Efforts at improving the social security system have been greatly impeded in recent years by an ongoing economic crisis that has been exacerbated by the presence of a large external debt.

REFERENCES

Board of Directors. (1989, September). Social Security System. Personal correspondence.
Ministry of Health. (1989, September). Personal correspondence.
Rosenberg, M. B. (1979). Social security policymaking in Costa Rica: A research report. *Latin American Research Review*, 1, 116–133.
Rys, V. (1990). *Trends and developments in social security—worldwide*. Regional Training Course on Social Security Administration, Kuwait. Geneva: International Social Security Association.
U.S. Department of Health and Human Services. (1990). *Social security programs throughout the world—1989*. Social Security Administration. Office of International Policy. Report No. 62. Washington, D.C.: U.S. Government Printing Office.

6

France

Jean-Louis Cayatte

Old-age pensions in France are provided under an extensive general system that is complemented by mandatory occupational pension programs. Both schemes are based on principles of social insurance and are funded by employer and employee contributions. The general program also includes income-tested benefits to the needy aged who do not qualify for a pension or whose pension amount is below a minimum level.

HISTORICAL DEVELOPMENT

As in most other industrial nations, the French system of income maintenance and health care protects workers against the risks of unemployment, accidents, disability, death, poor health, and old age. A family allowance that provides income to families with children has also been a major feature of the French social insurance system. There are a number of dominant social forces that have contributed to the development of a comprehensive system of social insurance. First is the fundamental concept of social protection based on historical paternalistic ideology, concern for the rights of laborers, and efforts to control wage costs. A second element has been successful reform measures of labor unions to promote benefits for both workers covered by the social security scheme and laborers who, for whatever reason, do not qualify for normal benefits. A third factor is the low birth rates in France, which have aided pronatalists and supporters of family policies in the development of family allowances. Finally, the system was influenced by the income maintenance policies of the regions of Alsace and Lorraine, which adopted Bismarckian principles of social insurance in 1880. These principles were to become important elements in French social security legislation that emerged between 1928 and 1930.

In recent years the system has been shaped by rising unemployment rates among young persons, which have contributed to policies aimed at reducing the working time of older persons by lowering the retirement age and encouraging early retirement (Baldenweck, 1987). Contributing to the problem is the changing balance of age created by a slowing birth rate and increasing life expectancy. The shifting demographic situation will lead to fewer persons below working age and more past retirement age in the future, although the ratio of wage earners to dependent members of the population is expected to stay about the same (100 to 127) until the year 2010.

GENERAL SYSTEM FOR EMPLOYED WORKERS

The first salaried workers to receive a retirement pension were sailors (1673), civil servants (1817), and military personnel (1831). In 1850, the National Retirement Fund was founded, which provided an annuity coupled with interest rates that were guaranteed by the state. Workers qualified for retirement benefits by contributing to the fund. A system of retirement benefits was introduced to cover miners and railroad employees in 1894 and 1909. Legislation to cover all workers was passed in 1910, but it was only partially implemented.

Another effort began in 1919 to establish a national system for all workers. It culminated in legislation in 1928 but, again, the law was not implemented. It was replaced in 1930 by legislation that created a system of contributory retirement pensions for all workers in industry and commerce. Only workers with income below a specified level were covered. Coverage was expanded in 1945 when income restrictions were eliminated. At the same time, however, benefit amounts were limited by a contribution ceiling.

Self-employed workers are covered by autonomous systems. These are distinguished by occupations, including industry and commerce (ORGANIC), artisans (CANCAVA), professionals (CNAVPL), and lawyers (CNBF). Other autonomous systems cover farmers and the clergy.

Coverage

The general system covers about 70 percent of all employees in the private sector, including domestic workers, salespersons, members of cooperatives, the self-employed, administrators of anonymous societies, artists, journalists, writers, practitioners, and prisoners. Nonemployed housewives and persons caring for an invalid family member may be voluntarily covered for old-age pensions. Women who receive a family allowance benefit are compulsorily included in the general scheme (USDHHS, 1990). Benefits for agricultural workers are financed under the general system but are administered separately, although contribution rates and benefit levels are the same. Salaried workers in the public sector are covered by a special system, as are miners and railway employees.

Qualifying Conditions

The age of first entitlement to an old-age pension is 60 to workers with at least 150 quarters of covered employment. In the special systems, the age can be lower, ranging from 55 years of age for miners and railroad workers to 60 for civil servants.

Financing

Old-age pensions under the general scheme are financed by contributions assessed on earnings below a ceiling. The rate of contribution is 15.8 percent, of which 8.2 percent is paid by the employer and 7.6 percent is paid by the worker up to a ceiling of 125,280 francs per year (one franc equaled U.S 16.9 cents as of December 30, 1989), which is about 1.6 times the 1984 wages of an average worker in manufacturing. An additional 0.1 percent of total earnings is assessed on employees for the surviving spouse's benefit. There is no government contribution to the old-age pension benefit.

Benefit Levels

The old-age pension is calculated as the product of a fixed rate times an average annual base salary. Since 1971 this base has been the average of the ten highest years of earnings adjusted to reflect inflationary trends. The contributions are revalued based on coefficients calculated by the National Old-Age Insurance Fund. Earnings after retirement are taxed according to the quarters of contributions and the age of retirement.

Since 1982 anyone who has contributed to the system is entitled to a minimum pension regardless of the amount of contribution. The minimum pension amount, which in July 1989 was 32,562 francs (USDHHS, 1990), represents 60 percent of the minimum guaranteed salary of active workers. There is also a maximum (63,240 francs) that prohibits a pension from exceeding 50 percent of the contribution ceiling. Pensions are revalued twice a year (in January and July) to reflect increases in national average wage levels.

A spouse's supplement is available only to persons who meet an income test. The amount of the benefit is 4,000 francs a year at age 65 if the insured had a minimum of 150 quarters of covered employment. If there is less than 150 quarters, the supplement is proportionately reduced.

A "solidarity" allowance is paid to low-income pensioners in the amount of 19,500 francs a year for single persons and 32,010 francs for couples. There is also a means-tested yearly allowance of 14,490 francs to low-income aged workers who are ineligible for a pension (USDHHS, 1990).

Survivor Benefits

A survivor benefit is payable to a widow, divorced or deserted wife, or widower at age 55 or at any age if disabled. The benefit is equal to 52 percent of the insured's pension plus an additional 10 percent for widows who reared three or more children. An income-tested allowance is payable to surviving spouses who are under age 55 and not disabled.

Administration

Social insurance is composed of five types of administrative units: (1) a National Sickness Insurance Fund (CNAM), with regional and local funds; (2) a national family allowance fund (CNAF), with local funds; (3) a national old-age insurance fund (CNAV); (4) a central agency of social security organizations (ACOSS) with a central treasury; and (5) URSSAF, which collects contributions for the three branches of insurance.

The CNAV assures the management of the old-age insurance base, including widows, of covered wage earners. It advises the government in matters of maintaining financial stability for the system. The CNAV is administered by a council of twenty-five members and various outside consultants. The members include fifteen representatives of social insurance programs who are elected from a list presented by diverse national organizations of wage earners (CGT, CGT-FO, CFDT, CFTC, CGC); six representatives of employers who are designated by the national organization of professional employers; two persons appointed by the minister of social security, one from a workers' organization and one from an employers' organization; and two retirees chosen by the other twenty-three members in consultation with national associations of retired persons.

COMPLEMENTARY PENSIONS

One important aspect of the 1945 legislation was to limit the benefit levels of employer-sponsored pension supplements. The National Council of French Employers established a system in 1947 to avoid this restriction through collective agreements with labor for complementary benefits for white-collar workers and management (cadres) (Horlick, 1980). This was the creation of the Association Generale Interprofessionelles de Retraite des Cadres (General Association of Retirement Institutions for Cadres) or AGIRC.

Blue-collar (noncadres) workers' demands for equal treatment were fulfilled in 1957 with the creation of the Union Nationale des Institutions de Retraite des Salaries (National Union of Retirement Institutions) or UNIRS. In 1962, the Association des Regimes de Retraites Complementaires (Association of Complementary Retirement Funds) or ARRCO was founded to unify all retirement provisions for wage workers in commerce and industry. The development of a system of compulsory complementary schemes has diminished the need for employer-sponsored retirement plans.

Financing

Both programs for cadres and noncadres are financed by payroll contributions under a pay-as-you-go system. The amount of contributions is based on the level of earnings within categories called tranches. There is a mandatory contribution rate for noncadres of 4 percent of earnings up to a specified earnings ceiling. The employer pays 2.4 percent of this tax and the employee pays 1.6 percent. If the employee has earnings above the ceiling, a voluntary supplement may be paid up to a second level (tranche) at the same contribution rates of 2.4 percent and 1.6 percent. There is an option for an additional voluntary supplement based on earnings above the maximum of the second tranche to the maximum level of the third tranche.

The mandatory contribution rate of 2.4 percent for employers and 1.6 percent for employees for earnings below the ceiling is the same for both cadres and noncadres. The rate payable for voluntary contributions, however, is higher. The second tranche, for example, requires 6 percent from employers and 2 percent from employees. For wage earners in the private sector, retirement income is acquired from two main sources: a pension base, which is paid under the general system of social security, and complementary pensions, which are paid by the conventional fund system.

Benefits

Benefits under the complementary system are based on adjusted career average earnings that are used as the basis to accumulate retirement points. These points are added together at the time of retirement and multiplied by the current value of a reference point based on a median of all covered workers for the previous year. The compulsory pension plans also provide for survivor benefits and orphan pensions. Companies with more than 100 workers are required to set aside each year an amount for a profit-sharing plan (IBIS, 1984). Benefits are payable at age 60 if the worker has at least 37.5 years of contributions.

SPECIAL PROVISIONS FOR WOMEN

The principle of old-age insurance rests on paid contributions during periods of paid employment. A woman who leaves paid employment to remain at home essentially gives up her pension. A woman who reduces her labor force activity also reduces her retirement benefit if her years of contributions total less than 37.5. Because of the disadvantageous position of women who leave the labor force or reduce their paid work activity, France has implemented a number of compensatory provisions for women, including the following measures:

1. A woman is credited for two years of contribution for each child that she rears.
2. The number of years of contribution required for a full benefit is reduced for workers who have at least three children.
3. Mothers in families receiving certain family allowances are automatically covered by the old-age general pension system.
4. Women caretakers of children or permanently disabled adults are also automatically covered by the old-age general pension system.
5. In 1985 all discrimination based on gender was eliminated and the term "woman" in the law was replaced with "single person." The absence of gender is applicable to both men and women.

SPECIAL PROGRAMS FOR AGRICULTURAL WORKERS

Social security coverage for agricultural workers has long been autonomous. This is explained by a strong tradition. Coverage has also been autonomous for agricultural workers because of the unwillingness of agricultural employers to pay social security contributions at the same rate assessed against industrial workers.

Agricultural coverage includes logging, fish hatcheries, forestry, rural artisans who do not employ more than two workers, agricultural contractors, and others. It is necessary to distinguish between mutual agricultural insurance companies that insure against accidents, hail, fire, and death of cattle, and the mutual agricultural societies that are the social security system in agriculture. The latter administers the old-age pension program and the occupational pension program.

Self-Employed Agricultural Workers

In order to qualify for a full pension an agricultural worker must be at least 65 (60 if disabled or a prisoner of war). A full benefit is granted if the worker has been active for 25 years. The benefit is prorated if employment is fewer years. The pension amount is proportionate to the contributions paid. Supplementary benefits are paid to workers who meet an income test under the National Solidarity Fund. An annuity is available under the Social Action Fund for the Management of Agricultural Structure.

Salaried Agricultural Workers

Although separately administered, the system of salaried agricultural workers is identical to that of the system for wage earners under the general system.

EARLY RETIREMENT

Early retirement was introduced in 1972 to cope with rising unemployment among younger workers. The new socialist government in 1981 introduced a series of measures that were designed to create employment for youth. This included "solidarty contracts" to create jobs and retirement provisions as early as age 55. The number of people retiring before age 60 subsequently doubled from 1981 to 1983. The high cost of the program, however, led to modifications at the end of 1983 that formally lowered the retirement age to 60 and reduced early retirement provisions (Baldenweck, 1987). Currently, the standard pensionable age for men and women with at least 37.5 years of covered employment is age 60. Various options exist to allow persons with fewer years of employment to receive a full benefit at age 60.

Prior to 1983, benefits paid between ages 60 and 65 were permanently reduced by 5 percent for each year before age 65. The term "early retirement" applies to anyone who receives a benefit before age 65.

Since 1935 workers in France have been able to receive a pension at age 60 if they are partially disabled. Up until 1972 eligibility was based on two-thirds disability or occupational incapacity. In 1972 the definition of disability was liberalized to 50 percent incapacity. If eligible for this pension, individuals receive a full pension as early as age 60, even if they lack the 37.5 years of coverage.

Before 1983 workers, primarily men, who held jobs in hazardous and arduous occupations were entitled to receive a full benefit at age 60. Implemented in 1976, this provision intended to alleviate unemployment among younger workers by opening up jobs. This provision became obsolete when the pensionable age was lowered to 60.

Women who have reared at least three children are eligible for full pensions at age 60 if they have been in covered employment for 30 years and have performed manual labor for five of the last 15 years.

Women with 37.5 years of coverage at age 63 from 1978 and age 60 from 1979 are eligible for a full pension.

Early awards are also made to persons under a variety of prepension inter-industrial agreements, subsidized by the government, to encourage older workers to leave the labor force before age 65.

In 1983 national legislation and industrial collective agreements effectively standardized the pensionable age by eliminating most of the special public and private provisions for entitlement to benefits before age 65 by lowering the standard pensionable age for full benefits to age 60. This action was designed to address the inequities of lower benefits for some individuals and to continue to encourage older workers to leave the labor force in order to open up job opportunities for younger persons (Tracy and Adams, 1989). A 1982 ordinance created a "solidarity contract," which provides a payment of 70 percent of wages to workers age 55 and over until they are entitled to an old-age pension.

Insured workers who defer retirement are entitled to an increase in their pension benefit of 2.5 percent of earnings for each quarter that retirement is postponed beyond age 65. Since 1983 workers with less than 37.5 years of coverage may accumulate a 10 percent increase in benefits for each year beyond age 65.

PERSONAL SAVINGS

In theory, savings do not provide any national source of resource reserves but, in reality, supplementary retirement funds do hold reserves to avoid creating excessive differences among income classes. It is true, however, that since 1945 personal savings have been very small. One reason for this is that the old-age pension system is viewed by workers as a savings system that does not require additional efforts to set aside income for the future. But studies conducted on the relationship between retirement and savings have given contradictory results. Nevertheless, some recent efforts have been made to establish a national system of savings.

BLUE-COLLAR WORKERS

Historically, businesses had their own retirement pension systems based on the perception that they had a duty to humanely dismiss old workers who had become low producers in order to assure some stability among employees. Although most retirement funds were created at the initiative of employers, wage earners who quit work before retirement age typically lost their rights to a pension and a number of persons were laid off before the age of retirement. These abuses have not been possible since the end of the nineteenth century as the integrity of the pension is maintained for any wage earner who leaves an employer.

CLEARING THE RIGHT TO EMPLOYMENT

Solidarity contracts have traditionally sought to provide younger workers with the right to employment. Public policy support for this position is substantiated by recent retirement age policies and flexible retirement options that attempt to open up job opportunities for young persons by retiring older workers. The lowering of the age so that a worker can receive a full pension at age 60 instead of 65 since April 1983, combined with the impossibility of raising the tax for long-term workers, has contributed greatly to the practice of retiring early.

INCOME-TESTED SUPPLEMENT

The social insurance system provides for a minimum level of income for both pensioners and persons who are ineligible for a pension. These income-tested benefits are made as ''old-age allowances'' to qualifying pensioners and their spouses. A lower minimum income is guaranteed to low-income aged who do not meet the contributory requirements for an old-age pension.

SUMMARY

The French system of old-age insurance is characterized by firmly entrenched social insurance principles reinforced by a belief in paternalism and workers' rights. These principles have been advanced by forceful support from trade unions, which have sought not only to promote benefits for covered workers but also for persons who, for whatever reason, may not have participated in the labor force. The provision of a minimum "solidarity" allowance reflects a commitment of applying the concept of a "social minimum" to the aged.

The French system has several unusual features, including mandatory complementary occupational pensions for both white- and blue-collar workers, a standard retirement age that is lower than that in most other industrial nations, and a variety of provisions designed to compensate women for special risks and reduced covered earnings.

REFERENCES

Andreani, E. (1986). *Les retraites*. Paris: Editions la Decouverte.

Babeau, A. (1985). *La fin des retraites*. Paris: Hachette.

Baldenweck, M. (1987). *Age, vieillissement et societé*. Paris: Comite pour l'amenagement du temps de travail et de loisirs en region d'ile de France.

Dupeyroux, J. J. (1988). *Droit de la sécurité sociale*. 11th ed. Paris: Dalloz.

France: Coping with an ageing society. (1988). *Social and Labour Bulletin*, 2, 243–246.

Horlick, M. (1980). *Private pension plans in West Germany and France*. Research Report No. 55. Social Security Administration. Washington, D.C.: U.S. Government Printing Office.

International Benefits Information Service. (1984). *IBIS Profile—France*. Chicago: Author.

Les dossiers de l'IRES. (1983, November). *La Protection Sociale*.

Tracy, M. B., and Adams, P. (1989). Age of first pension award under social security: Patterns in ten industrial countries, 1960–1986. *International Social Security Review*, 42 (4), 447–461.

U.S. Department of Health and Human Services. (1990). *Social security programs throughout the world—1989*. Social Security Administration, Office of International Policy. Research Report No. 62. Washington, D.C.: U.S. Government Printing Office.

7

Federal Republic of Germany

Heinz-Dietrich Steinmeyer

In the nineteenth century social conditions in Germany underwent a dramatic change. The population increased from 23 million at the start of the century to 56 million at the end. This increase was in conjunction with an abnormal increase in the urban population as people moved to the cities to get jobs in new industries. The migration had an adverse effect on the ability of families to help members who were in need. People were poor, the jobless rate was high, and wages were low. For most there was no chance to build up personal savings to order to have a source of income in the case of unemployment, old age, disability, or illness (Zoellner, 1982).

This was the background when Bismarck proposed a comprehensive social security system in 1881, which included protection against old age and invalidity, sickness, and work injury. Bismarck wanted to calm social tensions, split labor, and consolidate imperial Germany (Stolleis, 1980).

By 1889 the parliament had passed an act concerning disability and old-age insurance (Gesetz betreffend die Invaliditaets-und Alterversicherung). The legislation covered all wage earners (blue-collar workers) and salaried employees (white-collar workers) with salaries not exceeding 2,000 German marks per year. It was preceded by the Health Insurance for Workers Act (Gesetz ueber die Krankenversicherung der Arbeiter) of 1883 and the Accident Insurance Act (Unfallversicherungsgesetz) of 1884.

In 1911 these three acts were consolidated into the Reich Insurance Code (Reichsversicherungsordnung). In the same year a special old-age and invalidity insurance system for white-collar workers was established (Angestelltenversicherungsgesetz).

Miners have a special social insurance system that has a long tradition dating back to the sixteenth century. During the seventeenth to the nineteenth centuries this system gradually became a social security system. It remained more or less untouched when Bismarck established the German social security system. A uniform act on social security for miners became law in 1923 (Reichsknapps-chaftsgesetz) (Steinmeyer, 1986b). In 1957 a special social insurance system for farmers was established (Steinmeyer, 1986e). Self-employed craftsmen were first covered by the old-age, disability, and survivor insurance system on a compulsory basis (Gesetz uber die Altersversorgung fuer das Deutsche Hand-werk) in 1938 (Steinmeyer, 1986c).

In the same year the entire system of funding was changed by shifting from a full-reserve basis to a pay-as-you-go basis. This reform, which put the benefits on a higher level in order to maintain the standard of living in retirement, is regarded as the most important innovation of the German social insurance system since its establishment (Ruland, 1986).

In 1972 the so-called flexible retirement age was introduced, which permitted individuals to retire at age 63 and receive an old-age benefit without actuarial reductions (Rentenreform-gesetz 1972). The same act provided an opportunity for the self-employed to be covered on a voluntary basis. In 1981 a social insurance system for self-employed artists and publicists was established (Kuen-stlersozialversicherungsgesetz) (Schulte, 1986). Following a 1975 decision of the Federal Constitutional Court (Bundesverfassungsgericht), the West German parliament had to reform the system of widow and widower benefits to make them more equitable and gender-free. This reform came into force on January 1, 1986 (Hinterbliebenenrenten und Erziehungszeitengesetz).

MAIN PROGRAM FEATURES

Under the general pension insurance system all employees except civil ser-vants, judges, and soldiers are covered on a compulsory basis. The self-employed are compulsorily insured if they are craftsmen, farmers, artists, publicists, or select small businessmen. In addition there is the possibility of voluntary insur-ance (Bley, 1988; Brooke and Zacher, 1983). The pension insurance scheme provides benefits in the case of old age, death, incapacity to perform a particular job (occupational invalidity), incapacity for work generally (general invalidity), and vocational or medical rehabilitation (Steinmeyer and Tracy, 1985).

Qualifying Conditions for Old-Age Pensions

To qualify for an old-age pension the insured generally has to be 65 years of age. An additional requirement is an insured period of 60 months. This require-ment may be met by a combination of the months of payroll contributions, periods of service in the military during World War II, periods without em-ployment resulting from the war (Ersatzzeiten), and years of child care (Kin-dererziehungszeiten).

People usually retire before age 65. They can retire at age 63 and receive benefits without actuarial reduction if they have 35 years of insurance including not only years in which payroll taxes were paid and Ersatzzeiten, but also periods of pregnancy, rehabilitation, unemployment, apprenticeship, and education at general schools, vocational schools, or colleges and universities after age 16 (Ausfallzeiten). In this period of 35 years of insurance there have to be 180 months during which payroll taxes were paid or during which the insured served in the military during World War II or suffered unemployment as a result of the war. This early retirement option is called "flexibles Altersruhegeld" (flexible old-age pension) and is a result of the reform of 1972. More than 70 percent of the insured opt for it. There is an earnings test for this benefit that imposes a penalty for earnings of more than 1,000 Deutsche Marks (DM) a month or work for more than two months or 50 days.

Women can retire at age 60 if they have 180 months of insurance (excluding Ausfallzeiten). This differentiation between men and women has been held constitutional by the Federal Constitutional Court because it compensates women for rearing children and running households.

Persons who are seriously disabled, incapable of working, incapable of performing a particular job, or unemployed for at least 52 weeks during the preceding one and a half years are eligible for an old-age pension at age 60. They also need to have 180 months of insurance.

Survivor Pensions

Survivor pensions are paid to widows, widowers, and orphans. This system underwent a reform in 1985. Previously, widow benefits were paid in any case if the insured husband died, whereas a widower received a benefit only if his wife was mainly responsible for supporting him. In 1975 this was held to be unconstitutional by the Federal Constitutional Court. Under a new law passed by parliament in July 1985 (effective January 1, 1986) there is equal treatment of widows and widowers with respect to survivor benefits. For those widows and widowers with earned income or receiving another public pension the survivor pension is reduced if other income exceeds DM 1013.40 per month in 1989. The amount of a widow's or widower's benefit is 60 percent of the amount of an occupational invalidity pension and 60 percent of the amount of a general invalidity pension if the widow/widower is 45 or older, disabled, or has to care for a child (von Maydell, 1986).

Benefit Levels

Since the reform of 1957, the aim of the West German pension insurance system is to maintain, together with other sources of income such as private pensions, the standard of living the retiree had before retirement. Therefore the former wages are reflected by the benefit level of the individual retiree.

In order to equalize benefits for people with high earnings at the beginning of their career and people with high earnings at the end of their career, the percentage of gross earnings in relation to the average of the gross earnings of all insured people is calculated for each year of insurance. The next step is to determine the average of the individual's earnings in relation to the earnings of all insured persons (the personal assessment basis [persoenliche Bemessungs-grundlage]). It is expressed as a percentage of the average income of all insured people.

Since it is an insurance scheme, the years of insurance are taken into account to calculate the benefit. For this purpose not only those periods for which con-tributions were paid are taken into account but also Ersatzzeiten and Ausfallz-eiten. Finally, there is a coefficient for the years (Jahreskoeffizient or Steigerungsbetrag) that distinguishes among different kinds of benefits. For old-age pensions and disability benefits in the case of incapacity for work, it is generally 1.5 percent. In order to reflect the general income situation of the insured, the average income of all insured in the year of the retirement of the individual is taken into account (the general assessment basis [allgemeine Be-messungs-grundlage]) and put in relation to the personal assessment basis.

In general, only those earnings are taken into account that do not exceed a certain ceiling of the general assessment basis. The general assessment basis for 1989 was DM 30,709. For insured people with more than 25 years of insurance (excluding Ausfallzeiten and voluntary insurance) the personal assessment basis for years before 1973 is at least 75 percent of the general assessment basis (Rente nach Mindesteinkommen [pension based on minimum earnings]).

Therefore the benefit formula for the monthly benefit is:

(personal assessment basis × general assessment basis) × (years of insurance × coefficient for the years) ÷ 12

For example, assume a male individual retired on July 31, 1989, at age 65 after 40 years of employment. In the first 20 years his earnings amounted to 90 percent of the general assessment basis. That means for 1958 his earnings were DM 4,087.80 per year whereas the general assessment basis was DM 4,542. In the last twenty years his earnings were 120 percent of the general assessment basis. Therefore, his personal assessment basis is 105 percent. So his benefit level is calculated as follows: 105% (personal assessment basis) times DM 30,709 (general assessment basis for 1989) times 40 (years of insurance) times 1.5% (coefficient for the years for old-age pension) = DM 19,346.67 divided by 12 = DM 1,612.22. Therefore, the individual in the example will receive a monthly old-age benefit of DM 1,612.22 in 1989.

The average replacement rate after 40 years of insurance is about 65 percent of the net income after 45 years of insurance (Ruland, 1986).

The benefits are adjusted annually on July 1 by a special Pension Benefits Adjustment Act (Rentenanpassungsgesetz), if the general assessment basis of that year is different from the year before. In principle, the adjustment has to follow the increase of the net income of the people employed. Retirees are thus able to maintain their standard of living in case of inflation.

Administration

The pension insurance program is administered by a number of different institutes. The program for salaried employees is administered by the Federal Salaried Employees' Insurance Institute (Bundesveisicherungsantalt fuer Angestelle), the program for wage earners by 18 state insurance institutes (Landesveisicherungsantalten). In addition there is a special institute for seamen (Seekasse) and another special institute for national railway employees (Bundesbahn-Veisicherungsanstalt). The federal institutes are supervised by the Federal Insurance Agency (Bundesversicherungsamt) and the Federal Minister of Labor and Social Affairs, while the state insurance institutes are supervised by the states.

All these institutes have the right of self-administration, which means that there is an assembly (Vertreterversammlung) that consists of an equal number of employers and employees. It elects the directors and the governing body, who make up the budget and control the management of the institute. Supervision by the Federal Insurance Agency (Bundesversicherungsamt), the Federal Minister of Labor and Social Affairs, and the states is generally limited to whether the institutes are following the law.

Special Provisions for Women

In Germany the pension insurance system was established 100 years ago when the role of women was considerably different from now (Steinmeyer, 1986a). Women were typically considered housewives dependent on their husbands for income. As a result the German pension insurance system emphasized the protection of a woman after her husband's death. During the past several decades the role of women in society and the economy has changed considerably. Increasingly, women spend a considerable portion of their lives in the workforce. The pension insurance system, therefore, has had to react.

In a contributory system people who are not employed, such as women homemakers, usually do not receive pensions on their own right but as dependents. In addition, women who drop out of the labor force for a period of time to care for children ultimately receive smaller pensions because benefits are related to years of employment. Also, women typically receive smaller pensions due to the fact they usually earn less than men.

For decades this was widely accepted since the majority of women were housewives whereas men were the breadwinners. After retirement the husband and wife lived on his pension and in the case of his death the widow received a widow's benefit. Moreover, divorce was far less common than today. Consequently, the pension insurance system of the Federal Republic of Germany did not provide adequate protection in case of divorce. These provisions came under discussion when the role of women in the economy and society changed and when the divorce rate increased dramatically.

The first step in equalizing the treatment of men and women was made by the Federal Constitutional Court in 1975. The court found that different provisions for widows and widowers were unconstitutional. Consequently the federal government established a commission of experts to propose solutions for improving the treatment of women under the social security system (Sachverstaendigen-kommisson, 1979).

Realizing that the social protection for divorced women was insufficient, the Federal Republic of Germany introduced earnings sharing/credit splitting in the case of divorce (Versorgunggsausgleich) as part of the Marriage Reform Act of 1976. The idea of earnings sharing was brought into the discussion by Planken in 1961 (Planken, 1961).

Under earnings sharing, marriage is treated as an equal economic partnership in which accumulated assets, including social security earnings credits, are divided equally between spouses in case of divorce. Husbands and wives receive benefits based on equal shares of combined earnings records irrespective of their homemaking and breadwinning responsibilities during the marriage (U.S. Department of Health and Human Services, 1985). All pension entitlements are subject to sharing, including private pensions, pensions for civil servants, life insurance, and public pensions. In general, all these pension entitlements accumulated by both spouses during the marriage are divided equally between spouses.

The commission of experts rejected the idea of a homemaker pension. The commission found that if the pension was mandatory it would increase the financial burden for employees because they would have to pay contributions for their own old-age pension and for the pension of the homemaker. If voluntary, those people opting for it would generally be those who are better off financially and, therefore, least in need of coverage. Nevertheless, the commission favored the idea of crediting periods of child care.

Progress toward extending the principle of earnings sharing to ongoing marriages was halted by economic difficulties and the resulting efforts to trim the budget. Instead, the government proposed modification of the existing system of widow and widower pensions in order to comply with the decision of the Federal Constitutional Court. To improve the situation of women, crediting years of child care was introduced. Under the new law one year is credited to a mother for each child—or a father if he reared the child. The additional cost of this is financed from general revenues and not from contributions of the insured. Critics argued that one year for each child does not improve the treatment of women substantially since they usually have to drop out more than one year in order to care for a child.

Special Programs and Institutions

The special system for miners covers any employee who is working in the mining industry, whether in the mine itself or in the office. The system includes

health insurance and pension insurance. The pension insurance for miners provides, besides benefits under the general system, the so-called Bergmannsrente
(miner benefit). This benefit is similar to disability benefits and is exclusively
for employees who worked in the mine itself. Since mining is a very strenuous
job, many miners after a number of years are unable to perform their mining
job and as a result have a loss of income although they are still capable for work
under the provision of the general invalidity pension and the occupational invalidity pension. The Bergmannsrente is designed to compensate for this loss
of income.

As early as the 1960s the mining industry—especially the coal-mining sector—
had to adjust its production to a new and more limited market. For miners over
age 55 who have lost their jobs the system provides a special benefit called
Knappschaftsausgleichsleistung (miner compensation benefit); this benefit has
elements of both a redundancy payment and an old-age benefit.

The average amount of benefits for miners is higher than in the general system
due to the higher coefficient for the year. For example, for old-age pensions it
is 2 percent. Social security for miners is administered by the Bundesknappschaft.
Its assembly (Vertreterversammlung) is different from those in the general system. Whereas in the general system employers and employees each have 50
percent of the seats in the assembly, the mining employees have two-thirds and
the employers one-third.

The special program for farmers covers self-employed farmers, their relatives
if they work on the farm, and their survivors. Agricultural workers were covered
by the general system from its very beginning. The old-age benefit for farmers
is a flat-rate benefit. The farmer has to pay contributions for a period of at least
180 months and receives (in 1989) DM 607.00 if married and DM 404.90 if
unmarried. The benefit is adjusted annually at the same rate as benefits in the
general system. The amount of the old-age benefit for relatives is half the amount
of the old-age benefit for the farmer. Pension insurance for farmers is administered by a number of agricultural pension institutes (Steinmeyer, 1986c).

Special Groups

Handicraftsmen are compulsorily insured during the years when they are working as employees. The Pension Insurance for Handicraftsmen Act forces the self-
employed to continue pension insurance on a compulsory basis until they have
paid contributions for at least 216 months. This provides a floor of protection
for self-employed handicraftsmen in old age. The program is administered by
the State Insurance Institute since the handicraftsmen worked as wage earners
before they became self-employed (Steinmeyer, 1986b).

The 1981 Social Insurance for Self-Employed Artists and Publicists Act ex-
tends compulsory pension insurance under the program for salaried employees
to these persons. The program is administered by an institution known as Kuen-
stlersozialkasse. It has to collect the contributions and transfer them to the Federal
Salaried Employees' Insurance Institute that grants the benefits (Schulte, 1986).

Funding Provisions

The different pension insurance programs are mainly financed by contributions that are 18.7 percent of gross incomes up to a certain assessment limit in the general system. One-half of the contribution is paid by the employer, the other half by the employee. The contribution assessment limit in 1989 was DM 73,200 (DM 6,100 per month). A subsidy of about 17.5 percent of total cost of the general pension insurance system is paid annually by the federal government.

In the pension insurance scheme for miners the contribution rate is 23.5 percent. The employer pays 15 percent and the employee pays 8.5 percent. These contributions cover only 16 percent of the total cost of pension insurance for miners. The remaining 84 percent is covered by a subsidy of the federal government and by payment of other pension insurance institutes. The pension insurance system for farmers has a flat-rate contribution of DM 220 per month (1989). The subsidy of the federal government amounts to 80.3 percent of the total cost of this system of pension insurance.

Relationship to National Budget

In 1986 the total amount of benefits in the general system (including miners) was DM 159.5 billion. In the pension insurance system for farmers it was DM 2.85 billion. This was 9.2 percent of the GNP for the general system and 0.2 percent for the pension system for farmers (Sozialbericht, 1986).

POLICY ISSUES

Demographic Problems

The main policy issue on pension insurance in the Federal Republic of Germany can be phrased as structural reform (Strukturreform). This reform is necessary due to the demographic changes that will affect the system in the next century.

While the ratio between those who are paying contributions and retirees was 100 to 48 in 1985, it will be 100 to 80 in 2020, 100 to 103 in 2030, and 100 to 107 in 2040 (Mueller, 1985). Maintaining the present replacement rate would require a contribution rate of 27.1 percent in 2015 and 36.7 percent in 2040 without any reforms (Kolb, 1987).

Therefore, a number of reform proposals are under discussion. There are radical suggestions to substitute the existing system with one that provides only a basic floor of protection. These proposals would mean that people have to build on other assets like occupational pensions, life insurance, and savings for retirement.

In March 1989 the governing political parties (Christian Democrats and Free Democrats) together with the oppositional Social Democrats introduced a bill in parliament to reform the pension system effective January 1, 1992 (Retenreformgesetz 1992). This act is designed to solve the financial and demographic problems of the next two decades and will be the most comprehensive reform of the social insurance system since 1957. Its major features are an increase in the retirement age after the year 2000 and an increase in the federal subsidy to 20 percent of the total cost. The benefit formula will be revised in order to introduce improvements for people who care for children or for an elderly or infirm relative. The scheduled increase in the retirement age means removing the current early retirement provisions and reestablishing age 65 as the standard retirement age. This will be accomplished by actuarially reducing benefits payable before age 65 and by improving the rate by which benefits are increased for payment deferred beyond age 65. The contribution rate is projected to increase from 18.7 percent in 1989–1992 to 21.4 percent in 2010 (Ruland, 1989). Critics argue that this reform does not go far enough since it only deals with the problems of the next two decades and not with the subsequent years.

Coverage of Women

There has been little discussion of women's coverage since the 1985 act was passed. Due to the system's financial problems, proposals have no chance for realization.

Early Retirement

As a means of reducing unemployment, the 1984 Preretirement Plans Act created a basic framework for collective agreements that are primarily financed by the employer (65%) who can apply for an additional allowance of 35 percent by the Federal Labor Institute (Bundesantalt fuer Arbeit). The requirement for this allowance is that the job vacated by the preretiree is filled by an unemployed person. Under this program, which has been elected by about 70,000 persons, an employee can retire at age 58.

This was only a temporary measure: the program was phased out on December 31, 1988. A continuation was under discussion, but the federal government recently decided not to continue the program.

The Preretirement Plans Act was followed by the Old-Age Part-Time Retirement Plans Act (Altersteilzeitgesetz) effective January 1, 1989. Under the provisions of this act, workers who are at least age 58 can retire on a part-time basis. This act is similar to the Preretirement Plans Act; it also provides an additional allowance by the Federal Labor Institute supplementary to the benefit paid by the employer and was created as a measure to reduce unemployment among younger workers. Part-time employment is also viewed as a means to ease the transition to retirement. This act will phase out on December 31, 1991, since provisions on part-time retirement will also be part of the 1992 reform.

OCCUPATIONAL PENSIONS

Occupational pensions play an important role in the West German old-age income security system. In 1984 72 percent of all employees in manufacturing industry and 26 percent of all employees in commerce were covered by pension plans. Sixty-seven percent of all manufacturing enterprises and 30 percent of all commercial enterprises had pension plans. The average monthly benefit amount in 1982 was DM 310 (Sachverstaendigenkommission, 1983). The total amount of occupational pensions paid was DM 11.94 billion in 1986 (Sozialbericht, 1986).

SUPPLEMENTARY AND INCOME-TESTED PROVISIONS

The ultimate safety net in the West German social security system is social assistance (Sozialhilfe), which provides basic protection and guarantees everyone a minimum income. This system is means-tested. Along with other means-tested supplements, it provides subsistence assistance to ensure an adequate standard of living (Hilfe zum Lebensunterhalt).

Social assistance has importance for those retirees whose pension insurance benefits are low. This affects women especially. It is also important if a retiree needs permanent or long-term institutionalized care. Most retirees are unable to cover the costs of permanent care with their pension benefits. Social assistance has to fill the gap.

SUMMARY

The West German insurance system, which originated in the nineteenth century, is quite complicated. It provides a relatively high level of protection. The development of the system during the last decade can be described as filling the last gaps of protection by including self-employed artists and publicists and by improving the protection of women. The main problem is financial and is primarily a result of dramatic demographic changes. The system must make decisive changes in order to survive the challenges of the future.

REFERENCES

Bley, H. (1988). *Sozialrecht*. 6th ed. Frankfurt: Metzner-erlag.

Brooke, R., and Zacher, H. (1983). *Social legislation in the Federal Republic of Germany*. London: Bedford Square.

Kolb, R. (1987). Kuenftige strukturen der gesetzlichen renterversicherung?: Notwendigkeiten und machbarkeit. In *Beratungs-Gmbh fuer altersversorgung, Betriebliche altersversorgung 1987*. Wiesbaden: Arbeit und Alter Verlag.

Maydell, B. von (1986). Witwenrente. In B. von Maydell (ed.), *Lexikon des rechts/ sozialrecht*, 434–438. Neuwied/Darmstadt: Hermann Luchterhand Verlag.

Mueller, H. W. (1985). Zur deomgraphischen komponente als indikator fuer die finan-zentwicklung der rentenversicherung. *Deutsche Rentenversicherung*, 724–744.

Planken, H. (1961). *Die soziale sicherung der nicht-erwerbstaetigen frau*. Berlin: Duncker and Humblot.

Ruland, F. (1986). Rentenversicherung. In B. von Maydell (ed.), *Lexikon des Rechts/ Sozialrecht*, 227–265. Heuwied/Darmstadt: Hermann Luchterhand Verlag.

———. (1989). Die rentenreform 1992. *Neue Zeitschrift fuer Arbeitsund Sozialrecht 1989 Beil*, 2, 3–27.

Sachverstaendigenkommission Alterssicherungssyteme. (1983). *Vergleich der Altessi-cherungssysteme und empfehlungen der kommission-gutachten der sachverstaen-digenkommission*. Berichtsband, Bonn: Der Bundesminister fuer Arbeit und Sozialordnung.

Schulte, B. (1986). Kuenstlersozialversicherung. In B. von Maydell (ed.), *Lexikon des Rechts/Sozialrecht*, 190–193. Neuwied/Darmstadt: Hermann Luchterhand Verlag.

Steinmeyer, H. D. (1986a). Social security reform: Its consequences for women in in-dustrialized and developing countries. *Compensation & Benefits Management*, 3, 413–418.

———. (1986b). Handwerkerversicherung. In B. von Maydell (ed.), *Lexikon des Rechts/ Sozialrecht*, 143–146. Neuwied/Darmstadt: Hermann Luchterhand Verlag.

———. (1986c). Landwirtschaftliches sozialrecht. In B. von Maydell (ed.), *Lexikon des Rechts/Sozialrecht*, 194–202. Neuwied/Darmstadt: Hermann Luchterhand Verlag.

Steinmeyer, H. D., and Tracy, M. B. (1985). Rehabilitation program issues in the Federal Republic of Germany. *Journal of Rehabilitation*, 51, July–August–September, 39–41.

Stolleis, M. (1980). Hundert jahre sozialversicherung in Deutschland: Rechtsgeschicht-liche entwicklung. *Zeitschrift fuer die gesamte Versicherungswissenschaft*, 155–175.

U.S. Department of Health and Human Services. (1985). *Report on earnings sharing implementation study*. Washington, D.C.: Social Security Administration.

Zoellner, D. (1982). Germany. In P. A. Koehler and H. F. Zacher (eds.), *The evolution of social insurance, 1881–1981: Studies of Germany, France, Great Britain, Austria, and Switzerland*, 1–92. London: Francis Pinter.

8

German Democratic Republic

Paul Adams

Social insurance in the German Democratic Republic (GDR) has been closely tied to the demands of economic policy.[1] The GDR was founded in 1949, and its early years were a period of severe economic difficulties due to the result of wartime destruction, the loss of markets and sources of raw materials in the postwar division of Germany, and expropriations by the Soviet Union. In the process of postwar reconstruction, of rebuilding and restructuring industry and the military, social provision for the old and the disabled received low priority (Michalsky, 1984).

The government's difficulties were exacerbated by the large-scale exodus from East to West Germany, which resulted in a heavy loss of professionals and skilled workers and an overall decline of population from a peak of 19.1 million in 1947 to 17.1 million by the end of 1962 (Strassburger, 1984). After the closing of its borders and the building of the Berlin Wall in 1961, which prevented present and future workers, but not retirees, from leaving, the GDR experienced sustained economic growth and rising living standards. Despite problems of heavy foreign debt, slow growth, and low capital investment, it remained the richest and most successful of the centrally planned economies. In late 1989, however, political and demographic changes were under way, which were to lead the following year to the dissolution of the GDR as a political entity and its absorption into the Federal Republic. The following account first describes the old age insurance system of the GDR and then discusses briefly the steps that are being taken to absorb it into Federal Republic's social insurance system.

The demographic status of the GDR reflected both patterns common among European countries and factors specific to the GDR. Wars and a high sex differential in peacetime mortality produced an elderly population that was predominantly female. The experience of a baby boom followed by low fertility has resulted in a temporarily favorable situation in terms of social security financing. The GDR's dependency ratio reached an all-time low in 1985, with 65 percent of the population of working age, 19 percent children, and 16 percent of pensionable age. The proportions stayed at this level through 1987, and the number of pensioners was expected to decline (Buettner et al., 1987; Panorama DDR, 1988b; German Democratic Republic, 1988). Since the GDR had a very high female labor force participation rate (slightly over 90 percent), the proportion of social security contributors to beneficiaries was high (Bundesministerium fuer innerdeutsche Beziehungen, 1987; German Democratic Republic, 1988). As in the Federal Republic of Germany and many other advanced industrial countries, however, this situation was expected to be reversed in the next century, when the cohorts who recently entered the workforce reached retirement age. As a result of low birth rates over an extended period, there were expected to be fewer workers to support this enlarged population of retirees, who would have accrued pension entitlements based on a full lifetime of covered employment. These demographic problems were to be exacerbated by the renewed exodus of young professionals and skilled workers, together with their children, in 1989.

From its origins under Bismarck, German social insurance developed into a complex system of different insurance groups, programs, and benefit levels. After World War II, a major reform of social security was accomplished in the Soviet-occupied zone (the territory out of which the GDR would be formed). A single, universal comprehensive program replaced the prior system of different insurance programs for different occupational categories and for different contingencies (Hentschel, 1983). In 1951 responsibility for control and management of social insurance was given to the trade union federation, the Federation of Free German Trade Unions (Freier Deutscher Gewerkschaftsbund, FDGB). Those members of the workforce not controlled by the FDGB, including the self-employed, farmers, lawyers, and freelance workers, had been covered since 1956 by a state insurance system, at first called the German Insurance Institution (Deutsche Versicherungsanstalt) and, from 1969, State Insurance of the GDR (Staatliche Versicherung der DDR). The benefits under the two insurance carriers were substantially the same.

In the first two decades of the GDR, benefits were low relative to wages, but the system was costly to the state because many workers became entitled to pensions with only brief periods of contribution and because the ratio of elderly to workers increased. As the economic and demographic situations improved, benefits were raised and became increasingly differentiated to reflect differences in earnings and years of covered employment. Since 1968, pensions had been increased at regular intervals, although without being indexed, to reflect increases in the productivity and earnings of the workforce. A voluntary supplementary pension program (freiwillige Zusatzrenten-versicherung, FZR) was introduced in its present form in 1971, following an earlier version started in 1968. At first it enabled workers to opt for additional pension entitlement based on their monthly earnings between M 600 and a threshold of M 1,200. The upper limit was abolished in 1977, except for the self-employed.

MAIN PROGRAM FEATURES

The social insurance system of the FDGB covered wage and salaried employees, as well as students and apprentices (about 88 percent of the workforce in all), while the state insurance scheme covered the self-employed, members of agricultural and other cooperatives, and independent professionals (Bundesministerium fuer innerdeutsche Beziehungen, 1985). The voluntary supplementary program enabled workers with earnings above M 600 per month to take out additional coverage, entitling them to a supplementary pension and higher cash benefits during sickness and maternity.

The social insurance scheme was comprehensive, including coverage for old age and dependents, sickness, maternity, accident, and disability. Unemployment was not covered, since the right to employment is constitutionally guaranteed.

Qualifying Conditions for Old-Age Pensions

The normal retirement age was 65 years for men and 60 years for women. Miners were able to retire up to five years earlier, depending upon the number of years above five that they have worked as miners. In order to qualify for an old-age pension, a worker had to accrue fifteen years of insurance, or five in the case of a miner or a worker who was at least age 50 when first covered (Panorama DDR, 1988a).

The minimum of fifteen years of covered employment required to qualify for an old-age pension was reduced for women who had at least five years of insurance coverage and had reared three or more children. They were credited with one extra year of coverage for each child reared (Panorama DDR, 1988a).

Benefit Levels

Benefits were calculated by adding to a flat base of M 140 an additional sum based upon earnings and years of employment. One percent of average covered monthly earnings (2 percent in the case of miners; 1.5 percent for health and social service workers, railroad, and postal workers) for each of the last 20 years before retirement was multiplied by the number of years of insurance. Only income on which social insurance contributions were paid, that is, up to M 600 per month, was taken into account in this calculation. Periods of training, military service, leave from work while in receipt of maternity benefits (Babyjahr) or disability or accident pensions, and periods of unemployment up to 1945, were treated as covered periods of insurance in the calculation of benefits. When benefits were calculated for women who had been employed for the minimum period required to qualify for benefits, credit was given for additional years of coverage according to the number of children born. One year per child was credited for women with one or two children, three years per child for women with three or more (Panorama DDR, 1988b).

Flat supplements, unrelated to prior earnings, were paid for a spouse aged 60 or unable to work who was not entitled to a pension. This supplement amounted to M 200 per month (*Neues Deutschland*, December 1, 1988). A similar supplement to old-age pensions, as well as to disability and accident benefits, and war-disability pensions, was paid for dependent children and students, the amount varying according to the ages and number of children.

For every year of contribution to the voluntary supplementary scheme (FZR), pensioners received an additional 2.5 percent of average monthly earnings over M 600. For example, 25 years of an average income of M 1,000 would give a supplementary benefit of M 250 per month (25 × .025 × 400 = 250). Average monthly retirement pensions under the compulsory scheme were M 380 in 1987, compared with M 200 in 1970. Pensioners who had opted for voluntary supplementary insurance received an average monthly pension of M 476 in 1987 (Panorama DDR, 1988b).

The GDR had a complex system of minimum benefits. In 1989, the basic minimum monthly old-age and disability pension for those with less than the qualifying minimum of years of insurance (normally 15 years) was M 300 (USDHHS, 1990). The minimum pension then increased according to years worked, from M 340 after 15 years to M 470 after 45 or more years of covered work. Women who had borne five or more children and had a claim on old-age pensions or disability benefits from covered work received a minimum benefit at the highest level, M 470 (*Neues Deutschland*, December 1, 1988).

Survivor benefits, payable to an aged or invalid surviving spouse or to a widow caring for a child, amounted to 60 percent of the basic pension of the insured, but were also subject to a minimum. Minimum survivor benefits were M 330 for a widow or widower, M 165 for half-orphans, and M 220 for full orphans (*Neues Deutschland*, December 1, 1988).

The maximum retirement benefit under the compulsory scheme was determined by the earnings base of M 600 on which contributions were paid while working. The normal maximum benefit under the compulsory scheme was M 140 plus 1 percent of M 600 times 50 (the maximum years of insured work that could be taken into account). This calculation yielded a maximum of M 440. For miners and other groups of workers with special provisions the maximum would be higher. Beyond the low maximum ensured by the compulsory scheme, pensions depended upon prior contributions to the voluntary supplementary program.

Benefits were not automatically adjusted to inflation, but were increased periodically by a resolution of the political leaders. Thus an increase, applying especially to minimum pension levels, was announced in a joint resolution of the SED (the ruling Socialist Unity party) Central Committee, the FDGB Central Executive Council, and the GDR Council of Ministers, passed on November

30, 1988, and took effect on December 1, 1989 (*Neues Deutschland*, December 1, 1988).

Administration

The FDGB, under the central direction of its national executive committee, administered the social insurance program for blue- and white-collar employees. Directors were appointed at every level (national, county, district, and municipal), who were responsible to the FDGB committee at that level for administration of the program.

There was a high level of "self-administration" of social insurance. Every trade union group elected a representative who was responsible for social insurance matters. These representatives were guided by their social insurance council, a body appointed by the trade union branch committee to ensure the proper transfer of contributions and benefits, and to solve specific problems. Special arrangements existed within the FDGB program for miners, railroad employees, and postal service workers.

The State Insurance System (Staatliche Versicherung der DDR), which administered both compulsory and voluntary supplementary social insurance for those who were not production or office employees, was the responsibility of the minister of finance. The minister appointed a director-in-chief (*Hauptdirektor*) who managed a system of county, district, and local offices. Honorary advisory committees were appointed by the directors at each level from those insured under the state system.

Both the FDGB and the State Insurance System had complaint commissions at every level. These commissions handled disputes about such matters as benefit entitlements, and their decisions could be appealed up to the level of the county (*Bezirk*) commission. There was then the option of petitioning the central complaint commission, which had the power to annul lower-level decisions up to one year after they are announced.

The administration of social insurance in the GDR depended heavily on the voluntary, unpaid work of the various committees of the insured. In the FDGB scheme, almost 400,000 workers participated in this way and thereby helped to keep administrative costs to less than 0.5 percent of social insurance expenditure (Panorama DDR, 1988a).

Special Provisions for Women

The GDR had a complex array of measures that supported women in general and childrearing in particular. As we have seen above, credit was given for the number of children a woman had borne, both in assessing the minimum period of employment she needed to qualify for a pension and in calculating the amount of her benefit. The other provisions most directly related to the old-age insurance system were the five-year differential retirement age, credit for maternity leave from employment in the calculation of benefits, and provisions for dependent, surviving, and divorced spouses. Dependent spouse and survivor benefits went disproportionately to women, simply because, as elsewhere, women in the GDR were more likely to be dependent on and to outlive their spouses (German Democratic Republic, 1988; Buettner et al., 1987).

In certain circumstances, women with no record of paid employment were entitled to a pension. Women who had borne five or more children, but who were not otherwise eligible for a pension, received a minimum pension of M 330 when they reached retirement age. For women who had borne five or more children and were eligible for a pension by virtue of compulsorily insurable work, the minimum pension is M 470 (*Neues Deutschland*, December 1, 1988). These measures gave expression to the official view, according to which child-rearing was regarded as no less important a social contribution than paid employment.

Pensioners were entitled to an allowance of M 200 for retired spouses who did not have their own pension. They also received a children's allowance of M 60 for any dependent child. The surviving spouse of a pensioner who was the main breadwinner at the time of death was entitled to a pension that was 60 percent of the pension of the deceased, but in any case no less than M 330. If the surviving spouse was eligible for a pension in her or his own right, then the higher pension was paid in full, plus one-quarter of the lower pension. Surviving spouses were also entitled to 60 percent of the supplementary (FZR) pension of the deceased, in this case without regard to who was the main breadwinner. Divorced persons of retirement age who had been entitled to support from their former spouse and who were not eligible for a pension in their own right, received continued support from the old-age insurance system, up to a maximum of M 330, from the death of the former spouse. To be eligible for this benefit, the survivor had to have reached retirement age and the deceased former spouse had to have been eligible for a pension. The benefit was paid in the same amount as the former spouse's support obligation, up to the M 330 maximum.

Financing

The compulsory insurance program for old-age, survivor, invalidity, sickness, maternity, work-injury, and unemployment benefits was financed by contributions from employees and employers, with a substantial subsidy from the national budget. Employees paid 10 percent of their gross earnings, firms paid 12.5 percent of payroll (22.5 percent in the case of mining enterprises). Pensioners who continued to work did not pay the mandatory social insurance tax, but their employing firms continued to pay the employer's contribution. The maximum earnings for contribution purposes in 1989 was M 600 a month (USDHHS, 1990).

In 1987, the total expenditure of the FDGB-run program, for production and office employees, amounted to 30.123 billion marks. This was financed by revenues of 16.067 billion marks from employee and employer contributions and a subsidy from the national budget of 14.056 billion marks (46.7 percent of the total). The national budget subsidy came mainly from profits made by nationally owned enterprises (German Democratic Republic, 1988; Panorama DDR, 1988a). These expenditure figures covered a wide range of benefits in addition to old-age insurance. The largest expenditures were for pensions (13.48 billion marks in 1987), health care (6.8 billion marks), sickness benefits (3.95 billion marks), and medications (2.83 billion marks) (German Democratic Republic, 1988; Panorama DDR, 1988a). The increase in benefits that took effect in 1989, the fortieth anniversary year of the GDR, were expected to require additional national budget spending of more than 2 billion marks (Panorama DDR, 1989).

The produced national income of the GDR in 1987 was 261 billion marks. Social insurance expenditures consumed 11.5 percent of this total (German Democratic Republic, 1988).

POLICY ISSUES

As an intergenerational arrangement, old-age insurance may be seen as a closed system in which active workers both support present-day retirees and rear the children who will support them in old age (Adams, 1989). Demographic structure may therefore be of particular importance for the long-term financial stability of old-age insurance systems. Policy analysts in the GDR recognized that although the demographic dependency ratio at the end of the 1980s was favorable, the long-term outlook was uncertain. Thus leading East German demographers argued that there was an immediate need to consider measures to counteract the very dramatic future problems that would arise from the dependency ratios in general and from old age dependency in particular (Buettner et al., 1987).

The exodus of GDR citizens, mostly young and well-trained, that was taking place in the GDR's final year could only exacerbate these concerns. Emigration of young adults and their children, and the probable impact of the loss of professional and skilled labor, amplified the long-term consequences of a low birth rate for the social insurance system. These developments were unlikely to be offset either by immigrant labor (for example, from Vietnam) or by the emigration of East German retirees, who were entitled under West German law to a pension based on the putative earnings they would have.

UNIFICATION

As the full unification of the two German states approached, the problems of transition to a unified social insurance scheme and the phasing out of the East German system emerged as the preeminent policy concern. The treaty of May

18, 1990 between the two German states established a monetary, economic, and social union (International Labour Office, 1990). (The treaty for *political* union was signed on August 31, 1990.) It provided for the absorption of the GDR's pension insurance system into that of the Federal Republic, with a five-year transition period to protect the rights of persons approaching pensionable age.

The supplementary and special pension schemes were abolished as of July 1, 1990; accrued claims and entitlements are transferred to the pension insurance fund, and potentially excessive benefits are under review. As a result of the July 1, 1990 changes, contribution rates are essentially the same in both parts of Germany, but the contribution ceiling in the former GDR is about 38 percent of the ceiling applicable in western Germany. This differential in contribution ceilings corresponds to the difference in average gross income of employees in the two parts of Germany. Current pensions are fixed at a net replacement rate of 70 percent of average net earnings in the GDR after 45 years of coverage. The voluntary supplementary pension insurance scheme is discontinued, but basic individual pensions are upgraded on the basis of the pension of an average wage earner in the GDR, graduated according to year of entry, who has paid full contributions to the voluntary supplementary scheme over and above his or her compulsory social insurance contributions. If the beneficiary is not entitled to any upgrading on this basis, a pension is paid in deutsche mark (DM) corresponding to the amount of the former pension in GDR marks (M). The intent is that pensions and contribution ceilings in eastern Germany will be brought into line with those in the rest of the Federal Republic as income levels reach parity.

The Unification Treaty, signed on August 31, 1990 and with effect from October 3 of that year, specifies a number of temporary early retirement and other provisions for persons employed in the territory of the former GDR, to be phased out at the latest by the end of 1995. For persons whose pension under the statutory pension scheme begins in the period from January 1, 1992 to June 30, 1995, the treaty provides for payment of a pension at least as high as they would have received in the GDR on June 30, 1990, without regard for payments from supplementary or special pension schemes. Such persons will receive a pension in the Federal Republic if they would have been entitled to one under the pension law of the GDR, valid until June 30, 1990.

NOTES

The author would like to acknowledge the assistance of Dr. Ulrich Lohmann, Max Planck Institute for International and Social Law, Munich.

1. The primary source for this account is Staatssekretariat fuer Arbeit und Loehne (1988). In the text, English-language sources have been emphasized where available.

REFERENCES

Adams, P. (1989). Family policy and labor migration in East and West Germany. *Social Service Review*, 63, 245–263.

Buettner, T., Lutz, W., and Speigner, W. (1987). *Some demographic aspects of aging in the German Democratic Republic*. Working Paper No. 87–116. Laxenburg, Austria: International Institute for Applied Systems Analysis.

Bundesministerium fuer innerdeutsche Beziehungen (Federal Republic of Germany). (1985). *DDR Handbuch*. Cologne: Verlag Wissenschaft und Politik.

———. (1987). *Materialen zum Bericht zur Lage der Nation im geteilten Deutschland 1987*. Bonn.

German Democratic Republic. (1988). *Statistisches Jahrbuch 1988*. Berlin (GDR): Staatsverlag der Deutschen Demokratischen Republik.

Hentschel, V. (1983). *Geschichte der deutschen Sozialpolitik, 1880–1980*. Frankfurt: Suhrkamp.

International Labour Office. (1990). *Labour law documents* 1990/3. Geneva: author.

Michalsky, H. (1984). Social policy and the transformation of society. In Klaus von Beyme and Hartmut Zimmerman (eds.), *Policymaking in the German Democratic Republic*, 242–272. New York: St. Martin's.

Panorama DDR. (1988a). The GDR's social insurance scheme. *Dokumentation* 8-VI–50/5.3 (2).

———. (1988b). *GDR answer to the UN secretary-general: Facts and figures on material security in the German Democratic Republic*. Berlin (GDR).

———. (1989). *Is economic growth a guarantee for material security? Economic and social policy in the GDR*. Berlin (GDR).

Strassburger, J. (1984). Economic system and economic policy: The challenge of the 1970s. In Klaus von Beyme and Hartmut Zimmerman (eds.), *Policymaking in the German Democratic Republic*, 109–143. New York: St. Martin's.

U.S. Department of Health and Human Services. (1990). *Social security programs throughout the world—1989*. Social Security Administration. Office of International Policy. Research Report No. 62. Washington, D.C.: U.S. Government Printing Office.

9

Ghana

Florence Amattey

At the time of independence from the British (1957), Ghana's economy was dominated by agricultural production, which employed almost 60 percent of the labor force. Both the manufacturing and industrial sectors were small and undeveloped, with only 4 percent of the Gross Domestic Product and 4 percent of total employment respectively.

The government that took over from the British colonial administration emphasized modernization and a number of other economic measures of far-reaching consequence. Among these measures was a drive for industrialization and improved living conditions. The strategy for growth was based on a five-year development plan (1959–1964), which marked a turning point in the government's determination to achieve industrialization and to liberate Ghana's economy from foreign domination. High priority was given to the establishment of factories of varying sizes to meet the demand for manufactured commodities and to provide employment for the growing number of middle-school graduates migrating to the urban areas in search of jobs.

As a result of these measures, dramatic economic growth was experienced from 1959 to 1962. This was followed by a decline between 1963 and 1965, coupled with a chronic balance-of-payment deficits and a modest growth in the economy during the period prior to the introduction of social security in 1965.

BACKGROUND

Demographic and Social Conditions

From 1960 to 1970 there were numerous changes that affected many aspects of life in Ghana, especially a population expansion and a shift to urban employment.

From 1960 to 1970 the total population increased from 6.7 to 8.6 million or 36 persons per square kilometer. The 1970 population reflected a very young age distribution (44.5 percent were under fifteen years of age). On the other hand, the population aged 60 years and above was 5.1 percent. The net result of this situation was to create a high dependency burden on the economically productive age groups.

During this period, the rural population fell from 77 to 71 percent. Most of the shift took place in employment areas concentrated in the regional capitals. For instance, while the national annual rate of increase of population was 2.7 percent, it was 5.6 percent in the Greater Accra region. About 90 percent of the country's industrial establishments and almost all the government offices are in Accra.

Legislative History

As a result of the industrialization policies of the government in the early 1960s, many jobs were opened to rural migrants who came to urban areas. Many workers became dependent on a money wage and lost much of the kinship support they had enjoyed within the village or extended families. Thus, when income was interrupted as a result of old age, sickness, accident, or invalidity, workers became destitute. This led the government to give serious deliberation to the provision of a social security scheme for the working population. In 1960 the president announced that the government was considering the establishment of a national pension and insurance scheme for all workers irrespective of their employers.

A national committee was formed to provide the necessary framework for establishing a national social security scheme. The findings and recommendations of the committee submitted in 1961 were to establish a national pension and insurance scheme to cover all daily employees and nonpensionable civil servants and other workers, whether employed by the government or the private sector.

The National Social Security Fund

The 1961 recommendation for an insurance-based system was not implemented. Instead, in 1965 provident fund legislation was adopted under the National Social Security Fund (NSSF) to protect workers against sickness, invalidity, and old age, and to protect dependent widows and orphans from destitution in the event of the death of the breadwinner.

The scheme is a compulsory provident fund for employees of firms with five or more workers, including public employees. Voluntary participation is allowed for smaller firms and for self-employed persons. The provident fund was introduced with the intent that it would be transformed into a social insurance pension program after five years. When replaced by a pension scheme, benefits were to become payable on the occurrence of the same risk contingencies, but consist of regular periodical payments instead of the lump-sum payment under the provident fund. It was envisaged that the scheme would have enough reserves and experience to undertake the conversion from a provident fund to a social insurance scheme by 1972.

At the end of 1989, financing the provident fund was based on employee contributions of 5.0 percent of earnings and employer contributions of 12.5 percent of payroll. The contributions also fund a sickness benefit (USDHHS, 1990). A lump-sum amount equal to the accumulated employee and employer contribution, plus at least 3 percent compound interest, is payable to men at age 55 and to women at age 50 (ages 50 and 45, respectively, at the employee's request). The employee does not have to be retired to receive payment (Dudley, 1988).

The 1965 act placed legal responsibility for management of the scheme in the hands of the State Insurance Corporation, but initially it was the Labor Department that started the program by undertaking the registration of employers and their employees. Later in 1965 the Ministry of Pensions and National Insurance assumed management but, when it was abolished after only one year, the government appointed an advisory board to act in a consultative capacity to aid the State Insurance Corporation to administer the affairs of the fund.

In 1972, the government promulgated legislation (NRCD 127) that reorganized the social security system under the Social Security and National Insurance Trust (SSNIT) as an independent autonomous institution with a board of directors. The law gave great impetus to the scheme and sought to improve management and extend coverage but maintained the program as a provident fund.

Under the 1965 act and the 1972 social security decree, the scheme was applicable to any establishment with not less than five workers. Civil servants who were covered by the government colonial scheme, the police service and prison service, were originally exempt from coverage. In 1973, the government passed a decree (NRCD 190) which allowed voluntary affiliation of independent workers as well as those not covered. This decree also brought pensionable and nonpensionable officers in public service into the scheme. At retirement these officers have their superannuation benefits, consisting of their civil service pension from December 31, 1971, and their social security benefits from January 1, 1972. The transfer of these categories of workers into the national scheme was a major change in coverage.

At the inception of the scheme, the number of registered workers was 335,325 while the number of employers stood at 3,082. By the end of 1972, membership had risen to 617,000 workers and 7,000 employers. This increase in membership was largely the result of the transfer of the pensionable and nonpensionable public service officers into the scheme. By the late 1980s the membership had risen to 1.5 million employees.

The Social Security Act is in force throughout the country. The administration has its headquarters in Accra, where the bulk of the members are concentrated. There are 11 regional offices, nine of which are coterminous with the nine political regions of the country. The two additional regions were created in the twin city of Accra/Tema to cater to the working population in these areas. There are also 42 district offices in almost all the district headquarters of the country. Since the opening of these offices, the scheme has had nationwide coverage. As of December 1987, there were a total of 53 social security offices in Ghana.

PROPOSED NEW PENSION SCHEME

In 1982, the government set up a committee to review the whole social security scheme aimed at exploring ways of converting the program into a social insurance pension system. The primary reason for the interest in conversion is to guarantee income protection against inflation. Such protection is viewed as impossible under the provident fund system. The accumulated interest payable with total employee and employer contribution does not keep pace with price increases and, since the total benefit is paid in a lump sum, it has no future increase in value.

A social insurance scheme was proposed by the committee and was to have been promulgated in January 1989 (International Social Security Association, 1989) but it had not been activated as of December of that year. Notwithstanding, the public is being prepared for the eventual introduction of the new pension scheme through such means as the distribution of informational pamphlets (Public Affairs Department, 1989).

Main Program Features

When implemented, the proposed new scheme will apply to all nongovernment employees and self-employed persons and have the following provisions.

Full pensions payable at age 60 and a reduced pension payable as early as age 55 at 60 percent of the full pension amount will be available. Contributions will be levied on remuneration at the rate of 5 percent for workers and 12.5 percent for employers for a total of 17.5 percent. There will be a self-employed contribution rate of 17.5 percent of income. Nonpayment of contributions will be subject to a 3 percent penalty on outstanding amounts.

In order to qualify for a benefit, workers must have a minimum of 240 months of contributions. Contributions to the NSSF will be counted in the computation of the qualifying period. Workers will also be eligible for an invalidity benefit with a minimum qualifying period of 12 months of contributions in the last 36. The benefit amount is the same as for an old-age pension.

The benefit will be based on 50 percent of the last three years' average salary before retirement. Benefits are increased by 1.5 percent of the last three years' average salary for each year of work beyond the minimum qualifying period of 240 months. The maximum pension amount is 80 percent of the average of the last three years' salary based on 480 months of covered employment. Benefits will be adjusted to changes in wages or prices on an annual basis.

If the worker dies before age 72, the unexpired portion of pension will be paid to surviving dependents. If the worker dies after age 72, no payment is made. If death occurs before retirement, arrangements will be made for the payment of the pension that would have been payable up to age 72.

CIVIL SERVICE PENSION SCHEME

The civil service pension scheme was introduced in 1950 under the colonial administration and is governed by the Pension Ordinance Captioned 30. At present, the scheme covers pensionable officers of the civil service. This includes any officer declared covered by the government, a list of whom is published in the National Gazette. The scheme provides for noncontributory retirement pensions and gratuities. The scheme is designed not only to reward past service but also to attract workers and to encourage them to continue to stay in government. Teachers were brought into the scheme in 1955.

Benefits and Eligibility Conditions

Pensions are awarded at the retirement age of 60. Under voluntary retirement, males may be awarded a pension at age 50 and females at age 45. In all cases the employee must have completed a minimum period of 10 years' service. The pensionable age for teachers is age 50.

A pension is also awarded in circumstances pertaining to either reorganization of a department or abolition of certain positions by the government to allow for improvements or greater efficiency in administration. In such circumstances those who are affected and cannot be effectively reemployed are retired and awarded full pension in addition to an abolition allowance even though they have not attained the statutory retiring age.

Retirement on Medical Grounds

Officers who, due to ill health, are not capable of rendering further services are awarded pension by reason of their infirmity. In this respect, the infirmity has to be certified by a board of three government medical practitioners, two of whom must have declared the employee unfit for further service.

Premature Retirement

There are three conditions under which government employees can retire prematurely. When a serving officer is installed as a chief in his locality he may then apply to retire voluntarily, but his application must be supported with documentation from the "king makers" to prove that the applicant is the rightful candidate. A second instance is where a worker wants to retire and enter into the priesthood. The same documentation procedures must be followed except that the head of the religious body or denominational head has to confirm the appointment. Officers may also voluntarily retire for personal reasons, but each case is treated on its own merits.

Calculations of Pensions

Since 1975 the rate of calculation of civil service pensions is based on the number of months served divided by a constant of 480, multiplied by the final pensionable amount. The amount of pension to be paid may either be made in full or the pensioner may opt to have one-quarter of the pension converted into a lump sum amounting to twelve and a half times the pension.

Marriage Gratuity

A female officer with no less than five years' service who retires because of marriage while in service is granted a marriage gratuity payable at the rate of one-eighth of a month's pensionable amount for each completed month of total service.

Death Gratuity

A death benefit is payable to the estate of a civil servant who dies in service. The gratuity is calculated at the rate of one-half of full pension multiplied by twenty.

Additional Pension

An additional pension is awarded in cases where the officer retires as a result of abolition of post or department. The addition is at the rate of one-sixth of pensionable emolument for each complete period of three years' pensionable service.

HEALTH CENTERS/POSTS

The Social Security and National Insurance Trust has long understood that providing medical care for workers is among the most important economic benefits of a social security scheme. The trust has not found it convenient or possible, however, to support a medical care program. Nonetheless, the trust has been committed to some sort of contribution to bolster government efforts in medical care. This is demonstrated by its embarkation upon the construction of health centers in selected rural towns in the country so that eventually the Ministry of Health, which is responsible for public health care, will take on the operation of these health centers. The trust has contributed some of its funds toward the construction of eight health centers.

EQUITY HOLDINGS

Since the creation of the social security scheme, the National Insurance Trust has also helped to finance industry and commerce. Realizing the need for long-term capital investment, it provided part of the equity shares in the establishment of the nation's Bank for Housing and Construction and in the Ghana Plant Hire Pool Company. The trust in 1976 provided the total share for the establishment of the Social Security Bank, which is the only Social Security Bank in Africa. Apart from providing loans to employers for the expansion of their businesses, the bank provides institutional arrangements whereby workers buy durable essential consumer goods on hire purchase from the bank's consumer department, which has now been turned into a limited liability company. As of now the trust has shares in a total of 11 companies.

INVESTMENT IN HOUSING

The trust has also been involved in addressing basic housing needs in Ghana. This need has been rendered more urgent by population growth, urbanization, and industrialization. The trust has augmented government efforts to provide housing, especially in urban areas where the need is most acute, by constructing units throughout the country. Most of these housing units have been completed and are occupied by contributors. As of December 1988, the trust had spent 2.8 billion cedis in this program.

POLICY ISSUES

Coverage of Agricultural Workers

While employees in agricultural establishments employing five or more workers are covered under social security, the large number of self-employed agricultural workers in the production of cocoa, sheanut, and coffee, along with other cash crop farmers in the country, fall outside the provision of the scheme. Nevertheless, since these workers play a vital role in the national economy, the government has initiated legislation to provide them with social security coverage and other related welfare schemes. Under section 26 of the Ghana Cocoa Board Law, the cocoa board is required to establish a contributory insurance scheme for cocoa, coffee, and sheanut farmers within the framework of the social security scheme. In the same law, section 27 enjoins the board to establish a welfare fund to be known as the "farmers welfare fund," which is to provide for development projects.

Since the promulgation of this law there have been various committee meetings involving farm representatives, the cocoa board, the State Insurance Corporation, and the Social Security and National Insurance Trust to work out the modalities for the implementation of the scheme. It is hoped that when the scheme is begun it will be gradually extended to cover all other farmers within the agricultural sector.

Rural Areas

Rural areas, according to the national statistical services bureau's definition, are ones with population of less than 10,000. The areas falling under this definition are dominated by agricultural and fishing industries. Generally speaking, there are two types of rural workers: those working for wages on agricultural farms and other establishments, and self-employed peasant farmers and fishermen. The former are covered under the social security scheme if they are employed in establishments with five or more workers. The large number of self-employed workers in rural areas of the country, however, fall outside the scope of the scheme. Currently, there is no stated policy regarding the administration of the scheme in rural areas.

CONCLUSION

The social security scheme in Ghana has made steady progress since its inception in 1965. Membership, which initially started with a little less than 400,000 workers, has been extended to cover 1.5 million workers. The proposed conversion to a social insurance system represents the culmination of years of planning and is designed to address the needs of members for long-term contingencies such as old age and invalidity.

The decision taken by the government to institute a separate scheme for self-employed agricultural farmers is a particularly worthwhile action since it will guarantee an economic future for this category of workers and will also help to curtail the influx of young farmers from rural areas to urban centers in search of white-collar jobs.

REFERENCES

Dudley, S. (1988). Profile on Ghana: New social security system proposed. *Benefits & Compensation International*, 17(11), 13.

International Social Security Association. (1989). *Presentation des changements: Ghana.* Unpublished research document.

Public Affairs Department of the Social Security and National Insurance Trust. (1989). *SSNIT pension scheme.* Accra: Author.

U.S. Department of Health and Human Services. (1990). *Social security programs throughout the world—1989.* Social Security Administration. Office of International Policy. Research Report No. 62. Washington, D.C.: U.S. Government Printing Office.

10

India

Fred Groskind and
John B. Williamson

As the world's largest parliamentary democracy, India is faced with an enormous challenge in developing a comprehensive social insurance system for its people. Between 75 and 80 percent of a population that exceeds 800 million live in villages where agriculture is the main activity. Almost half of the more than 500,000 villages had yet to get electricity as of 1983 (Daruwalla, 1983; Hardgrave, 1980), much less any form of state-sponsored social security coverage. Indeed, the social insurance programs of India limit their coverage largely to the organized sector of the labor force (Gupta, 1986; Williamson and Pampel, 1989).

This extremely limited social insurance coverage is due in large part to the relatively low level of economic development in India. According to World Bank figures, Indian Gross National Product per capita was $340 in 1988, compared to $3,600 in Korea and $21,020 in Japan (World Bank, 1990). In the early 1980s, the Indian government estimated that ''48.1 per cent of the Indian population lives below the poverty line defined as a minimum daily calorie intake of 2400 per person in rural areas and 2100 in urban areas'' (Johri, 1982:105). In fact, the average daily caloric supply per person in India scarcely increased between 1965 and 1985, moving from 2,100 to 2,126 calories over the two decades. In contrast, Korean caloric supply increased from 2,255 to 2,806 and U.S. supply increased from 3,292 to 3,682 over the same twenty-year period (World Bank, 1990).

These economic conditions will be difficult to alleviate in the future, given the continued high fertility rate, which stood at 4.4 children per woman of childbearing age in 1986. While this is a significant reduction from 6.2 children in 1965, it compares unfavorably with China's reduction from 6.4 to 2.3 and the U.S. reduction from 2.9 to 1.9 during the same time period. Further, low birth weight babies constituted 30 percent of all births in India in 1984, compared to 5 to 6 percent of births in industrialized market economies (World Bank, 1990).

Since population dynamics have such a dominating effect on social planning in India, it is important to provide a more detailed demographic context for the social welfare programs that are currently in place. The demographic information below is drawn from Martin (1988), except where noted. Life expectancy, although still low by Western standards, has risen dramatically since independence was won from Britain in 1947. Expectation of life at birth had risen to 55.4 years for the 1980–1985 period, compared to only 38.7 years for the 1950–1955 period.

In part because of this relatively low average life expectancy, the proportion of the Indian population of age 65 and older was only 4.0 percent in 1980, compared to 11.5 percent in the most developed countries of the world. Even so, India has the second largest elderly population on earth. And according to United Nations projections, the absolute number of elderly in India will almost double between 1980 and 2000, from 28 million to 54 million, and more than double again by 2065, to 119 million, accounting for 9.7 percent of total population by that time. In 1981, only about 18 percent of the over 65 population lived in urban areas.

The total Indian population stood at 798 million in 1987 (25 percent of whom lived in urban areas) and was projected to reach just over one billion by the year 2000 (World Bank, 1989).

Historically, the vast majority of Indian people have relied on their own "independent social security system," consisting of the self-sufficient village community, the joint (extended) family, craft guilds, the caste system, and the organization of charity (Mamoria and Mamoria, 1983; Sinha, 1980). Such a system is said to have provided for the ill, the unemployed, and the elderly. According to Mamoria and Mamoria, "most of these institutions either disintegrated or lost their significance gradually after the advent of industrialization in the 19th century" (1983:32). It is estimated that three-quarters of elderly Indians still live with their children (Martin, 1988).

Although the first mill was started in Calcutta in 1838 and large-scale factories were introduced in the 1850s, the first legislated protection of workers of any substance did not occur until 1923, when the Workmen's Compensation Act was passed. Generally regarded as the first social insurance measure in India, Mamoria and Mamoria insist that since it placed the burden solely on the employer for payment of compensation for injury or death, the first true social insurance measure, involving tripartite financing by employers, employees, and government, did not take place until after independence, with enactment of the Employee's State Insurance Act in 1948. A retirement benefit program, restricted to civil servants and government railway workers, however, was instituted in 1925, providing a lump-sum payment to workers or their families (Sinha, 1980).

The Employees' State Insurance Act, passed in 1948, was based on a report made in 1944 by B. P. Adarkar. This report was recognized as a landmark plan for sickness insurance and for a comprehensive social security system for labor. According to Mamoria and Mamoria, "this was the first social insurance scheme that was prepared in this country" (1983:36). It introduced a compulsory system of sickness, maternity, employment injury, and survivor coverage for employees in the organized sector.

In 1952, the Employees' Provident Fund and Miscellaneous Provisions Act was passed. It is financed by employer and employee contributions and provides a lump-sum payment to workers upon retirement or to dependents in case of early death. The EPFS was preceded by the Coal Mines Provident Fund and Bonus Schemes Act of 1948, which was the first national private-sector provident fund plan, but applied only to coal miners. After demand increased for extending such benefits to workers in other industries, the state of Assam passed the Assam Tea Plantations Provident Fund Act in 1955, covering tea workers; the national legislature passed the Seamen's Provident Fund Act in 1966.

In 1971, the Employees' Family Pension Scheme was enacted. It is the only national pension scheme in India and the first social security program to include a national government contribution.

The Gratuity Act, passed in 1972, mandated a fund to be financed solely by employers providing another lump-sum payment to covered workers on retirement or on leaving a position after five years of employment. Previously, gratuity payments were given to workers on a voluntary basis by individual employers as a reward for services (Sarma, 1981).

In 1976 the Employees Deposit Insurance Scheme was enacted, setting up life insurance for workers covered under Provident Fund provisions. It is financed by an employer tax and a government contribution.

Social insurance benefits for civil servants and other government employees are distinct from the benefits for private employees and are not addressed below. It is worth noting, however, that receipts and expenditures for public employees have slightly exceeded those for private-sector employees. For example, in 1982–1983, receipts for public employees were 24 billion rupees compared to 22 billion for those in the private sector; expenditures were 15 billion compared to 8.5 billion, respectively. (In December 1983, U.S. $1 equaled 10.49 rupees. At the end of 1989 one U.S. dollar equaled 14.95 rupees.) These figures reinforce the view that, currently, social insurance in India functions less as a national safety net than as a fringe benefit for an elite set of government employees and for workers in the organized segment of the private sector—the former receiving the majority of expenditures, despite their small numbers.

SOCIAL INSURANCE PROGRAM FEATURES

The various legislative acts that have been passed by the Indian government during this century provide benefits in the following categories of social insurance: (1) old age, invalidity, and death; (2) sickness and maternity; (3) work injury, and (4) unemployment compensation. India currently has no family allowance program.

The coverage, qualifying conditions, and benefit levels of the old-age, invalidity, and death programs are described below. The information is drawn from summary data in *Social Security Programs Throughout the World—1989.* (USDHHS, 1990), except where noted.

The central programs directed toward old-age needs are the Provident Fund Scheme, the Family Pension Scheme, and the Gratuity Scheme (Gupta, 1986).

The Provident Fund, begun in 1952, covers employees of firms that have been established at least three years. Excluded are employees earning over 2,500 rupees a month. Employees covered by equivalent private plans may be contracted out.

Eligibility for the old-age benefit begins at age 55 (or earlier if out of covered employment for six months with 15 years of contribution, if leaving the country permanently, or a miner). An invalidity benefit goes to covered workers who become permanently disabled (at least 25 percent of capacity), with coverage of up to two years. Survivor benefits are granted in case of the death of the insured before retirement if the last monthly salary of the insured was less than 1,500 rupees.

Cash benefits for retirement, invalidity, and survivors are in the form of a lump-sum payment and are equal to total employer and employee contributions paid in, plus 11.5 percent interest.

The Provident Fund is financed by contributions of 8.33 percent of earnings from employees and 8.33 percent of payroll from employers. Employees contribute 10 percent of earnings in factories with 50 or more workers. Employers contribute 10 percent of payroll in factories with 50 or more workers, plus 0.65 percent of payroll for the cost of administration of the Provident Fund. There is no government contribution.

The Employees' Family Pension Fund, begun in 1971, covers Provident Fund members. It is the first pension for survivors of employees in the private sector to be instituted in India. The fund provides a monthly pension up to a maximum of 19,825 rupees for family members if the worker who died was a member of the plan before age 25 and contributed for one year. To receive a retirement benefit from the fund, a worker must have been a member before age 25, reached the age of 60, and contributed for at least three months. Further, there is a withdrawal benefit if the worker leaves employment for reasons other than death before the age of 60 (Sinha, 1980).

Different benefit formulas apply, depending on the length of membership in the fund. Generally, a lump-sum amount is provided equal to the total employer and employee contributions paid in plus 7.5 percent interest, up to a maximum of 9,000 rupees.

The Family Pension Fund is financed by taking 1.16 percent of the Provident Fund contributions from both employer and employee. Government contributes 1.16 percent of payroll plus the cost of administering survivor benefits.

The third major component of the old-age package is the Gratuity Fund, initiated in 1972. Financed solely by the employer, it covers employees of firms, factories, mines, and plantations with 10 or more workers. To qualify for the benefit on termination of employment, a worker must have been employed continuously for at least five years, except in the event of total disability or death. The cash benefit consists of a lump-sum payment equal to 15 days' wages for each year of continuous service, up to a maximum of 50,000 rupees.

The Employees' Deposit Linked Insurance Scheme of 1976 initiated a life insurance plan for Provident Fund members, whereby designated beneficiaries receive an additional benefit equal to the average balance in the Provident Fund account of the deceased over the preceding three years, up to a maximum of 10,000 rupees. Employees do not contribute to this plan; employers contribute at the rate of 0.5 percent of employee pay plus 0.1 percent toward administration. The central government contributes 0.25 percent of payroll plus 0.1 percent toward administration.

Regarding retirement benefits for employees earning wages above the legal ceiling set by the Employees' Provident Fund Scheme, it is customary for employers either to extend coverage to them under the existing scheme or to establish company-sponsored funds outside the scheme. The gratuity plan is likewise extended voluntarily to those not technically eligible for the state scheme. Further, many employers set up private pension plans for management-level employees (*International Benefit Guidelines*, 1987).

Administration of the Provident and Family Pension Funds is provided through the Ministry of Labor of the central government. Boards of trustees at the central and state levels—composed of representatives of government, employers, and employees—manage the funds. Regional committees are appointed by the central government where state boards do not yet exist. In general, Provident Fund commissioners at the central, regional, and state levels are responsible for day-to-day administration (Gupta, 1986).

Administration of the Gratuity Fund is usually under the control of state governments and appointed labor commissioners. The central government and its regional labor commissioners manage gratuity funds for firms owned or operated by the central government and for firms having branches in more than one state.

POLICY ISSUES

According to Johri, "the basic problems of the Indian social security system are a) its relatively narrow population base and b) its fragmentary legal and organizational character" (1982:117). As mentioned, benefits are only available to workers and their dependents in the organized sector of the economy, which consists of about 10 to 15 percent of the total labor force. This lack of protection of the rural population is despite the fact that agriculture accounted for almost one-third of India's GDP in 1986 (World Bank, 1990).

Further, it is estimated that the organized sector is able to absorb only about 11 percent of additions to the labor force each year. Thus, "the remaining 89 percent have either stayed on farms or been absorbed into the unrecorded or unspecified 'informal' sector" (Johri, 1982:108).

The vast majority of the Indian population, in short, remains outside of any government system of social security. Over 500 million citizens continue to rely on traditional, joint family protection or community protection. Instead of comprehensive social insurance policies, which are beyond the economic and administrative capacities of the nation to implement, the national and state governments focus on policies for economic development of the unorganized sector. According to Gupta,

the system of social protection available to the rural population is in the form of allotment of land to the tiller; health schemes and encouragement to doctors to serve rural areas; advancement of loans on easy terms through lead banks; social services through community development programmes which are corollary to social security; extension of E.S.I. Scheme to mechanized farms; the generation of employment through the scheme of decentralization of industries, cottage and small scale industries; development of infrastructural facilities like road, transport, ration shops, free education to children, adult education and means of entertainment; (and) clearance of slums. (1986:321)

Regarding the fragmentary character of the social insurance system that is in place, most critics argue for some form of integration of its components. Mamoria and Mamoria, for example, claim that "integration of the various measures of social security under the auspices of a single organization . . . is the most vital need of the country" (1983:40). Given that there are "gaps and defects in the working of individual schemes," according to Gupta, however, "integration will amplify the problems and further complicate the system as the integration of diseased limbs carries nowhere" (1986:312).

Several major problems and challenges confront the Indian government, in addition to integration of programs and extension of programs to the rural population.

As life expectancy increases, and the elderly population jumps from 30 million to over 100 million by 2025, a gradual shift from lump-sum payments to ongoing pensions is needed (Gupta, 1986; Sinha, 1980). An initial problem in such a shift is providing adequate pensions to older workers who have not contributed substantial sums to a pension scheme. Also, an expanded administration would be difficult to accomplish, not only because of the cost involved, but also because of inadequate training of social security administration personnel (Gupta, 1986).

Several state governments have begun modest pension plans for the most destitute elderly, those without any income and without relatives, but it is estimated that only about 10 percent of the over 60 population will receive any assistance "when all the state schemes have been fully implemented" (Johri, 1982:116–17).

There is very little government contribution to any of the social insurance programs other than a sharing by state government of a part of medical care. For the most part, the burden for the cost of retirement, invalidity, and survivor benefits is placed on employers and employees.

Cost of living adjustments are not yet legislated, so that there is devaluation of the amounts that are returned to workers upon retirement.

CONCLUSION

Although the social insurance model of the industrialized nations was available to the Indian government both during British imperial rule and as it began formulating its own social policies after independence, the Provident Fund model was chosen for several reasons. First, during most of the years of colonization, India was primarily "an industrial raw material supplier" for Britain (Sinha, 1980). Administration of a complex system of social security for aging Indian workers was not a priority under such conditions. Second, given the country's blatant poverty, the model of the developed countries was seen as too large a burden on the underdeveloped economy of India, even after independence. Third, even the less costly Provident Fund approach was initially viewed as a drain on scarce capital by employers. Similarly, "workers were concerned about the employees' contributions, which many viewed as an unacceptable tax on their already low wages" (Williamson and Pampel, 1989:19). Fourth, the Provident Fund's lump-sum payment is not at all redistributive, as pension schemes typically are. The Provident Fund approach may thus be more suitable in a nation where religious and ethnic tensions run high, creating distrust among groups. Lastly, once established, the lump-sum component of the Provident Fund scheme proved popular among workers, creating little public demand for an alternative system. This is not to mention the difficulties involved in shifting to an entirely different social security system, once the Provident Fund scheme was in place.

Despite the range of social insurance programs initiated since the 1920s by the national government, expenditures for all programs, both in the public and private sector, accounted for only 1.5 percent of Gross Domestic Product in 1982–1983. For perspective, the United States spent 13.9 percent of its GDP on social insurance in that year; West Germany spent 24.5 percent.

Regarding the likelihood of moving toward a more comprehensive social insurance system in the near future, economic conditions and demographic trends argue strongly against it. As Sinha wrote in 1980, "owing to obvious difficulties, which are almost fundamental, like (the) poverty of the country, incomplete development of the country's resources, problems of cost, administration, etc., one may hardly dream of introducing any such comprehensive and full-fledged social security schemes (as Britain's) in India under existing conditions" (p. 210).

In sum, although India has made progress in developing policies for the economic security of its workforce in the organized sector since independence was won, there are powerful forces working against significant improvement. Johri puts it bluntly: ''Basically, social security has retained the character of a privilege or an addition to the pay packet of employees in the organized sector. The large majority of the population receives no protection and there is no proposal to extend the coverage of existing schemes beyond their intended limits'' (Johri, 1982:117).

REFERENCES

Daruwalla, R. K. (1983). The benefits environment in India. *Benefits International*, 19–24.

Gupta, N. H. (1986). *Social security legislation for labour in India*. New Delhi: Deep and Deep.

Hardgrave, R. L. (1980). *India: Government and politics in a developing nation*. 3 ed. New York: Harcourt Brace Jovanovich.

International Benefit Guidelines. (1987). *India*. New York: William M. Mercer International.

International Labour Organization. (1988). *The cost of social security: Twelfth international inquiry, 1981–83*. Geneva: International Labour Office.

Johri, C. K. (1982). Social security in India: Issues and prospects. *Labour and Society*, 7(2), 105–120.

Mamoria, C. B., and Mamoria, S. (1983). *Labour welfare, social security, and industrial peace in India*. Allahabad: Kitab Mahal.

Martin, L. G. (1988). The aging of Asia. *Journal of Gerontology: Social Sciences*, 43(4), S99–S113.

Sarma, A. M. (1981). *Aspects of labour welfare and social security*. Bombay: Himalaya.

Sinha, P. K. (1980). *Social security measures in India*. New Delhi: Classical.

U.S. Department of Health and Human Services. (1990). *Social security programs throughout the world—1989*. Social Security Administration. Office of International Policy. Research Report No. 62. Washington, D.C.: U.S. Government Printing Office.

Williamson, J. B., and Pampel, F. C. (1989). *Old age security developments in India*. Paper presented at the 29th International Congress of the International Institute of Sociology, Rome, June 12–16.

World Bank. (1990). *World Development Report 1990*. New York: Oxford University Press.

11

Indonesia

Sentanoe Kertonegoro

In Indonesia, social insurance schemes are provided under a 1969 Law on the Basic Provisions on Manpower. Article 15 of this law gives the federal government responsibility for administering the nation's social insurance system, including sickness, maternity, old-age, death, invalidity, and unemployment programs. The programs, however, are being implemented in stages based on need, and administrative and financial viability. Currently, programs for government employees, armed forces personnel, and private- and state-enterprise workers are in operation under a social insurance system known as ASTEK. Benefits include employment injury, provident fund, and death payments. A public enterprise, PERUM ASTEK, operates and administers the programs. Benefits are currently being extended to include health care.

SOCIAL AND POLITICAL BACKGROUND

Indonesia is the largest archipelago in the world, consisting of five main islands and about thirty smaller archipelagos totaling 13,667 islands of which about 6,000 are inhabited. The Indonesian archipelago forms a cross-road between the Pacific and Indian oceans, and a bridge between Asia and Australia. Indonesian cultural, social, political, and economic patterns have been strongly influenced by its geographical position.

The diverse nationalities who make up the Indonesian nation consist of a blend of multiethic as well as racial entities, each with its own cultural heritage and sociocultural manifestations. There are about 300 ethnic groups in Indonesia with more than 250 local languages. The national motto "Bhinneka Tunggal Ika" (unity in diversity) is reflective of this multiracial and multilingual society blending into one nation.

Economic Background

Since the government launched a successive five-year plan nineteen years ago, the Indonesian economy has undergone rapid growth. Agriculture has long been the dominant sector of the economy. During the past decade, however, significant structural changes have occurred as a result of development in manufacturing, transportation, trade, and banking, while the growth of the agricultural sector has lagged.

The process of industrialization followed by urbanization has resulted in more and more people working as employees for wages. Hired workers are almost completely dependent on a continuing flow of income to provide themselves and their families with the basic necessities of life. Any misfortune that interrupts their income can mean destitution and poverty. This had led to the need for income protection measures in the form of social security programs providing benefits and services in case of ill health, old age, invalidity, death, and unemployment.

The Demographic Situation

Based on the 1985 Inter-Census Population Survey, the population of Indonesia in 1985 was 164 million. This makes it the fifth most populous country in the world after the Peoples' Republic of China, India, the Soviet Union, and the United States. In the period 1980–1985 the population grew at a rate of 2.15 percent. In order to lower the level of fertility rate, various government programs of family planning have been launched. Under these programs, the annual growth rate in the 1995–2000 period is expected to be reduced to 1.9 percent.

One other significant demographic characteristic of Indonesia is that the population is unevenly distributed among provinces as well as among islands. Almost 61 percent of the total population inhabit Java, which is only 6.9 percent of the total area. The province of Jakarta is the most densely populated, with 13,365 people per square kilometer, whereas Irian Jaya is the least populated with only three people per square kilometer.

The population structure of Indonesia is skewed to a younger age group because of high birth rates among people aged zero to fourteen years which was estimated at 39.2 percent in 1985. In 1985 persons aged 55 and over constituted about 8 percent of the total population, but this is expected to reach 10 percent by the year 2000 (*ASTEK Statistik*, 1988).

Due to advances in medical care and technology, the death rate per one thousand of population is declining. As mortality rates decrease, the probability of surviving to retirement age and beyond increases. Between 1951 and 1971, life expectancy increased seven years, and between 1971 and 2000 life expectancy is expected to increase approximately thirteen years. Most of the gain in life expectancy is the result of improved survival rates of infants and young people. In addition, older people live several years longer.

Another significant event in the demography of Indonesia is the migration from rural to urban areas. This urbanization is the direct effect of industrialization, which attracts people to move from villages to cities in the hope of improving their living standard. Urbanization has created problems associated with crowded cities, such as slums, poor health, absence of clean water, traffic congestion, high crime rates, and high unemployment.

Labor and Employment

In general, the labor force consists of persons aged ten years and older who are actively engaged in economic activities. This includes persons who work at least one hour a day, are temporarily not at work (on leave, ill, laid off), and are seeking work. The labor force is expected to increase at an average annual rate of 2.79 percent during the fourth five-year development plan.

THE SOCIAL INSURANCE SYSTEM

As noted, the social insurance system in Indonesia is comprised of three separate schemes covering government civilian employees, armed forces personnel, and private- and state-enterprise employees. PERUM ASTEK, in addition to the three main programs of employment injury, provident fund, and death insurance, also provides health insurance and severance pay. The health scheme is in fifteen cities in Java and Sumatera covering 125,000 employees and 445,000 dependents working in 350 enterprises. The severance pay scheme is applicable to construction workers in the oil and gas industry and covers 3,682 workers in 69 companies.

Social Insurance for the Armed Forces

By definition, the military and civilian personnel in the armed forces are government employees whose salary is provided by the state budget. Accordingly, social insurance coverage for the armed forces is similar to that for civil servants especially with respect to the types of program and the rate of contributions.

A total contribution of 10 percent of earnings is deducted from the salary of armed forces personnel to fund pensions (4.75%), endowment insurance (3.25%), and health insurance (2.00%). The contribution is withheld directly from the state personnel budget and remitted to the appropriate administrative agencies.

The endowment insurance scheme for armed forces personnel is Asuransi Sosial Angkatan Bersenjata Republik Indonesia (ASABRI). It was established in 1971 and is administered by a state enterprise known as PERUM ASABRI.

Benefits provided under ASABRI include cash benefits, death benefits, funeral allowances, and a cash surrender value. A cash benefit is payable upon retirement.

The benefit is paid in the form of a lump-sum grant equal to five months of earnings immediately before retirement. Death benefits are given to the dependent if the worker dies before retirement; the amount is based on the deceased's average earnings over the seven months prior to death. The funeral allowance is fixed at a flat amount irrespective of the retiree's past earnings.

A cash surrender value is allowed in case a member's services are terminated for reasons other than death or retirement. This amount is determined by dividing the total number of contribution years by 20. In turn, the result is divided by the amount corresponding to five months' earnings immediately before service is terminated.

Social insurance schemes for government employees, armed forces personnel, the private sector, and state enterprises are provided under separate laws and regulations.

Social Insurance for the Private Sector

ASTEK (Asuransi Sosial Tenaga Kerja), the social insurance scheme for the private sector, has been in operation since 1978 (Johnson, 1982). It has nation-wide coverage that includes employees in private as well as government enterprises. Membership in ASTEK will eventually be compulsory but initially mandatory coverage includes only employees in enterprises with 25 or more workers and with a monthly payroll of at least one million rupiah (about U.S. $60). Before 1987 coverage required a payroll of at least 5 million rupiah in enterprises with 100 or more employees (Rys, 1990). Any enterprises can join ASTEK on a voluntary basis. In 1989 the scheme covered over 3.5 million employees and over 21,000 employers (ASTEK, 1989; ''Indonesia to See Development of Private, State Benefits,'' 1989). This coverage will gradually be extended over the years as the system matures until every gainfully employed individual is covered.

ASTEK is designed to protect employed persons against losses resulting from such risks as work-related injury or diseases, invalidity, old age, and death under workmen's compensation, provident fund, and death benefit schemes. The program may be broadened in the future to include health insurance. Workmen's compensation insurance was first implemented in 1939 due to the recognition that such protection is a basic right of workers. It is also comparatively inexpensive, since accidents at work leading to disablement or death do not happen that frequently, and, in its simplest form, ASTEK can be easily administered.

Income protection for old age is provided by a provident fund that consists of the accumulated contributions of the member and the employers, plus compound interest. It is paid in a single lump sum. There are several reasons why retirees prefer to receive their benefits in a lump sum (a hedge against inflation, the desire to own property, the provision of working capital to support a new life after retirement, and the difficulties brought about by poor communication and the consequent delays in the receipt of monthly benefits).

Under the provident fund, the total contributions of a member may be withdrawn whenever the worker attains the age of 55, is physically or mentally incapacitated from engaging in any further employment, or dies. Death benefits are payable to a beneficiary appointed by the covered employee in the event of the latter's death not related to work and before the age of 55. Death benefits are Rp. 600,000 regardless of the amount of the member's contribution.

The provident fund is financed by contributions from employees and employers amounting to 1.0 percent and 1.5 percent of covered earnings, respectively. In addition, the employer pays contributions for death benefits at the rate of 0.50 percent of wages. The employer also bears absolute liability for workmen's compensation and the contribution rate is divided into ten industrial risk classifications, ranging from 0.24 to 3.60 percent of employees' earnings.

Investments play a major role in ASTEK to generate income for provident fund benefits and operating and administrative expenses. The general criteria adopted in the investment of funds are basically the same as in any fiduciary institution, namely, safety, yield, and social and economic utility. Based on these criteria, most of the funds are invested in state bank time deposits that provide guarantees by the Central Bank with tax-exempted monthly interest. In addition, part of the investable funds are made available for regional development. Another part of the funds is offered for supplementary benefits, such as stock loans, housing loans, education, and worker barracks.

Stock loans are provided for members who wish to buy shares in their workplace offered at the stock market. Over 5,522 employees have purchased 388,640 shares worth Rp. 867.7 million. A house-ownership plan has been used to develop 2,030 low-cost houses. The housing loans are channeled through the House Ownership Credits (KPR) scheme of the Mortgage Bank (BIN) and the Regional Development Bank (BPD).

Scholarships for education have been granted to 10,000 children of ASTEK members worth Rp. 1.8 billion. Grants are Rp. 15,000 a month for each child for a duration of 12 months. Loans are also provided to labor cooperatives to strengthen their capital funds.

Social Insurance for Civil Servants

The social insurance program for government civil servants was implemented in stages, providing coverage for old-age (1978), savings (1981), and health care (1984).

The pension program is financed primarily from the state budget and a 4.75 percent contribution on earnings from employees. As a general rule, an employee is qualified for a pension upon reaching age 50 with at least 20 years of government service or other services recognized under the law. The compulsory retirement age is 56. A civil servant may also qualify for a pension prior to retirement age in the event of sickness and/or disability resulting from the performance of official duties. The amount of the monthly pension is the equivalent of 2.50 percent of the pension base for every year of pensionable service, with a maximum of 75 percent, but not lower than 40 percent of that base.

In the event of the employee's death before retirement, a monthly pension is given to the widow(s) or the widower, or to the children if there are no spouses. A pension is also given to the widow(s) or widower or to their children in the event of death of the retiree. Both pensions for the widow(s) or widower and the pension for the children is 72 percent of the pension base, if the employee dies before retirement. This is reduced to 36 percent of the base if death is after retirement. The pension base is the basic salary of the last month prior to the death or retirement of the employee.

The pension plan is administered by the Government Civil Servants Administration Board, which operates directly under the state secretariat. The board is not a centralized agency administering the entire operation of the plan. All applications for pension benefits emanate and, to some extent, are processed by different government offices in which prospective retirees are employed. Payment of benefit claims is entrusted to the regional branches of the Office of the State Treasury, which have the authority to pay.

Unlike the government pension plan, the Government Civil Servants Saving and Insurance Scheme, known as TASPEN (Tabungan dan Asuransi Pegawi Negeri), is financed solely from the contributions of employees who put 3.25 percent of their monthly take-home pay into the fund. TASPEN was established primarily to provide a lump-sum benefit to government employees on retirement or to their beneficiaries if death occurs before retirement.

The TASPEN plan is actually a modified form of endowment insurance, where the insurance amount, or the sum assured, varies as the employee's length of service and salary are increased. The lump-sum benefit is determined on a periodical basis and circularized in a schedule indicating the lump-sum amounts for employees in corresponding income brackets. A burial allowance, with the specific amount also announced from time to time, is included in the benefit schedule. In the event the employee should resign before retirement age, a cash surrender value equivalent to the total contribution years divided by 20 is provided.

Applications for benefit claims are processed by the TASPEN administration. The papers are checked against personnel files in TASPEN's recording division. If the papers are in order, payment is eventually made at the cash/bank and payment division of TASPEN's financial bureau. To expedite payment of claims of employees or their heirs in the remote islands of the archipelago, TASPEN has delegated the authority to Mayors and Regents to process payment of claims.

The third type of scheme is the health insurance covering not only active government civil servants but also retired employees as well as their widows and orphans. The retirees, widows, and orphans contribute 5 percent of their basic pension. Health benefits are provided in the form of medical services and reimbursements for medical and hospital expenses.

Occupational Pensions and Severance Pay

Private occupational pension benefits are somewhat common in Indonesia (Munro, 1988; P. T. Asuransi Jiwa Panin Putra, 1990). Benefits are typically based on one or two months of last year's salary or the average of the last three years' salary for each year of coverage with a maximum benefit ranging from 60 to 75 percent of final salary ("Indonesia to See Development of Private, State Benefits," 1989). Retirement age is usually 55 or 56. Widow benefits are usually provided and represent from 50 to 75 percent of the insured's pension.

Employers are also required to provide a termination of employment indemnity based on the years of service. One month's salary is paid for each year of employment up to four years and one additional month's salary for every additional five years of employment.

CONCLUSION

Social insurance in Indonesia is distinctly affected by demographic and social changes that are creating a growing need for income protection in an urbanized wage economy. Currently, there are three public insurance schemes that cover most government workers and armed forces personnel. Coverage is gradually being extended to workers in the private sector. The social insurance program for workers under ASTEK in the private sector limits mandatory coverage to large industries. Benefits cover old age, work injury, and death. Old-age benefits are in the form of a lump-sum provident fund that also provides for loans before retirement age.

REFERENCES

ASTEK. (1989). The development of ASTEK schemes. In *Factbook, 1988*, 12–17. Jakarta: Author.

ASTEK Statistik/Statistics 1978–1987. (1988). Jakarta: ASTEK.

Indonesia to see development of private, state benefits. (1989). *IBIS Review*, 4(1), 27–28.

Johnson, T. (1982). Benefits in Indonesia. *Benefits International*, 11(9), 16–19.

Munro, H. (1988). The development of pension funds in Indonesia. *Benefits & Compensation International*, 18(4), 19–25.

P. T. Asuransi Jiwa Panin Putra. (1990, January). *Social security provisions and occupational benefit plans in Indonesia*. Brussels: Area Benefits Network.

Rys, V. (1990). *Trends and developments in social security—worldwide*. Regional Training Course on Social Security Administration, Kuwait. Geneva: International Social Security Association.

Social Insurance System ASTEK. Indonesia: The social insurance system ASTEK. (1988). *Asian News Sheet*, 18(2), 14–16.

12

Israel

Leah Achdut and Jack Habib

Israel has aged rapidly since the establishment of the state in 1948. The percentage of the population over age 65 has risen from 3.5 percent in 1950 to 6.8 percent in 1970 to 8.6 percent in 1980.

Together with the rise in the elderly population, the ratio of aged (65+) to the working-age population (20–64) has also increased from 91 (per thousand) in 1955 to 177 in 1986. At the same time the total dependency ratio has remained fairly stable but is expected to decline dramatically in the future from one dependent person for every working-age person, to 0.79 working-age persons for every dependent in the year 2010.

The growth in the share of the elderly has naturally led to a significant rise in the importance of old-age assistance in the Gross National Product.

A concomitant process has been the decline in the labor force participation of the elderly. Labor force participation declined from 40 percent in the 1960s to 25 percent in the 1980s among males over age 65. Yet, the rate of labor participation remains high by international standards and the rate of market income in the total incomes of the elderly is also high.

Similarly, among the population in the preretirement years the rates of labor force participation also exceed by far those in most Western countries. Seventy-eight percent of males aged sixty to sixty-four are employed. By contrast, the rate of women's labor force participation is a very low 36.8 percent in the age group fifty-five to fifty-nine. At the same time, there has been a dramatic increase in labor force participation among women as a whole.

The pattern of access to pension rights in Israel is heavily influenced by the immigrant status of the majority of the elderly. Most elderly forfeited all pension rights in their countries of origin and had little time to accumulate such rights in Israel. This has affected significantly the access to occupational pensions and has been a major complicating factor in the design of pension systems in Israel.

Another factor affecting pensions has been a major change in basic economic conditions in recent years. After many years of rapid growth from 1953 to 1972 there was a marked slowdown after 1973. This was accompanied by an inflationary rate of 15 percent in the early 1970s to a peak of 445 percent in 1984. The introduction of a stringent economic policy has brought inflation back to a rate of 16 percent in 1987. The efforts to deal with rapid inflation have been a major preoccupation of Israeli policy makers and will receive special attention in this chapter.

The pension system in Israel has three tiers: a flat-rate benefit under social security (National Insurance Institute); a supplementary benefit under social security for those with low incomes, and a system of occupation wage-related pensions whose coverage has rapidly expanded and is today almost universal.

The National Insurance Law, which was enacted by the Knesset (the Israeli parliament) in November 1953 and came into force in 1954, created the legal framework of the social security system in Israel. The law designated the National Insurance Institute as the administrative body responsible for its implementation. Initially, the law provided only three categories of benefits: old-age and survivor, maternity, and employment injury.

Collection of insurance contributions for the old-age and survivor branch began in April 1954 and benefits to survivors were paid as of April 1954. The elderly began receiving benefits only as of April 1957 (after a qualifying period of three years).

Over the years many legislative changes were introduced in the old-age insurance scheme. These changes were characterized by the following overall trends:

1. The guaranteeing of a minimum income to low-income elderly, especially to those for whom the old-age benefit is their sole source of income under supplementary benefits program (1965, 1982)
2. The granting of benefits to those elderly who are not entitled by law (1963)
3. The strengthening of the universal elements of the benefit scheme by liberalizing the eligibility conditions to expand the coverage of the nonworking population; shortening of the qualifying period and exempting certain groups from such a period (1973, 1981); a more liberal definition of retirement tests (1970); and broadening the arrangements for the voluntary insurance of housewives (1973)
4. The linking of benefits to the average wage (1973–1975) and the introduction of automatic adjustment methods in order to prevent erosion in the value of benefits

MAIN PROGRAM FEATURES

Coverage

Under the Israeli national insurance system, every resident aged 18 or over is insured in the old-age pension scheme and obliged to contribute to the system, with two exceptions. New immigrants aged 60 or over upon their arrival in Israel and old people who were too old (reached the age of 67) to be covered on the day in which the National Insurance Law came into force are guaranteed special nonstatutory pensions that are financed by the government. Housewives who are not working outside their own household and whose spouses are insured, and widows already receiving a survivor pension or a work-injured dependent's pension are granted the option of voluntary insurance in order to enable them to preserve a continuity of insurance.

Qualifying Conditions

Entitlement to the old-age pension starts at age 70 and 65 for men and women, respectively, or at age 65 and 60 for those with income that does not exceed 50 to 70 percent of the old-age pension, according to the number of dependents.

Entitlement to an old-age pension is generally conditional on a minimum period of insurance: at least five out of ten years preceding the qualifying age, or 144 months whether or not they are consecutive. The latter possibility was introduced in April 1973 as part of a reform that was intended to extend the circle of those entitled to old-age (and survivor) pensions and especially to include women who work short and generally noncontinuous periods during their lifetime. In certain cases women are totally exempt from a qualifying period: divorcees, widows (who do not receive survivor or work-injured dependents' pensions), deserted wives (as defined by law), women whose husbands are not insured, and those who were at least 55 years old when they immigrated to Israel.

Benefit Levels

The national insurance old-age pension is fixed at a uniform rate as a percentage of the average wage (the average wage in January 1989 for purposes of calculating benefits was NS 1,762—one new shekel equaled U.S. $0.63) (USDHHS, 1990), which varies with the number of persons dependent on the elderly person for their livelihood. The pension is independent of the insured person's income at the time of employment, and is only loosely related to the duration of the insurance. In 1989 the pension rate for a single person was 16 percent of the average wage and 24 percent for a couple, with a 5 percent supplement payable for each of the first two dependent children. Also, an entitled person receives a seniority increment of 2 percent of the basic pension for each year above ten years of insurance, up to a maximum of 50 percent. In addition, a deferred retirement increment of 5 percent of the basic pension is paid for each year that retirement is postponed after the conditional age (65 for a man and 60 for a woman). The maximum deferment is 25 percent of the basic pension, that is, five years deferment of retirement.

In 1965, an income-tested supplementary benefit for the elderly was introduced, financed from general revenues but administered by the National Insurance Institute. With the supplementary benefit a single individual is entitled to 25 percent of the average wage, and a couple to approximately 40 percent.

At present, the updating of the old-age pension in accordance with changes in the average wage is carried out at the beginning of each year and each time a cost-of-living increment is paid to all wage earners in the economy. Linkage to the average wage is intended to ensure that the rise in the living standard of benefit recipients will not lag behind that of the general population.

Administration

The old-age and survivor branch of the National Insurance Institute has direct responsibility for the operation of the program. Claims are dealt with at forty-two local offices. The everyday treatment of claims—receipt, examination, and decision—is discharged by special claims officers. If the decision is negative the claimant may appeal to the labor court. If the decision is positive, the claims officer fills in a payment order, including a summary of the decision form for the central computer system at the head office.

Payments are usually made once a month, at the end of the month, to the bank account of the claimant, and in exceptional cases may be paid at post offices in order to make it easier for people who are not familiar with the banking system.

The processing of claims can be lengthy. If a decision is not made within three months of a claim's submission, the claimant is fully compensated for the decrease in the value of the benefit since the date of submission.

Financing

The financing of the benefits, while basically being a pay-as-you-go system, has elements of funding. The reserve fund normally maintained is quite high in relation to the benefit payments. It is subject to fluctuations according to the policy adopted by the institute's governing board. Since 1979 a ''coverage level'' has been set for each insurance branch, defined as the desirable ratio of asset accumulation to total annual expenditure. In branches that pay long-term benefits—of which old-age and survivor is a principal component—the minimum coverage level has been set at three times the annual expenditure, whereas the maximum coverage level should be six times the annual expenditure. In recent years the actual coverage level of the old-age and survivor branch has been, on the average, 3.5 expenditure years.

While the sole source of financing of the non-statutory old-age benefits and the supplementary benefits to the elderly is the government, the statutory old-age benefits are mainly financed by contributions paid by the insured population. The rate of insurance contributions for the employee in 1989 was 2.7 percent of earned income for old-age and survivor benefits, and 1.3 percent for invalidity up to a ceiling of three times the average wage. In addition, there was a contribution of 1.0 percent for long-term care (USDHHS, 1990). A provision for service benefits for the care of the elderly was implemented in 1988 (Israel: Implementation of the long-term insurance scheme, 1988). The employer's contribution is 1.65 percent of payroll for old-age and survivor pensions, 0.25 percent for invalidity, and 0.05 percent for long-term care. The contribution rate for a self-employed individual is 4.35 percent of old-age and survivor, 1.55 percent for invalidity, and 0.15 percent for long-term care up to four times the average wage. Contributions to the old-age and survivor branch constitute 28 percent of the total national insurance contributions.

Under the National Insurance Law, the government participates in the financing of the statutory and old-age and survivor benefits by supplementing the contribution collections by 15 percent of employee and employer contributions. Another source of financing old-age and survivor benefits is the interest payment on the institute's reserve funds. In recent years, the breakdown of the financing sources of old-age and survivor has been, on the average, as follows: collection of contributions—60 percent, government participation in financing statutory benefits—8 percent, government payments to nonstatutory benefits and to supplementary benefits to the elderly—19 percent, and income from interest—13 percent.

OCCUPATIONAL PENSIONS

The Israeli occupational pension scheme is based on work-related pension entitlements and is intended to provide retired workers with income support proportionate to the income level they had while employed. It consists of two main systems. The first is a budgetary noncontributory pension system, covering civil servants and municipal employees and funded from the current budget of the state and municipalities. The second is a funded contributory scheme, organized and administered primarily by the Histadrut, the General Federation of Labor, operated as provident funds and financed by employee and employer contributions as negotiated in collective bargaining agreements.

The budgetary pension system includes old age, survivor, and disability provisions and benefits, while the contributory-funded systems may include old-age benefits exclusively, although increasingly they are comprehensive as well. The exact benefit and entitlement packages are negotiated periodically in collective labor agreements, but generally pension benefit rates depend upon seniority in the scheme and can amount to as much as 70 percent of the preretirement wages. Following a pensioner's death, his widow receives a pension equivalent to 60 percent of his pension during her lifetime. Widowers receive 30 percent of the wife's pension, and orphaned children receive 20 percent each until age 21. The survivor pension may amount to a full pension.

The eligibility age for a pension is 60 for women and 65 for men in both the national insurance and occupational pension schemes. Certain groups such as teachers or construction workers may receive a pension at earlier ages. With the exception of civil servants, there is, in Israel, no compulsory retirement age under law. Rather, the retirement age is anchored in collective bargaining agreements. In the budgetary pension framework of the civil services, the retirement age is the same for men and women, that is, age 65.

In the Histadrut funds, the retirement age, until 1967, was 65 and 60 for men and women, respectively. In 1987, women were given the option, under a state law, to retire between the ages of 60 and 65. This law, which is binding in all employment places in Israel, is likely to enable women who will retire in the future to accumulate the qualifying period for a pension (ten years) as well as to gain higher pension levels by accumulating more years of insurance.

The work-related pension schemes have gradually extended their coverage of the working population. Thus, a considerable part of the retired population, and especially those leaving employment in the early years of the state, were not covered by work-related pension schemes and do not receive such pensions. The large influx of adult immigrants who entered the labor force at a late age, if at all, exacerbated this problem so that even those in covered industries may not have worked sufficient years to be eligible for benefits or receive significant benefits. Recent surveys indicate that about 40 percent of the elderly population receive a work-related pension in addition to the National Insurance Institute pension. Among those, only a small proportion have accumulated the maximum (70 percent) pension rate. Most of those receiving such pensions have accumulated considerably lower rates, with the average level currently only about 50 percent of average wages (Achdut, 1981).

It is expected that in the future an increasing proportion of the employed will be able to retire with occupational-based pension entitlements. Data from a recent survey on pension insurance coverage among wage and salary employees and members of cooperatives in Israel (Central Bureau of Statistics, 1982) show that 81 percent of the employees (83 percent of male and 78.5 percent of female employees) reported being covered by some sort of work-related pension scheme under collective bargaining agreements. About half of those covered reported coverage by one of the General Federation of Labor (Histadrut) pension funds; just over one-fifth (22 percent) reported being covered under direct budgetary pension arrangements, while the rest were found to be covered by other kinds of pension coverage such as "private" provident funds. Of critical importance for this discussion is the near-universality of the occupational pension coverage of female employees at these ages. About half of those not covered are in the 18–34 age group (at the beginning of their career cycle) and almost one-fifth are elderly males (aged 65 +).

Nevertheless, several problems still remain. Since the occupational pension is not compulsory, the self-employed (consisting of 20 percent of all workers in Israel) are often uninsured. Moreover, although the present coverage rate of employees is relatively high, there are significant differences in coverage rates among the various economic branches: 43 percent in personal services, 63 percent in industry and commerce, 89 percent in public services, and 97 percent in electricity and water.

The less organized the branch (and, as is usually the case, the lower the wages paid to workers), the lower the coverage rate. Also, the prevailing arrangements allow the withdrawal of the accumulated funds upon the termination of employment and may not allow the transfer of rights from one place of employment to another. In view of the above, it appears that only an obligatory legal framework will be able to ensure universal pension coverage, as well as continuity of insurance rights.

INCOME-TESTED PROVISIONS FOR THE ELDERLY

The basic old-age (or survivor) benefit paid by the National Insurance Institute is low and cannot guarantee an acceptable standard of living. Originally, this pension was meant to constitute the initial tier on which the occupational pension would be added so that the two-tier system would guarantee a fair living to the retirees. In practice, however, due to the problems of the occupational pension system mentioned above, the basic old-age pension remains the only or major source of income for considerable proportion of the elderly population.

As noted, an income-tested benefit—the supplementary benefit program—to guarantee a minimum income was introduced in 1965. In the early 1970s, however, it became evident that benefit levels were inadequate. Therefore benefit levels were increased as part of a general reform. In 1982, the program was included under new Income Support Law that was designed to provide a minimum income to all low-income groups in a special branch within social security.

The guaranteed minimum income level is fixed as a percentage of the average wage per employee: 25 percent for a single person, 37.5 percent for a couple, with additional increments of 5 percent for each of the first two children. These minimum income levels correspond approximately to the poverty line in Israel at 40 percent of the median family income per standardized person (using a need equivalence scale to weight family size). In 1975, almost 50 percent of all the elderly and survivor (most of them old) pension recipients were entitled to income supplements. That percentage declined gradually to 35 percent in 1988 mainly as a result of the increase in the proportion of the elderly who receive occupational pensions. This trend can be expected to continue in the future.

Nevertheless, the benefits paid by the National Insurance Institute still constitute the single most important source of income for a majority of the elderly population. As can be seen in Table 12.1, national insurance benefits constitute 90 percent of the gross income of the lowest quintile of elderly families and 84 percent in the second quintile. Occupational pensions become significant only for those in the third quintile and above and never exceed 30 percent of total income.

Table 12.1
Composition of Gross Income of Elderly Employees by Income Source and by Quintiles (in percentages)

Income Source		Quintiles				
	All	1	2	3	4	5
Employment income	13.6	1.7	2.0	7.1	11.0	20.1
National Insurance transfer payments	32.0	89.1	83.8	49.5	28.3	10.6
Occupational pensions	21.0	3.4	6.4	23.3	29.3	22.0
Other income	33.4	5.8	7.8	20.1	30.4	47.3

POLICY ISSUES

Maintaining Living Standards

The problem of maintaining the standard of living of the elderly has been on the agenda of Israel's social policy makers since the early 1970s. The policy that emerged attempted to prevent an erosion in the value of the benefits relative to the average wage by means of automatic updating rather than by means of recurring amendments.

While this policy succeeded in maintaining the relative level of benefits up to 1977, it failed to cope with the subsequent acceleration of inflation. One weakness of the automatic updating system was that benefits were updated in accordance with an *estimate* of the average wage and not in accordance with the *actual* average wage at the time of adjustment. This estimate, which was based on the three last known average wages, could serve as a good approximation of the actual wage as long as there were only small changes in wages or prices. At high rates of inflation, however which reached a monthly average of almost 20 percent in 1984, even a three-month lag in known wages could cause a significant erosion in benefits. Another weakness of the system stems from the infrequency of updating: during the period between two consecutive updatings, the benefits eroded at precipitate rates as inflation accelerated.

To prevent an erosion of national insurance benefits, continuous changes have been introduced since 1978 in indexing procedures and in particular in those used for maintaining the benefits of the lower-income population groups.

The basic old-age benefit has been updated according to the changes in the average wage. The linkage arrangements, however, have not always succeeded in maintaining the ex post value of benefits in relation to wages. This is primarily due to the timing of updates in relation to rate of wage increases and the use of approximate wage data due to the lag in information on actual wages. In order to address this problem a unique measure was undertaken in 1984 in response to the development of a particularly large gap between the planned and ex post level of benefits in relation to wages. Since December 1984, a "floor" has been determined for the level of the basic benefit at 15 percent of the actual average wage for a single person. If it turns out that the benefit paid (according to the average wage under the law) is less than the "floor," the elderly will receive the difference retroactively.

COVERAGE OF WOMEN IN THE NATIONAL INSURANCE SCHEME

While coverage under the first tier—the national insurance scheme—is universal with respect to the family unit, it is not necessarily so with regard to individuals within the family. Under the National Insurance Law, all men, regardless of their family status and labor force status, are covered. Divorced, single, or abandoned women are covered even if they do not work, but married women who do not work and whose husbands are insured are not covered. Approximately 93 percent of men aged 65 and over receive an old-age pension in their own right compared with 50 percent of women aged 60 and over.

The voluntary insurance arrangement that applied to housewives does not provide an adequate solution to the unequal treatment of this group under the law, and has been a source of controversy. Some argue that this arrangement should be replaced by compulsory insurance for all housewives. The arguments made for introducing compulsory insurance for housewives involve both issues of principle as well as practical considerations.

It is argued that there can no longer be an objection to insuring housewives on the grounds of the absence of paid wages, since the national insurance system has been extended to cover other nonworking individuals and it is not a pure contributory system. Moreover, the old-age benefit is, as we have noted, a flat-rate benefit designed to provide a minimum income. In a full income-related pension system the possibility of obligating payments by housewives would be much less realistic. It should be emphasized that recent legislation in Israel— the General Disability Law (1972), the Accident Insurance Law (1980), and the Community Long-Term Care Insurance Law (1982)—has adopted the concept of universal insurance regardless of employment status, insuring housewives as well.

Awareness of voluntary insurance among housewives is very low. In addition, some choose not to join the voluntary arrangement because of the financial burden it imposes on the family. Only about 1,000 housewives have, at present, purchased voluntary insurance. Obviously the introduction of compulsory insurance would have to consider the additional burden on the family and whether special rates should be set.

The voluntary insurance option enables the housewife to acquire rights relatively "cheaply." Under the present arrangement, women who have insured themselves voluntarily are entitled to withdraw at any time. They may thus acquire insurance rights after payments for a relatively short qualifying period, whereas employed insurees must pay their insurance contributions during the whole period of their employment.

At present, there is a lack of uniformity with regard to the treatment of the housewife under the national long-term benefit laws. Thus, a disabled housewife receiving disability benefits is not eligible for these benefits nor for an old-age pension upon reaching the age of 60. The inclusion of housewives under the old-age and survivor branch will assure a continuity of rights over the disabled housewife's life cycle, in the same way as such continuity is preserved for other recipients of disability benefits.

In view of the above, there is now an increasing tendency among policy makers to equalize the status of the housewife under the old-age and survivor branch. Due to budgetary constraints these changes are bound to take time. Yet, the problem of the disabled, elderly housewife may be resolved in the near future, as it relates to a relatively small population.

REPLACEMENT RATE AND COST

At the present time there is no statutory or other connection between the two tiers of the Israeli pension system; each tier is financed independently of the other and each pays a pension regardless of the eligibility for a pension in the other.

Many recent studies (Habib and Factor, 1981; Antler and Kahana, 1948) indicate the existence of a theoretically high replacement rate; a retired person entitled to full pensions under both tiers may receive a higher level of net income than before retirement. The National Insurance Institute pension is presently completely exempt from income tax, while one-third of the occupational pensions are also tax-exempt.

The calculation of the replacement rate, however, is complicated by the fact that a significant portion of wages are not covered (such as care allowances). These may represent significant components of total wages for some groups and significantly reduce effective replacement rates. Moreover, it should be stressed that all the studies that have arrived at high replacement rates refer to the pension system at the height of its maturity when it guarantees a full pension to every insuree. At the present time, as mentioned earlier, most retirees are entitled to low-level occupational pensions so that in practice the high replacement rate is received by a relatively small group of pensioners. Yet, as the system matures, more and more retirees will be entitled to full benefits.

An analysis of the demographic situation in the next three decades (Vermus, 1984) indicates that the ratio of the labor force to pensioners will not rise until 2020. The maturation of pension entitlements at present replacement rates, however, would lead to a major expansion of the share of the total pension payment in GNP from the present 8 to 10 percent to 21 percent of GNP. Therefore a reduction of the replacement rates underlies many proposals for an overall reform toward the integration of both pension tiers within an obligatory framework of a state law. These proposals also generally include provision for introducing more progress either by more fully taxing pensions or by expanding the weight of the flat-rate component in total pensions.

CONCLUSION

The social security system in Israel has developed a nearly universal network of entitlements to retirement benefits that both guarantees a minimum income to all elderly who have not been able to accrue adequate earned retirement benefits, and at the same time offers a high level of earnings replacement for the elderly with full seniority. At the same time, the system is relatively young. As a result, the majority of the elderly have accrued little or no wage-related pension benefits and an unusually large percentage are at the minimum income level. This has created an ongoing dilemma. On the one hand, there has been pressure to enhance the level of basic benefits to meet the needs of those with limited benefits. On the other hand, extending benefits to these groups may lead to unreasonably high benefit levels to those who have accrued extensive seniority.

The second major problem that has complicated planning in the pension system has been the question of wage components not included in the wage base for pensions. These components are generally subject to special rates of taxation, and therefore have become a significant proportion of compensation in Israel. As a result, it has been particularly difficult to evaluate the adequacy of pension benefits, to establish fairly uniform levels of adequacy. This problem, which is shared by all countries, has loomed particularly large in the Israeli context. As the system matures, pressure is building for a basic reform in the system that will reduce the level of full benefits while extending the components of wages that are included in the pension base, at the same time enhancing the relative component of the flat-rate social security benefit within the pension benefit mix, in order to ensure and even enhance progressivity of the system as a whole.

Another issue with which the Israeli system has had particular experience has been the attempt to protect pension benefits against inflation. The large variation in the rates of inflation over time coupled with the unusually high rates of inflation achieved in the mid–1980s, brought about the need for constant revision in the indexing arrangements. The Israeli system has displayed a great deal of flexibility and ingenuity in making these adjustments. Also, despite periods of very severe economic restraint there has been a steady commitment to maintaining the level of minimum benefits to the elderly—both protection from inflation as well as to maintenance of their relationship to average wages. Even during the periods of severe economic restraint, when real wages declined dramatically, the minimum income guarantees were maintained in real terms.

REFERENCES

Achdut, L. (1981). *Annual review, selected years* (in Hebrew). Jerusalem: National Insurance Institute.

Achdut, L., and Carmi, M. (1980). *Retirement and well-being among the elderly.* Jerusalem: National Insurance Institute.

Antler, Y., and Kahana, Y. (1984). The influence of the structure of taxation on the free entry of the worker and the pensioner (in Hebrew). *Economic Quarterly.*

Central Bureau of Statistics. (1982). *Survey on pension insurance coverage* (in Hebrew). Jerusalem.

Habib, J., and Factor, H. (1981). Issues in the evaluation of proposals for a national pension law (in Hebrew). *Social Security*, 21, 89–99.

Israel: Implementation of the long-term insurance scheme. (1988). *International Social Security Review*, 41(4), 438–440.

U.S. Department of Health and Social Services. (1990). *Social security programs throughout the world—1989.* Social Security Administration. Office of Research and Statistics. Office of International Policy. Research Report No. 62. Washington, D.C.: U.S. Government Printing Office.

Vermus, N. (1984). The burden of pension insurance (in Hebrew). *Economic Quarterly*, 258, 84.

13

Ivory Coast

Prosper Koffi Kouassi

Various socioeconomic factors have shaped the thirty-year legislative history of old-age pensions under social insurance in the Ivory Coast. The Ivory Coast has over 10 million inhabitants, 54 percent of whom are less than 20 years old. The population is largely rural (58%) in spite of a considerable migration that has led to a rapid urbanization. The growth rate of urbanization increased from 32 percent in 1975 to more than 40 percent in 1985. In addition to a yearly national growth rate of 3.1 percent, the in-migration rate is 1.3 percent a year.

The development of social insurance coverage and benefits has been significantly influenced by a limited GNP and a national income per capita of only U.S. $1,308. Much of the nation's limited resources have been used for the development of health infrastructures throughout the country instead of old-age benefit programs.

Economic constraints and health priorities have had a major impact on the extent to which wage earners are covered by social insurance. Wage earners are covered by the National Contingency Fund or NCF (CNPS), which began with the creation of a system of family allowances in 1956. This was followed in 1958 by an Employment Injuries and Occupational Diseases (EI/OD) program administered by private insurance companies. Each of these systems was grouped under the National Contingency Fund (Caisse Nationale de Prévoyance Sociale) in 1968.

The insurance system for civil servants and government workers dates from legislation in 1952 that organized the French West Africa Pension Fund (La Caisse de Retraite de l'Afrique Occidentale Française). This law has been modified over the years by a series of decrees covering cash sickness benefits, accident insurance, and life insurance benefits.

GENERAL OLD-AGE PENSION SYSTEM

Retirement benefits are payable to wage earners affiliated with the National Contingency Fund. Benefits include an old-age pension, survivor benefits for widows and orphans, disability pensions for wage earners who are legally recognized as unable to work, an allowance to former wage earners who were active before the creation of the fund, and a lump-sum benefit allowance to every insured worker's beneficiaries (widows and orphans) in the event of the insured's death.

A pension is awarded to workers who have reached the age of 55, with the possibility of an early award at age 50. In case of the latter, the retirement pension is reduced by 5 percent for each year before age 55. In addition, the worker must have ceased all wage-earning activity, have been in covered employment at least 10 years, and have made contributions to the NCF for at least three years.

Financing

Pensions are funded by employee contributions of 1.6 percent of earnings and by employer contributions of 2.4 percent of payroll. The maximum monthly earnings for contribution purposes is 1,497,555 francs (1989) (one franc equaled U.S. $0.03 in 1989) (USDHHS, 1990).

Pension Benefit Amounts

The amount of an old-age pension is about 1.33 percent of average earnings times years of coverage and periods of incapacity (USDHHS, 1990). The pension is increased by 10 percent for each child under age 16 up to a maximum of 30 percent.

Survivor Pensions

Widow Pensions. A widow benefit of 50 percent of an insured's pension is paid only if the deceased worker was a beneficiary of an old-age or disability pension or fulfilled the conditions for entitlement. The widow must have contracted a civil marriage at least two years before the death of the worker and be at least 50 years old for full benefits. Benefits are payable at age 45 but the pension is reduced by 5 percent per year. The conditions relative to the length of marriage and to age are dropped if the widow has at least one dependent child.

Orphans. Twenty percent of an insured person's pension is paid to each full orphan up to a maximum of 100 percent of the pension. An orphan must be the child of both the mother and the father, and have survived the parent as a beneficiary. Payments are continued until the child is 16 or, if in school, age 21.

Solidarity Allowance

A solidarity allowance is paid to wage earners who are 55 years old, have at least ten years of earnings, and have ceased working. This benefit is designed to provide a benefit to older workers who were employed primarily before the present system began (IBIS, 1985).

Old-Age Settlement

A lump-sum allowance is awarded to workers who do not meet the qualifying conditions for a standard retirement pension if they have less than ten years of covered employment, have contributed for at least three years, have ceased work, and have reached age 55. Personal contributions are reimbursed to every wage-earning worker contributing for less than three years and withdrawing from the scheme.

CIVIL SERVANT AND PUBLIC EMPLOYEE SYSTEM

Retirement benefits paid to civil servants and public employees include a seniority pension (normal pension for the civil servant/public employee who has made a career in the civil service) and a proportional pension.

Seniority Pension

The civil servant/public employee must have stopped working, reached age 55 (age 60 for the civil servant and public employee in certain categories), and have thirty years of active service. The age requirement is waived for disabled workers and workers with professional inadequacy, provided that the worker has not been guilty of a professional misdemeanor or dismissed due to job reductions. It is possible for women civil servants to reduce the age of entitlement by one year for each child up to a maximum of six years.

Proportional Pension

A proportional pension is awarded to workers who have fulfilled only one of the two necessary requirements in order to receive a seniority pension. In order to have the right to such a pension, it is necessary to either reach the age limit without entitlement to the seniority pension, or else have at least fifteen years of service.

Moreover, the civil servant allowed to retire because of disability, who does not qualify for a seniority pension because of the thirty-year service requirement, has the right to a proportional pension regardless of age or length of service.

Retirement Benefits for Temporary Civil Servants

Temporary civil servants are awarded a retirement benefit when reaching age 55 with at least 15 years of active service. The annuity may be granted without age or length of service requirements for temporary agents dismissed because of disability resulting from the execution of their duties.

Survivor Benefits

Survivors include the wife or wives of the worker, orphaned children, and widowers of female civil servant/public employees. Pensions payable to survivors include widow or widower pensions, orphan pensions, and provisional pensions for the survivors of missing civil servants.

Widow Pensions

In order for a widow pension to be paid, the death of the husband must be certified, and the death must occur while the husband has a right to a pension or at least has not lost his rights. In addition, the widow must have been legally married, or in case of divorce or bodily separation, the divorce or separation must have been pronounced to the exclusive benefit of the wife, and the divorced woman must not have remarried before the death of her first husband.

Ordinarily, the marriage must have been contracted at least two years before the husband ceased activity. This condition is dropped when one or more children are born of the marriage or if work stoppage is due to a disability.

Widower Pensions

To be entitled, a widower must satisfy the requirement of two preceding years of marriage, be stricken with a disability or incurable illness making him definitively unfit for work, and not have his own resources that, being added to the pension, would put them above a minimum living wage. The pension ceases to be paid to the widower who remarries or has a common law marriage.

Orphan Pensions

Orphan benefits are restricted to children aged 21 and under unless the child is permanently disabled. The child must be legitimate, an acknowledged illegitimate child, or adopted.

Pensions for the Assignees of Missing Civil Servants

Dependent benefits are payable when a civil servant who was the holder of a pension of lifetime disability annuity has been missing more than one year. If the missing beneficiary was the holder of the rights to a pension on the day of disappearance, and a minimum of one year has gone by since this day, a pension may be allowed, temporarily, to the dependents. The provisional pension is converted into a definitive pension when the death is officially established or the absence has been declared by passed judgment on the strength of res judicata.

Financing

The civil service retirement system is financed by both contributory and non-contributory funds. Contributions are made by both employers and wage earners to finance old-age, disability, and survivor pensions. Benefits for health care are financed by employee contributions, which are assessed on earnings up to a ceiling of CFA 212,233. The contribution rates consist of 6 percent payable by the worker and 12 percent payable by the state. The rate of contribution for medical care is 3 percent of salary on a ceiling of CFA 212,233.

CURRENT ISSUES

Financing

On the whole, the financial equilibrium of the system managed by the National Contingency Fund is not threatened in the short term since the cost of the benefits only absorbs a relatively small part of resources. For example, in 1986, benefits paid out represented only 57.62 percent of the year's contributions. The financial situation of the organization is comfortable. This is explained in large part by the newness of the system.

Retirement Benefits

Retirement benefits under NCF have been the object of particular attention since 1982, when efforts to reform the system were first initiated. The purpose of the reform was to simplify the method for calculating benefits, improve the level of benefits, and create new benefits. Although the first objective has encountered no obstacles, the second has been blocked by financial constraints. The program's resources are insufficient to support the desired improvements.

Coverage of Farm Workers

In theory, farm workers employed in the modern sector (large industrial plantations) are covered by the social security scheme managed by the NCF. In actual practice, however, these workers are only covered for workmen's compensation.

Utilization of Reserves

A major objective regarding insurance fund reserves is to shelter money from monetary depreciation. There is also a policy of using the funds to promote more participation in development projects. In accordance with this policy, half of the reserves are placed in public funds that allow the state and certain public institutions to have capital at hand in order to finance development.

Administrative Problems in the Rural Zone

One policy objective for the five-year period from 1986–1990 was drawing the NCF and its users closer together. Since 1986, authorities have undertaken the relocation of the structures by installing regional headquarters, agencies, and welfare information centers in rural areas.

Civil Servants System

A major problem with the civil servants system is that it does not have an autonomous management. The scheme's receipts and expenses, therefore, are registered within the civil service's budget. This structure makes it difficult to separate the system's management from the state.

CONCLUSION

Limited economic resources and a higher priority for the establishment of a health infrastructure have played significant roles in circumscribing the development of old-age benefits under social insurance in the Ivory Coast. As in other former French colonies, income programs have also focused more on family allowances and workmen's compensation. Old-age pensions are paid as monthly annuities, in contrast to the lump-sum benefits of the provident fund schemes of former British colonies, but are limited to a small number of wage earners and civil servants who work in urban areas. The old-age pension system for wage earners is financially strong because, as an immature system, there are few current recipients.

REFERENCES

Bakayoko, A., and Ehouman, S. (1987). Ivory Coast. In J. Dixon (ed.), *Social welfare in Africa*, (69–99). London: Croom Helm.
IBIS. (1985, December). *Ivory Coast: Social security*. IBIS Briefing Service, 22–24. Chicago: Charles D. Spencer.
U.S. Department of Health and Human Services. (1990). *Social security programs throughout the world—1989*. Social Security Administration. Office of Research and Statistics. Office of International Policy. Research Report No. 62. Washington, D.C.: U.S. Government Printing Office.

14

Mexico

Emilio Rabasa-Gamboa

Interest in social security in Mexico dates from the Revolution of 1910, which included a provision for a program in Article 123 of the Constitution. It was not until 1944, however, that the Social Security Act of 1943 made the program a tangible reality. Moreover, until 1973 the system was restricted to wage and salary workers. In that year, a coverage was extended through the Mexican Social Security Institute (IMSS), which was entrusted with the task of providing direct health care for low-income groups in rural areas.

As a corollary to the services provided by the IMSS to the country's working community, the state also organized a system in 1959 to protect civil servants, with the establishment of the Institute of Social Security and Services for Civil Servants (ISSSTE). This program covers 7.5 million civil servants and their families. The information presented here, however, is concerned only with the IMSS.

BACKGROUND

The enactment of a legal system to protect the rights of workers, particularly those related to work injuries and diseases, and to those derived from work environment conditions, became a concern for the government around the turn of the century. It was not until after 1907, however, that this concern was articulated in the plans and proposals of leaders and ideologists of the Revolution.

The Flores Magon brothers, who in 1906 formulated the Mexican Liberal party's basic charter, recognized that there was a need for employers to pay cash benefits for work injuries, to prohibit children under age 14 from employment and to provide safe and healthy working conditions.

Proposals to ensure pensions for disabled workers and their families were made by many leaders of the social movement who contributed to the Mexican social security doctrine. When the new Constitution was written in 1917, these ideas were addressed by the members of the Constituent congress, in Article 123, which states:

It is considered socially useful to establish people's insurance funds, for invalidity, for life insurance, for involuntary cessation of work, accidents and others with similar aims; therefore the federal and state governments should encourage the organization of institutions of this nature to introduce and develop protection for the people. (Inter-American Center for Social Security Studies, 1987:7066d)

The federal characteristics of the Constitution, however, led to the proliferation of different social security schemes from one state to the other. As a result, the Constitution was amended in 1929 to have a nationwide and unitary system to meet both the health and income insurance needs of the working population, especially in cases where work injuries could endanger their livelihood.

As a result of this amendment, several attempts were made in the ensuing years to implement a federal social security scheme to protect all Mexicans in times of hardship, orphanage, widowhood, in sickness and unemployment, and also in old age. Many factors, however, prevented the adoption of such a program until the Social Security Act of 1943. That act created the Mexican Social Security Institute (IMSS) to administer the program and to enforce the constitutional precept that workers and their families had a right to health, income, and social benefits.

As noted, services offered by IMSS were limited to the wage-earning urban communities. It was only in the mid–1950s that the limitations of this policy became clear and attempts were made to expand welfare coverage to the rural population. This began on a limited scale with agricultural workers in the northern states of Sinaloa, Sonora, Baja California, and Tamaulipas. There was additional momentum when sugar-cane cutters and producers were covered in 1963.

As a result of IMSS's sustained growth, further efforts were launched in 1970 to expand social security benefits to other population sectors. This involved the compulsory coverage of such groups as the Nayarite State Tobacco Company and the State of Yucatan Sissal Treatment Plant workers.

In 1973 a crucial step was taken to implement a "social solidarity program" that would provide medical services to the country's rural community through the institute's existing infrastructure. The program was targeted to low-income individuals and was funded by the federal government.

This inclusion of medical care under the IMSS program is a unique feature that has become characteristic of many Latin American social security systems. The service provides a wide range of medical care services, including preventative, curative, hospital, pharmaceutical, and rehabilitative services. In addition to cash and medical benefits, there are supplementary benefits for workers and their families. These include health and educational programs such as improvement of nutrition, nursery and recreational centers, and cultural and sports pro-grams.

These comprehensive programs have generated a broadly interconnected net-work of medical, social, and administrative units, as well as a procurement system of drugs, medical supplies, instruments, furnishings, and equipment, which have stimulated national industries and economic activities growth.

SOCIAL SECURITY COVERAGE

Access to social security is made possible by two schemes defined in Article 6 of the Social Security Law: the compulsory program and the voluntary program.

The compulsory program is especially important since it incorporates the economically active population under social security coverage. This represents basic income protection for 34.5 million people. Individuals covered by this system include industrial, agricultural, trade, cooperative, and community work-ers and peasant organizations—more than 60 percent of the population (Inter-national Benefits Information Service, 1988).

The IMSS basic programs provide protection for the following risks: work injuries, sickness, and maternity; invalidity; old-age severance and death; and nurseries for the children of insured women.

The voluntary program allows workers the option of acquiring additional protection for both medical coverage and cash benefits. Supplementary medical insurance may be purchased individually or collectively to provide in-kind ma-ternity and sickness benefits to families of insured persons or other individuals not included in the compulsory program. Additional cash benefits may also be purchased to acquire higher benefits than those provided under the compulsory program.

Eligibility for old-age benefits are age 65 and a minimum of 500 weeks of contributions.

There is also an old-age severance pension that is payable when the insured worker does not have gainful employment after age 60. In order to qualify for this benefit, the insured worker is required to have a minimum of 500 weeks of contributions, have reached age 60 and be unemployed.

Finally, at the death of an insured worker, disabled pensioner, old-age, or old-age severance insured worker or pensioner, the IMSS will provide the fol-lowing benefits: widow pension, orphan pension, survivor pension, welfare to widowed pensioner, and medical care.

Funding

The IMSS operating system is built on careful actuarial studies that ensure and anticipate the timely and efficient delivery of services and benefits workers are entitled to during various stages of life. The system is funded by a tripartite system of compulsory contributions from workers, employers, and government.

Table 14.1
Contribution Rates by Program

	Sickness & Maternity	Work Injury	OASDI	Nurseries	Total
Employers	6.30	2.01*	4.20	0.92	13.43
Employees	2.25	----	1.50	----	3.75
Government	0.45	----	0.30	----	0.75
Total	9.00	2.01	6.00	0.92	17.93

*Average contributions in five categories of firms.

Table 14.2
Proportion of Expenditures by Program

Program	Proportion (percent of total)
Sickness & maternity	50.5
OASDI	33.7
Work injury	11.0
Nurseries	4.8
Total	100.0

The compulsory nature of the system ensures the coverage of all individuals who have a labor relationship with an employer. The employer is responsible for the insurance of workers and the retention of contributions, which are delivered to the institute on a monthly basis. The law sets forth the services and benefits that the insured worker is entitled to in each of the four insurance programs (Patino, 1986).

Revenue collected for the employer-employee and government contributions, as well as sums employed to pay for the costs of the services and benefits provided to the insured workers, are organized in compliance with two basic components: sources of funds and financial programs.

Sources of Funds. Employers, workers, and government contributions cover social security's operating costs. Contributions are based on total earnings. Employers contribute 15.53 percent for all categories of coverage, employees 4.50 percent, and the government 0.90 percent for a total of 20.93 percent (TPF&C, 1989; USDHHS, 1990) (Table 14.1).

Most insurance program revenues are allocated to sickness and maternity insurance (50.5 percent) (Table 14.2). Expenditures for old-age, invalidity, severance, and death benefits account for 33.7 percent of total program costs, work injuries 11.0 percent, and nurseries 4.8 percent. The maximum earnings for contribution and benefit purposes was 10 times the minimum wage in the Federal District, which in January 1989 was 259,000 pesos per month (one peso equaled U.S. $0.04 in 1989).

Financial Programs. These programs are defined as a set of accounting, statistical, and actuarial techniques, which properly applied, allow for the establishment of programs and strategies to ensure the delivery of services and benefits within a financial balance.

The basic features of the actuarial strategy are based on immediate, medium- and long-term expenses. Immediate expenses are allocated to medical services, nurseries, funeral grants, and temporary disability grants due to sickness, maternity, or work injuries. They are the basis for the formulation of annual budgets, called "annual distribution financial programs," which are used to balance revenues and expenditures in the short term through yearly budgets.

The program is charged with ensuring workers' future rights under disability and old-age pensions, as well as widow and orphan benefits in the annual distribution financial program. Therefore, a program has emerged to financially balance the medium- and long-term funding of benefits involved in current insurance, in predetermined periods of time, through anticipated capitalization.

In short, IMSS operates on the two aforementioned financial programs, which have proven their ability and flexibility to ensure the compliance of the tasks of coverage and social security for the national community.

BASIC FEATURES OF IMSS

Medical Benefits

Medical benefits are the main institutional services. They are organized in three care levels, staggered according to the seriousness and degree of specialization demanded by the workers' conditions. These levels also correspond to the three different types of medical units.

The activities of the first level are undertaken in 1,216 so-called "family medicine units" (UMF), where common disorders curable through preventive medicine are treated. About 85 percent of health complaints are cared for at this level.

The second level is provided in 209 regional general hospitals" that have all the resources available to treat the four basic medical specialties: pediatrics; gynecology; general surgery; and internal medicine.

Finally, those cases in which medical specialists determine the need to conduct tests and provide high specialty care are treated at the third level. Service is provided in "specialty hospitals" located in ten national medical centers, strategically distributed throughout the country.

Cash Benefits

Cash benefits are basically geared to protect the covered population's income subsistence in accordance with the provisions of the Social Security Act. These benefits are: grants, pensions, overall indemnity, family allowances, welfare, annual cash bonuses, provisions of lump sums to pensioners, and marriage and funeral grants.

The old-age pension is 35 percent of average earnings during the last 200 weeks of contribution, plus 1.25 percent of earnings per year of contribution beyond 500 weeks. The pension is increased by 15 percent if there are no dependents (USDHHS, 1990). The maximum pension is 100 percent of earnings if the worker has 2,000 or more weeks of contribution. The minimum is 70 percent of the minimum salary in the federal district. Beneficiaries receive a Christmas bonus of one month's pension. Dependent benefits consist of 15 percent of the pension amount for a wife and 10 percent for each child under age sixteen. The pension is adjusted according to changes in the minimum wage. Widow benefits were increased in January 1989 from 50 to 90 percent of the old-age pension of the insured and the funeral grant was doubled from one to two months' minimum wage (Rys, 1990).

Social Benefits

The purpose of social benefits under IMSS is to promote community health, prevent sickness and injuries, and contribute to raising the standard of living. They are also designed to foster, in both individual and social terms, the proper use of leisure time.

IMSS's programs are geared to offer the following social benefits and services to the community as a whole: hygiene promotion, sanitary and first aid education, nutritional and housing improvements, cultural activities in 73 theaters, sports activities in 9 facilities, technical and work training courses in order to increase income levels in 166 social security centers, and four resort facilities oriented to the family integration and social coexistence.

SPECIAL PROGRAMS

The Expansion Program

Social security expansion is being sought through legal mandate, as provided in Article 14 of the Social Security Law, that sets forth the implementation of compulsory social security. The law also empowers the institute to expand coverage according to the social and economic conditions of the various regions and to initiate services in the municipalities where they are not in operation.

The expansion program is becoming a reality as services are being extended to noninsured persons. Making benefits available to new social areas has allowed for modified programs, especially designed for individuals—urban and rural—with partial capacity or health and income needs.

Social Solidarity

Social solidarity programs formally appeared in 1973 as part of IMSS's institutional tasks. The purpose was to expand the universality of care of the IMSS by taking welfare services to the most impoverished population cores of the country. Their contribution, when they lack the economic capacity to pay cash to cover social security costs, is provided through actions of specific benefit to the community, such as work projects to improve nutrition.

Medical Care

Medical care and welfare are provided through a wide network of rural medical units, field clinics, and hospitals of the IMSS-COPLAMAR program (Inter-American Center for Social Security Studies, 1987; Soberon et al., 1986). The federal government is responsible for the funding of these services, particularly in rural areas. The programs are supported by IMSS's infrastructure and logistics and IMSS is responsible for their management and development.

Occupational Indemnity Benefits

Under Mexican labor law there are two types of termination indemnities required of all employers. One type is a severance pay that is paid for involuntary retirement on account of age, which is equal to three months' pay plus 20 days' pay per year of service. The other type is a seniority premium that is payable for any termination, including retirement and death. The premium is equal to 12 days' pay per year of covered employment up to a maximum of two times the minimum wage (International Benefits Information Service, 1988).

Many employers with formal occupational pension plans offer a pension payment option to termination indemnities. This allows employers to take advantage of tax deductions for plan contributions that are not allowed for severance pay until actually paid (Sander and Mendoza, 1987). About 40 percent of industrial businesses in Mexico have funded pension plans, most of which require 10 years of service for eligibility to benefits. The typical retirement age for full benefits is 65 but most plans permit early retirement with a reduced benefit.

CONCLUSION

The Mexican social security program has had a strong historical movement toward the development of comprehensive income and health care coverage for both urban and rural, employed and unemployed populations with the general goal of "social solidarity." The roots of these aspirations stem from the Constitution of 1910, although progress toward fulfillment of these goals has been sporadic. Major events include the Social Security Act of 1943, the commitment to expand coverage to the rural population in the mid–1950s, the "social solidarity program'' of 1973, and the extension of medical care through joint programs such as the IMSS-COPLAMAR.

While considerable success has been achieved in extending primary health care to rural areas under IMSS, the extension of old-age pension coverage to rural workers, especially those engaged in agriculture, has not progressed at a comparable rate. There remains, however, a clear social and legal commitment to continue to expand income and health care coverage to the entire population as resources allow.

REFERENCES

Inter-American Center for Social Security Studies. (1987). *Primary health care under Mexican social security: The experience of the IMSS-COPLAMAR Programme.* Geneva: International Labour Office.

International Benefits Information Service. (1988, August). *IBIS profile—Mexico.* Chicago: Charles D. Spencer.

Patino, E. M. (1986). Estructura financiera del instituto Mexicano del seguor social: Cuestión social. *Revista Mexicana de Seguridad Social,* No. 4–5.

Rys, V. (1990). *Trends and developments in social security—worldwide.* Regional Trading Course on Social Security Administration, Kuwait. Geneva: International Social Security Association.

Sander, G. B., and Mendoza, F.J.C. (1987). Paying with chuchulucos: Creativity in compensation in Mexico. *Benefits & Compensation International,* 17(6), 7–12.

Soberon, G., Frank, J., and Sepulveda, J. (1986). The health care reform in Mexico: Before and after the 1985 earthquakes. *American Journal of Public Health,* 76(6), 673–680.

TPF&C. (1989, April). *International Issues,* 7. Issue No. 112. London: Author.

U.S. Department of Health and Human Services. (1990). *Social security programs throughout the world–1989.* Social Security Administration. Office of Research and Statistics. Office of International Policy. Research Report No. 62. Washington, D.C.: U.S. Government Printing Office.

15

Sweden

Richard M. Coughlin and Richard F. Tomasson

Sweden is often regarded as the epitome of the modern welfare state.[1] Although relatively late to industrialize and lagging behind many other nations in embarking on the road to social welfare in the late nineteenth century, as early as the 1930s Sweden was acclaimed the democratic model of the welfare state (Childs, 1936). This reputation was further secured by the rapid expansion of social welfare and related programs during nearly a half-century of uninterrupted rule by social democratic governments committed to principles of economic equality and social solidarity. The hiatus in social democratic dominance from 1976 to 1982, when a coalition of the nonsocialist parties ruled, did little to undercut Sweden's commitment to social welfare. Indeed, the largely failed attempts at social policy retrenchment by bourgeois governments during this period served if anything to underscore the depth of public support for the Swedish welfare state (Heclo and Madsen, 1987).

PRINCIPLES OF UNIVERSALISM, SOLIDARITY, AND EQUALITY

In Sweden as elsewhere, social insurance programs bear the traces of multiple political philosophies, actors, and interest groups that have shaped the development of the welfare state over the past century (Heclo, 1974). More than other nations, however, Sweden's approach to the welfare state reflects the dominant role of social democracy. While not articulated as a formal philosophy, the social democratic "image of society," to use Castles's (1978) apt term, has guided a distinctive approach to social insurance and other programs of the welfare state in Sweden. This approach is based on principles of universalism, solidarity, and equality.[2]

Universalism in Swedish social insurance is embodied in the coverage of virtually the entire population under provisions of public programs. It is taken for granted in Sweden that comprehensive public programs will provide the safety net of social and economic protection for the population. In social insurance, health care, social services, and education in Sweden, the public sector is large and the private sector small.[3] Although the past decade has seen increased discussion about supplementing public programs with private initiatives—but *not* replacing them in the manner of privatization policies of the United Kingdom—the principle of comprehensive social programs administered by public agencies is still strongly endorsed by the Swedish public (Svallfors, 1989).

The principle of solidarity is closely linked to universalism in social insurance. Besides its frequent use in social democratic rhetoric, solidarity in the Swedish context refers more generally to a sense of collective purpose and common fate transcending individual success or failure in the market economy. While most discernible in the area of collective bargaining over wages, solidaristic principles play an important part in a broad range of social and economic policies in Sweden. Sweden's small size, high degree of ethnolinguistic homogeneity, highly unionized labor force, and vulnerability to the vicissitudes of the world economy have all been suggested as sources of solidarity (Esping-Andersen, 1985; Heclo and Madsen, 1987; Einhorn and Logue, 1989; Milner, 1989). Evidence from public opinion surveys suggests that attitudes in Sweden are strongly influenced by normative factors that mediate the impact of narrow economic individualism (e.g., Zetterberg, 1979; Hadenius, 1986). Attempts to import into Sweden ideologies stressing individual free choice as an alternative to collectively provided social benefits have not enjoyed much success.

Finally, in combination with the first two principles, an overreaching goal of social and economic policy in Sweden is the pursuit of equality—or, more accurately, the effort to reduce the inequalities generated by the market economy. The principle of equality is a thread that has woven through the public debate in Sweden for many years. At times the question of equality has been the focal point of debate, culminating in the late 1960s with the extraordinary report issued by the committee on equality chaired by Alva Myrdal (1969). At other times the question of equality has formed the backdrop against which nearly all important social and economic questions have been debated. This attention to equality has apparently had an impact: in equality of results, Sweden ranks at or near the top among Western industrialized democracies; ideologically, the endorsement of egalitarian principles appears to be much broader and deeper among both the general population and business elites compared to other nations (Verba, Nie, and Kim, 1987; Coughlin, 1990).

OLD-AGE, SURVIVOR, AND DISABILITY PENSIONS

As early as 1884 a proposal from the Swedish Riksdag led King Oscar II to appoint a committee to study the question of social insurance (Elmér, 1960,

1986). The proposal from the committee for universal contributory old-age pensions, based mainly on German ideas, was put forth five years later but was not well received. It was not even debated in the Riksdag. Sweden at that time had only just embarked on the path to becoming an industrial society. A concern with old-age pensions, though, was continuously present from the beginnings of industrialization in this Lutheran monarchy, where the state had so early taken over many of the caring functions of the church. There was disagreement, however, as to what form public pensions should take. The passage of old-age pensions in Germany in 1889 gave additional impetus to the topic. A Bismarckian plan was introduced by a second committee in the mid–1890s, but got nowhere because of the opposition of the farmers, still one of the strongest elements in both the society and the Riksdag. In 1898 a much modified version of the original Bismarckian bill was again defeated.

Folkpension

In 1907 a fourth and decisive committee was established by a conservative government to continue to investigate various alternatives and to make proposals. Five years later, in typical Swedish fashion, the committee came forth with a series of comprehensive reports and some specific proposals. In 1913 a liberal government with support from the Social Democrats and the Conservatives adopted the core proposals of the committee, establishing the world's first universal and compulsory pension system. The system covered the entire population then under age 67. To this system was added the committee's proposal for a program to provide means-tested supplementary pensions (*pensionstillägg*) from general revenues for the poor and for those incapacitated for work regardless of age. As Heclo (1974: 194) observes, this legislation "was supported by but scarcely attributable to the advocacy of the political left."

This first Swedish *folkpension* (literally, "people's pension," often translated as "basic pension") was similar to that adopted in Germany a quarter of a century earlier (it was compulsory and contributions were income-related). It differed from the German system in most other ways. It was a premium revenue system wholly paid for by earners with no employer or government contribution; it covered all citizens; and it was administered by a centralized social insurance board rather than by associations of workers and employers. All citizens were to receive a pension upon reaching age 67, the established retirement age for civil servants. By contrast, the retirement age in Germany was 70. Beginning in 1914 all citizens aged 16 to 66 were to contribute. No provisions were made for those already aged, although they were covered for half pension supplements the following year. The program was not expected to become fully mature until 1956, 42 years after it went into effect (see Elmér, 1986; Heclo, 1974: 178–195).

The system legislated in 1913 remained in force with few changes until 1935, when pension and pension supplement levels were substantially raised. The system was now largely supported by general revenues and not workers' contributions. In the 1920s the Social Democrats had begun to agitate for higher pensions and this is one of the factors that contributed to their electoral successes in the 1930s.

In 1946, immediately after World War II, the Riksdag passed a major pension reform almost unanimously.[4] The reform replaced the system first legislated in 1913. It provided a demogrant of 1,600 Swedish kronor (Skr) to an eligible couple and SKr 1000 to a single individual at age 67 (one kronor equaled about U.S. $16.6 in 1989). There was no means test for the old-age pension, but there was for the disability pension. As a result of postwar inflation, the real value of these demogrants declined and in 1950 the Riksdag reacted by passing a bill indexing the *folkpension* to the Consumer Price Index. Sweden thus became the first country to index the benefits of its pensioners. In 1952 legislation was passed increasing the *folkpension* by an amount equal to the increase in real wages since 1946; a number of subsequent increases in the *folkpension* were made. In the same year the Riksdag also passed legislation providing means-tested municipal housing allowances, with each municipality deciding on the size of the grants and rules of payment. All of the political parties through the 1950s and 1960s favored increasing the amount of the *folkpension*. The vigor of the Conservative and the Center parties in advocating a bigger *folkpension* was enhanced by their opposition to establishing a compulsory supplementary pension system.

Supplementary Pension (ATP)

In the 1940s several motions were put forward in the Riksdag for government earnings-related pensions to supplement the modest *folkpension*. Most concerned with introducing such a system was the *Landsorganisationen* (LO), the confederation of trade unions, the most powerful interest group in Sweden and the most important influence on the dominant Social Democratic party. The issue of supplementary pensions had been brought up as early as the 1936 LO Congress (Molin, 1965). The earnings-related pension system for civil servants was the model for a similar scheme for the whole working population. In Sweden, as in most other industrial societies, civil servants had a developed and generous pension scheme before the general population.

In 1955 a National Commission on Pensions introduced a plan for an inflation-proof supplementary pension scheme. It was immediately supported by the LO and the Social Democrats, but was opposed by the three nonsocialist parties and most of the interest groups in the country. The issue of a compulsory government-operated, earnings-related pension scheme became the most bitterly fought political question of the next half-decade.

Because of the divided opinion on the question of supplementary pensions—even within the coalition government of Social Democrats and the Farmers' party (renamed, in the summer of 1957, the Center party)—the government decided on a referendum on the three most discussed alternatives:

1. Compulsory supplementary earnings-related pensions to be paid for by the employers and administered by the government. (This alternative, favored by the social demo-cratic government and the LO—with the TCO, the Central Organization of Salaried Employees, remaining neutral at the time of the referendum—received 46 percent of the vote.)
2. A voluntary supplementary plan administered by the government. (This alternative, supported by the Center party alone, received 15 percent of the vote.)
3. A voluntary supplementary pension system administered by a nongovernment agency under boards elected by employers and employees. (This alternative, favored by the Conservative and Liberal parties and the SAF, the Swedish Employers' Federation, received 35 percent of the vote.)

After the nonbinding and nondecisive referendum in which 72.4 percent of the electorate participated (with 4 percent submitting blank ballots), the coalition government resigned and was followed by a minority social democratic one. The new government then proceeded to introduce a bill for compulsory, gov-ernment-administered, supplementary pensions (*allmänna tilläggspensioner*, ATP), which was passed by the strongly social democratic Upper House, but was defeated by six votes in the Lower House. The social democratic government then dissolved the Lower House and an extra election was called. The results, by party alignment, resulted in the Lower House being equally split (115–115) in party support for ATP: 110 Social Democrats and five Communists in favor, the Conservatives, Liberals, and Center party representatives against. In February 1959 the government again introduced the ATP bill. It passed 115–114 because one Liberal member of the Lower House, Ture Konigsberg from Gothenburg, abstained from voting against the government's bill. It was by this narrowest of margins that the most costly undertaking in Swedish history was legislated.

After the victory for ATP, the Conservative and Center parties banded together in an attempt to have ATP rescinded. The Liberals, however, joined with the Social Democrats to oppose any attempt to abolish the program. That public opinion quickly moved in the direction of support for ATP is indicated by the setback the Conservatives suffered in the 1960 elections and the relative success of the Social Democrats and Liberals. A 1960 public opinion poll showed 76 percent of the respondents opposed to repealing the recently passed ATP Act, 22 percent in favor of repeal, and a mere 2 percent undecided (Coughlin, 1980).

ATP went into effect in 1960 and the first supplementary pensions were paid in 1963. In 1980 the system reached a certain maturity in that this was the first year in which those retiring at the official retirement age of 65 (lowered from age 67 in 1976) could receive full ATP pensions, an amount equal to 60 percent of average income during their 15 best years of indexed earnings. Eriksen (1981: 2) clearly summarizes the purpose of ATP as follows:

to enable retired employees to retain on the whole the same level of living as they had enjoyed during their active years and to prevent retirement from involving a substantial reduction of living standards. In other words, the *minimum standard* principle of the basic pensions scheme was to be superseded by a *loss of earning principle*. (emphasis added)

Base Amount

To understand how all pensions work in Sweden it is necessary to understand the concept of the base amount (*basbeloppet*). All government and most private pensions are based on this figure. Until 1982 it was adjusted in any month in which the Consumer Price Index had increased by an annual rate of at least 3 percent with a lag of two months. From 1982 it had been adjusted on an annual basis. The initial base amount was the general price level of September 1957, when it was set at SKr 4,000. By 1989 it had reached SKr 27,900 (USDHHS, 1990).

While the *folkpension* is awarded the individual wholly on the basis of being a citizen or resident national regardless of prior labor force status, ATP is based on one's earnings as a member of the paid labor force similar to the West German and American systems. Pensionable income for ATP purposes is calculated for gainfully employed persons aged sixteen to sixty-four. Only that amount in excess of the base amount in January of a given year up to an amount equal to 7.5 times this amount is treated as pensionable income for ATP purposes. There is no spouse supplement in the ATP program, but it does, like the *folkpension*, provide survivor and disability pensions.

Financing

In recent years nearly all the cost of the *folkpension* has been financed by employers and the self-employed with a small amount (barely 6 percent in 1987) financed from general revenues (Riksförsäkringsverket, 1988). Since 1983 payroll taxes for the *folkpension* have remained at 9.45 percent of total payroll, all of which is paid by employers.

In 1981 employers and the self-employed contributed 12.25 percent of ATP point earning payroll, having increased in steps from 3.00 percent in 1960. Beginning in 1982 contributions to the ATP funds became based on *total* payroll, in spite of strong opposition from employers, with the percentage contribution set at 9.4 percent. The ATP payroll tax increased by steps through the 1980s, reaching 11.0 percent in 1989.

Pension Benefits

The absolute level of pensions in Sweden is very high. In 1989 a single person at age 65 without any ATP would have received a *folkpension* of SKr 26,784 per year (USDHHS, 1990). A couple with similar characteristics would have had an annual income of SKr 43,800, again not taxable. In addition, such people would also be eligible to receive a municipal housing allowance. Additional benefits are available for the disabled.

At the other extreme, a single individual at age 65 with full ATP and always having earned the maximum number of ATP points would have a combined *folkpension* and ATP equivalent to slightly over $1,875 per month. At this income level, it is important to note, pensions are taxable as ordinary income, but with some special provisions. Remember also that the medical expenses of the retired in Sweden, although having nearly doubled since 1980, are still low by comparison with most other nations.

Less than one-third of the population over age 65 is eligible for means-tested municipal housing allowance. More than 40 percent of health care resources are devoted to the 16.4 percent of the population over age 65 (Ståhl, 1982).

Redistributive Impact

While the *folkpension* has some downward redistributive impact, ATP is hardly redistributive within generations. ATP is strictly an earnings-related system and there are some basic inequities in how the present formula will operate when the system is fully mature. The ATP formula will be disadvantageous to individuals with many years of ATP credit, mostly manual workers, but advantageous to those with few credited years over the maximum of 30 years, mostly women and professionals with lengthy educations. Extreme examples would be the worker who had 49 years of ATP credit (from ages 16 through 64) at a moderate and constant level of earnings compared with a woman dentist who did not begin to accumulate ATP credit until age 35 (after her two children were in school) and who had a constantly rising income, bringing her to an earnings level of 7.5 times the basic amount for 15 years at ages 50 to 64. The worker who contributed to ATP for 49 years would receive a modest ATP pension, while the dentist with 30 years of contributions would receive the highest possible ATP pension. The person with low or moderate but constant earnings is also at a disadvantage compared to a person with erratic earnings but a number of high years. There has been concern within the LO with the inequities inherent in the present formula, and it may be modified in the future.

Individuals eligible for a *folkpension* but who do not receive ATP or have ATP pensions of less than 48 percent of the basic amount qualify for a pension supplement (*pensionstillskott*). The pension supplement in 1989 was equal to the difference between 48 percent of the basic amount and the amount of ATP received. The purpose of this supplement is to provide support over and above the folkpension for those persons who were too old when ATP began, or who for some other reason did not receive ATP pensions or received small ones.

COLLECTIVELY BARGAINED PENSIONS

The old-age benefit system of Sweden has a well-developed third tier on top of the *folkpension* and ATP. Around 90 percent of blue-collar workers and a slightly smaller percentage of salaried workers are covered by private pension plans achieved through collective bargaining, so highly developed in organized Sweden. These private pensions supplement statutory pensions by amounts equal to about 10 percent of preretirement earnings for lower- and middle-income persons, but by greater percentages for the highly paid. Not surprisingly, a comparative study done by the Union Bank of Switzerland (1977) of old-age benefits in ten industrial societies (including West Germany, the Netherlands, and the United States) found Sweden to have the highest pensions on retirement at low-, medium-, and high-income levels. Swedish old-age pensions also provided the highest replacement ratios in a study of twelve industrial nations (Tomasson, 1984).

PENSION REFORMS

Since the passage of ATP in 1959, several retirement pension reforms have been introduced. The major reforms have provided for a more flexible age at retirement; (2) early retirement for those who have difficulty working or who have had long periods of employment; and (3) partial pensions. These reforms had their origins in government pension committee proposals but never became controversial political issues like ATP.

In 1964 it became possible to retire at age 63, when the official retirement age was 67, with an actuarially reduced *folkpension* and ATP. Since 1976, when the official retirement age was lowered to 65, it has been possible to retire as early as age 60. Pensions are reduced by 0.5 percent per month for each month under age 65, reducing pensions by 30 percent with retirement at age 60. In recent years, only about 2 percent of those aged 60 to 64 have opted for this alternative (Crona, 1981), because other alternatives became available. Also in 1964 it became possible to delay retirement to age 70. Deferring retirement after age 67 (age 65 from 1976) gives an increase in pensions of 0.6 percent per month to age 70. Delaying receipt of pensions to age 70 will increase both the *folkpension* and ATP by 36 percent at age 70. Only a small fraction of one percent of Swedes 65 to 69 have ever elected this option (Sweden, 1977).[5] The reason is that Sweden has no retirement test. One can receive a full *folkpension* and full ATP at age 65 whether employed or not and regardless of income.

Legislation from 1970 and 1972 made it possible to get disability pensions of the same amount as the *folkpension*, not actuarially reduced, on lenient grounds at ages 60 to 64. This relaxation of the disability rules was specifically intended for those who have arduous work or who are not in good health. Being over 60 and having been unemployed for a lengthy period (more than 450 days, about 22 months) is also grounds for receiving a disability pension. The Swedish name for disability pension is, by the way, *förtidspension* or early pension, less stigmatizing than the older Swedish term *invaliditetspension*. There are full, two-thirds, and half disability pensions, but the overwhelming majority of those aged

60 to 64 receive full pensions (Packard, 1982; Tracy and Adams, 1989). Pension supplements for those with disability pensions are double the normal *folkpension* supplement for those who receive no ATP, those with some ATP receiving correspondingly less. The rationale for this remarkable generosity is that those receiving disability pensions have been less able to build up ATP pension points and hence have greater need for supplementation.

The most important pension reform legislation of the 1970s was passed in 1974 and became effective July 1, 1976. The official retirement age in effect since 1913 was reduced from age 67 to 65, and the age limit for early retirement was reduced from 63 to 60. Statutes were also passed by the Riksdag to make partial pensions available at ages 60 to 64 and to allow individuals to take half of their *folkpension* and ATP as early as age 60 or to postpone half of either up to age 70. The same reductions and increases apply as with full pensions. Pension points for ATP are earned from employment at the same time that half-pensions are not claimed.

The most popular innovation in the Swedish pension system has been the introduction of the partial pension (*delpension*) on transfer to part-time work. This alternative gives individuals aged 60 to 64 the option of shifting to part-time employment and replacing 65 percent of lost income without reducing the amount of the pensions received at age 65. (Previous to 1981 the replacement rate was 65 percent; it was lowered to 50 percent by legislation put forth by the nonsocialist government in 1980 and then restored to 65 percent in 1987.) To be eligible to receive a partial pension an individual must have been receiving ATP pension-earning income for at least ten years after age 45 and meet certain other conditions that the great majority of Swedes aged 60 to 64 can meet. At first only employees could receive partial pensions, but from 1980 the self-employed, too, have been eligible. To receive a partial pension one must work a minimum of 17 hours a week and reduce one's work week by at least five hours. In the spring of 1981 some 30 percent of the eligible population aged 60 to 64 had opted for partial pensions with varying amounts of gainful employment. The partial pension itself together with earned income count for ATP pension points. Since 1980 the partial pension program has been funded by contributions of 0.50 percent of gross payroll by employers; this is double the 0.25 percent of payroll contributed before 1980. All of these various pension alternatives can be changed from month to month.

Two minor cutbacks became effective in 1981. First, the partial pension was lowered from 65 percent of lost income to 50 percent. This reduction did not apply to those who went on partial pensions prior to 1981, and in any case the amount was restored to 65 percent in July 1987. Second, the method of calculating the base amount was also changed by eliminating increases in energy prices, consumer price subsidies, and indirect taxes from the index. The effect will be to slow somewhat the rise of the base amount that affects the size of all pensions. Effective in 1982, adjustment of the base amount was changed to an annual basis. Also in 1982 the pensions of persons provided for in nursing homes were reduced and there was a tightening up on income tax regulations of the retired (affecting higher-income retirees).

Beginning in 1984 the old indexing system was reinstated, a campaign pledge made by the Social Democrats who returned to power after the September 1982 elections. To offset the past effects of the modified index, the government raised the base amount by SKr 300 to 1983 over what it would have been using the modified index. The once-a-year adjustment of the base amount, however, was not rescinded by the new government.

In recent years there have been no proposals to further expand the pension system. Reform efforts have focused on removing from the system all distinctions based on gender and marital status. Little has been done to modify the future costs of the system. In November 1981 the long-lived Swedish Pensions Committee presented its final report to the minister of social affairs, entitled *Familjepension* (Sweden, 1981). The report contained radial and rational proposals for changing the system of family benefits in the Swedish pension system. The committee argued powerfully and in detail for changes that it believed to be in accord with the changes that have occurred within the family and society.

In June 1988 the Riksdag finally passed reform legislation scheduled to go into effect on January 1, 1990. The new law is intended to improve the fit between the *folkpension* and ATP systems and changes that have occurred in the labor force participation of women, the composition of the family, and other social conditions. The widow pension will be gradually phased out under both the *folkpension* and ATP systems. The new law provides an adjustment pension payable for one year after the death of the insured to the spouse or cohabitant who has been married or lived with the insured for at least five years or if there are mutual children under age 12, or a special survivor pension payable to the surviving spouse or cohabitant who due to illness or unemployment is unable to support himself or herself. The amount of the pension will be a maximum of 96 percent of the base amount under the *folkpension* system and 40 percent of the deceased's ATP pension (20 percent if the child pension is paid out simultaneously). The new system of pensions for survivors is centered around support payments to minor children. Separate age limits in the *folkpension* and ATP will be standardized to provide the payment of benefits under both systems until the child reaches 18 years of age.

FUTURE PROBLEMS AND PROSPECTS

From an American perspective the cost of pensions in Sweden is staggeringly high. This is not only a consequence of the highest level of benefits among the industrial societies, but also of having a high proportion of the population 65 years or older (16.9 percent in 1985, according to the OECD, 1987a) and 60.1 percent of those aged 60 to 64 receiving pensions (in 1981, as reported by Packard, 1982). In 1980 it was estimated there were only 2.3 persons in the paid labor force for every person receiving a pension (Sweden, 1977). Total contributions for pensions in 1989 equaled about 26 percent of gross payroll, about 21 percent for statutory pensions (9.45 percent for the *folkpension*, 11.00 percent for ATP, and 0.50 percent for the partial pension) in addition to about 5 percent for additional pensions under collective agreements. Until 1983 the annual outgo of the ATP funds has been less than pension disbursements (SNPIF, 1983). The funds at present have large reserves, but these are projected to disappear by the late 1990s unless there are large increases in the scheduled ATP contribution rates.

The future will see a great escalation in the cost of pensions in Sweden, above all for ATP. Among the reasons for this are the increase in the proportion of older people. Sweden already has the largest proportion of population 65 years and older of any nation (OECD, 1987a). The projected increase in the elderly population, however, will not be as large as in most other industrial societies. Sweden's birthrate, low since the late 1960s, has experienced an unexpected increase in the late 1980s, from a low of 1.6 total fertility rate (average births per woman) in 1983 to 1.9 in 1989. This increase has required a revision in population projections for the next century (Johansson, 1989).[6] Nonetheless, despite these relatively favorable population trends there will still be major additional burdens on the public pension systems because of a large rise in the number of ATP pensioners as the system matures, an increase in female employment participation with more women earning ATP pension points, together with their greater life expectancy, and the very liberal pension alternatives available at ages 60 to 64.

The National Social Insurance Board has estimated that under the assumption of a 2 percent annual increase in real income, ATP contributions would need to be 11.0 percent of total payroll in the year 2000 and 13.3 percent by the year 2020. Assuming no increase in real income, the estimates jump to 16 percent in the year 2000, to 25 percent by 2020 (Eriksen, 1981), and to 32 percent by 2030 (based on a 1982 projection). Were there to be along-term decline in real income, the costs of ATP would be still higher, so high—as Tor Eriksen of the National Social Insurance Board has proclaimed—the system could no longer exist. We need to keep in mind that these estimates are for ATP alone and do not include the cost of the *folkpension*, partial pensions, or collectively bargained pensions.

ATP and other retirement systems based on indexed earnings—like the West German and American systems—are built on the assumption of long-term increases in real income. Without such an increase, these systems will become extraordinarily expensive in the future. With long-term decline in real income, they cannot survive in their present form for they would come to take an impossibly large share of total payroll. Almost as untenable is a situation whereby the retired population continually improves its economic situation relative to the economically active population. The beginnings of such a pattern have been seen in all of the industrial societies with indexed retirement systems, but probably nowhere has this proceeded farther than in Sweden, where the economist Ingemar Ståhl (1982: 116) has concluded "that 16 percent of all Swedes over 65 years of age consume 22 percent of total individual consumption—i.e., private and public consumption—less collective services, such as defense, crime prevention, and basic research." A recent report by another economist (Kruse, 1988) has expressed a similar concern about the stability of the pension system.

Finally, related to these questions is the issue of the future of income-related benefits under ATP. Unless action is taken soon, the vast majority of working Swedes will be eligible upon retirement for the maximum ATP benefit. In effect, the system will revert de facto to a flat-rate pension system—albeit a very generous and expensive one. The contemporary debate in Sweden over the future of ATP has had several interesting and, in one case at least, unanticipated consequences. First, as in other advanced industrialized nations, discussion of the funding problems that are likely to befall pension systems in the decades to come has caused a certain amount of alarm. Like their counterparts elsewhere, young Swedes are beginning to question whether they can depend upon public retirement schemes to provide adequate support when they retire. There has been increased interest in privately purchased insurance, a commonplace in many other nations but a novelty in Sweden's welfare state.[7] Second, discussion over the future of ATP has reopened political questions long considered dead. Some thirty years after the passage of ATP, the Center party, which opposed ATP from the outset, has put forth a proposal that would formally replace ATP with a flat-rate system (Centerns Riksdagsgrupp, 1989). While the prospects of the Center party's proposal are doubtful, the very fact of its existence at this time indicates the possibilities for instability created by the current and future crises of old-age pensions.

CONCLUSION

Old-age pensions in Sweden can be summed up in four words: comprehensive, generous, flexible, and expensive. The idea that Sweden is a welfare state leader is borne out by its performance in old-age pension policy. Among fifteen nations studied by Myles (1984), Sweden ranked first in an index of pension quality based on benefit levels, adjustment for inflation, coverage, flexibility, and lack of restrictive qualifying conditions. But success in this area of social insurance has not come cheaply. Since 1980, total government spending has consumed a larger proportion of Gross Domestic Product in Sweden than in any other OECD nation (OECD, 1987b). Pensions alone accounted for just over 15 percent of all government spending in 1988–1989 (Ministry of Finance, 1988). These high levels of spending have, of course, been accompanied by a correspondingly heavy tax burden. The question of high taxes is a perennial concern in Sweden, but recent studies suggest that antitax sentiments are diffuse and are not increasing (see Hadenius, 1986).

In recent years the discussion over Sweden's old-age pension programs, as in other nations, has been cast in the language of crisis and controversy (Rosa, 1982). The reality has been that social insurance programs have fared reasonably well in Sweden's welfare state. But the horizons of social policy are never entirely clear: the task of maintaining financial stability in the pension systems without undermining public confidence remains as much of a challenge in Sweden as elsewhere. In this respect, the problems Sweden faces bear a remarkable similarity to those confronting other nations, including that perennially "reluctant" welfare state, the United States.[8]

APPENDIX

Sickness Benefit and Parental Insurance

Sickness insurance provides compensation for earned income lost due to illness. The benefit, payable from the second day of illness, amounts to 90 percent of earned income up to SKr 209,250 annually in 1989 (USDHHS, 1990). Sickness benefits are taxed as ordinary income and qualify for future payments under ATP.

The sickness insurance benefit has been the focus of considerable controversy over the past decade. In 1982 the bourgeois government introduced and narrowly passed legislation increasing the waiting period to three days. This change was intended to reduce total spending by some SKr 1.4 billion annually—at a time when the government was running a SKr 77 billion budget deficit—and to discourage worker absenteeism (Heclo and Madsen, 1987). The increase in waiting days was bitterly opposed by the LO, whose members were less likely to be covered by private contractual sick-pay benefits and who thus would bear the brunt of the reform. Despite the fact that the three-day waiting period originated in national health insurance law in effect from 1955 to 1967, the social democratic opposition managed to portray the bourgeois government's reform as an attack on the welfare state. Shortly after their return to power in 1982, the waiting period for sickness benefits was once again lowered to one day.

Recently there has been growing concern over the increase in the number of sick days claimed by workers. After decreasing in the early 1980s sick days started to rise in 1985, increasing nearly 25 percent between 1983 and 1987, and more than 7 percent between 1986 and 1987 alone (Riksförsäkringsverket, 1988). The issue of sick days is significant not only because of the concomitant rise in sickness insurance benefits, but also because of concern over Sweden's relatively high rate of worker absenteeism. Major industrial enterprises such as Volvo routinely experience worker absentee rates of 20 percent, meaning that on average one in five workers reports in sick on any given day.[9]

Also part of the sickness insurance scheme is coverage for parents of newborns or younger adopted children. Sweden's parental benefits rank among the most generous and flexible of any nation. Parental cash benefits in connection with childbirth (*föräldrapenning vid barns födelse, FP*) was introduced in 1974, with a special benefit component (särskild föräldrapenning, SFP) added in 1978. Beginning in 1986 FP and SFP were combined into a single benefit. Parental insurance provides for 270 days of benefit paid at 90 percent of taxable income for either parent until the child's fourth birthday. In 1991 the benefit period is scheduled to increase to 540 days. In addition, both parents are eligible for cash benefits for ten days in connection with childbirth, and both parents are entitled to draw an allowance of up to 60 days before the delivery. For persons outside the labor force, the parental benefit is the flat-rate minimum of SKr 60 per day (Olsson, 1989a).

Parental insurance also provides for coverage of up to 60 days per year for each child under age 12 if the parent stays home from work due to the child's illness. The replacement rate is 90 percent, the same as ordinary sickness cash benefit.

Family Allowances

A basic child allowance (*barnbidrag*) of SKr 5,820 (1989) is paid for each child under 16 years of age. An extended child allowance is paid for children over 16 who are still enrolled in school. Beginning in 1982, families with three or more children received a supplement to the basic child allowance; as of 1983, the supplement was extended to children between the ages of 16 and 20 enrolled in school. The supplementary child allowance for three children amounts to half of the basic allowance and is increased by a full basic allowance for each additional child. Child allowance benefits are not indexed, but are periodically adjusted by parliamentary action. Child allowances are nontaxable.

In the case of parents living apart, low or missing child support payments are supplemented or replaced by a child maintenance award. In 1986, slightly over 14 percent of all children up to 17 years of age received some maintenance advance, averaging SKr 9,240 per year. Child maintenance awards are covered primarily by payments from the noncustodial parents, with the rest paid out of public funds.

Work Injury Insurance

Every person gainfully employed or undergoing education in Sweden is covered by national work injury insurance (*arbetsskadeförsäkring*). In most cases, the first 90 days of absence because of injuries incurred from work are treated the same as other illnesses, and are covered under sickness insurance. After 90 days the government social insurance office rules whether or not an injury is due to work. Certain diseases, such as asbestosis and eczema, are always decided by the social insurance authorities regardless of the length of the illness-related absence from work. If the illness is judged work-related, the insured person is eligible for extended compensation for loss of earnings and for medical and dental care. An insured person whose earnings have been reduced by at least one-fifteenth as a result of work injury is entitled to compensation in the form of an annuity based on qualifying income for sickness insurance. Work injury insurance is financed by an employers' payroll tax of 0.90 percent.

Unemployment Insurance

Since the 1930s Sweden has placed heavy emphasis on maintaining full employment. Indeed, the commitment to full employment is a central tenet of social democratic ideology and is one of the pillars of the Swedish welfare state (Olsson, 1989a; Heclo and Madsen, 1987). Sweden's rate of unemployment has always been low by comparative international standards. Since World War II it has generally remained below 2 percent (regarded in Sweden as full employment), peaking at 3.1 percent in the early 1980s. The reason for this extraordinarily low unemployment rate has been an active labor market policy that makes extensive provisions for employment counseling, retraining, relocation, job creation, and subsidized employment. Unemployment insurance is only a minor, but not insignificant, part of publicly sponsored employment policies. In 1984–1985, for example, outlays for unemployment benefits made up less than a third of all labor market expenditures (Olsson, 1989a).

Unemployment insurance is organized under the trade unions with supervision by the National Labor Market Board (AMS). Two-thirds of the labor force are covered by unemployment insurance schemes (Olsson, 1989a). Eligibility for unemployment insurance benefits is restricted to workers who have been members of a fund for at least 52 weeks. In addition, the individual must have been employed for at least 20 weeks during the twelve months preceding the loss of a job. Further, the unemployment must be involuntary and applicants must register at the local employment office and must be available for work. Declining any offer of a "suitable job" is grounds for denial of benefits, and Olsson (1989a: 297) characterizes the work test as "rather harsh."

Unemployment insurance benefits are earnings-related, and begin after a waiting period of five days. The maximum period benefits may be received is 300 days, but for workers between 55 and 60 the period is extended to 450 days. The maximum payment, which most unemployed workers receive, amounted to SKr 450 per day in 1989, about 70 percent of the average industrial worker's earnings. Persons not covered by unemployment insurance or who exhaust their insurance benefits are eligible to receive unemployment cash assistance, which in 1989 stood at SKr 158 per day. The duration of unemployment assistance benefits varies with age: 150 days for persons up to age 55, 300 days for persons 55 to 60, and unlimited for those over 60. Both unemployment insurance and assistance benefits are fully taxable.

NOTES

1. Parts of this chapter are drawn from Tomasson's (1984) paper on old-age pensions in four nations. A study grant from the Bicentennial Swedish-American Exchange Fund

enabled Coughlin to visit Sweden in 1989 to conduct interviews and obtain current data and other information used to prepare this chapter. The authors are grateful to Sten Johansson, Sven E. Olsson, and Stefan Svallfors for comments on an earlier draft. The authors alone are responsible for any remaining errors of commission or omission.

2. These three principles are given particular emphasis by Esping-Andersen (1985), but the list of distinctive principles associated with Swedish social democracy is open-ended. For example, Furniss and Tilton (1977) identify the following as values of the "social welfare state" (an ideal type most closely approximated by Sweden): equality, freedom, democracy, solidarity, security, and economic efficiency. Esping-Andersen and Korpi (1987) describe Scandinavian social policy as comprehensive, institutionalized, solidaristic, and divorced market criteria. Einhorn and Logue (1989) and Milner (1989) both contain extensive discussions of solidarity in Sweden's welfare state. Baldwin (1988) questions the assumption that the solidaristic welfare state is a specifically social democratic phenomenon.

3. Esping-Andersen (1985: 177) reports data from the mid–1970s showing private pension expenditures in Sweden as 11.7 percent of public pensions. This figure, however, overstates the size of the private pension sector since it includes the amount spent on occupational pension schemes achieved through collective bargaining. These schemes, Esping-Andersen notes, "cover all workers" (p. 178).

4. See Olsson (1989b) for a discussion of the role of the political parties in the 1946 reform. Olsson questions Baldwin's (1988, 1989) contention that the pension reform in the mid–1940s represented a significant departure from the Social Democrats' vanguard role in Swedish social policy.

5. About one percent opted for delayed retirement in 1977. A decade later, according to data reported by Tracy and Adams (1989), the figure had risen slightly to 2 percent.

6. Sweden's recent experience with a very high number of elderly as a proportion of the total population contains a positive lesson for other industrial societies. The Swedish case demonstrates that the dependency ratios projected for other nations in the early twenty-first century need not cripple the welfare state.

7. Increased interest in private pension plans may also have been stimulated by the generous tax deductions available to individuals purchasing such policies. The forthcoming tax reform will reduce these advantages.

8. Wilensky's (1965) characterization of the American welfare state.

9. Sweden's very low unemployment rate may be a factor in the nation's high rate of absenteeism. The Swedish labor force includes many workers (e.g, the semidisabled, those with alcohol abuse problems, etc.) who in other nations might well be unemployed or outside the labor force entirely. Such workers are likely to be at greater risk of calling in sick.

REFERENCES

Baldwin, P. (1988). How socialist is solidaristic social policy? Swedish postwar reform as a case in point. *International Review of Social History*, 33, 121–147.
———. (1989). The Scandinavian origins of the social interpretation of the welfare state. *Comparative Studies in Society and History*, 31, 3–24.
Castles, F. G. (1978). *The social democratic image of society*. London: Henley and Boston.

Centerns Riksdagsgrupp. (1989). *Förstärkt grundtrygghet: En rapport om möjligheter i pensionssystemets utveckling*. April. Stockholm: Mimeograph.

Childs, M. (1936). *Sweden: The middle way*. London: Faber and Faber.

Coughlin, R. M. (1980). *Ideology, public opinion and welfare policy*. Berkeley: University of California, Institute of International Studies.

———. (1990). The economic person in sociological context: Case studies in the mediation of self-interest. *Journal of Behavioral Economics*. Forthcoming, Summer.

Crona, G. (1981). Partial retirement in Sweden: Development and experiences. *Aging and Work*, 2, 113–120.

Einhorn, E. S., and Logue, J. (1989). *Modern welfare states*. New York: Praeger.

Elmér, Å. (1960). *Folkpensioneringen i Sverige*. Lund: CWK Gleerup.

———. (1986). *Svensk socialpolitik*. Stockholm: Liber.

Eriksen, T. (1981). *The cost of ATP—Some reflections concerning a pensions pledge*. Unpublished manuscript. Stockholm: National Social Insurance Board.

Esping-Andersen, G. (1985). *Politics against markets*. Princeton: Princeton University Press.

Esping-Andersen, G., and Korpi, W. (1987). From poor relief to institutional welfare states. In R. Erikson et al. (eds.), *The Scandinavian model*. London and New York: Sharpe.

Furniss, N., and Tilton, T. (1977). *The case for the welfare state*. Bloomington and London: Indiana University Press.

Hadenius, A. (1986). *A crisis of the welfare state?* Stockholm: Almqvist and Wiksell International.

Heclo, H. (1974). *Modern social politics in Britain and Sweden*. New Haven: Yale University Press.

Heclo, H., and Madsen, H. (1987). *Policy and politics in Sweden*. Philadelphia: Temple University Press.

Johansson, L. (1989). *P.M. OM 1989 ärs befolkningsprognos*. Mimeographed report no. 890407. Stockholm: Statistics Sweden.

Kruse, A. (1988). *Pensionssystemets stabilitet*. Stockholm: Regeringskansliets Offsetcentral.

Milner, H. (1989). *Sweden: Social democracy in practice*. Oxford: Oxford University Press.

Ministry of Finance. (1988). *The Swedish budget 1988/89*. Stockholm: Author.

Molin, B. (1965). *Tjänstepensionsfrägan*. Göteborg: Akademiförlaget-Gumperts.

Myles, J. F. (1984). *Old age in the welfare state*. Boston: Little, Brown.

Myrdal, A. (ed.). (1969). *Jämlikhet: Första rapport fran SAP-LO's arbetsgrupp för jämlikhetsfrågor*. Borås: Sjunhäradsbygdens Trykeri.

OECD. (1987a). *Labor force statistics*. Paris: Author.

———. (1987b). *Historical statistics: 1960–1987*. Paris: Author.

Olsson, S. E. (1989a). Sweden. In J. Dixon and R. P. Scheurell (eds.), *Social welfare in developed market countries*, 264–308. London and New York: Routledge.

———. (1989b). Working class power and the 1946 pension reform in Sweden. *International Review of Social History*, 34, 287–308.

Packard, M. D. (1982). Retirement options under the Swedish national pension system. *Social Security Bulletin*, 45(12), 12–22.

Riksförsäkringsverket. (1988). *Social försäkrings statistik: Fakta 1988*. Stockholm: Riksförsäkringsverket.

Rosa, J. J. (ed.). (1982). *The world crisis in social security*. San Francisco: Institute for Contemporary Studies.

Ståhl, I. (1982). Sweden. In J. J. Rosa (ed.), *The world crisis in social security*, 93–120. San Francisco: Institute for Contemporary Studies.

Svallfors, S. (1989). *Vem älskar välfärdsstaten?*. Lund: Arkiv.

Sweden. (1977). *Pensionsfrågor m.m.* Stockholm: SOU 1977:46.

———. (1981). *Familjepension, sammanfattning*. Stockholm: SOU 1981:61.

The Swedish National Pension Insurance Fund. (1983). *Annual Report for 1982*. Stockholm: Author.

Tomasson, R. F. (1984). Government old age pensions under affluence and austerity: West Germany, Sweden, the Netherlands, and the United States. *Research in Social Problems and Public Policy*, 3, 217–272.

Tracy, M. B., and Adams, P. (1989). Age of first pension award under social security: Patterns in ten industrial countries 1960–1986. *International Social Security Review*, 42(4), 447–461.

Union Bank of Switzerland. (1977). *Social security in 10 industrial nations*. Zurich: Economic Research Department, Union Bank of Switzerland.

U.S. Department of Health and Social Services. (1990). *Social security programs throughout the world—1989*. Social Security Administration. Office of International Policy. Research Report No. 62. Washington, D.C.: U.S. Government Printing Office.

Verba, S; Nie, N. H., and Kim, J. (1987). *Participation and political equality: A seven-nation comparison*. Chicago: University of Chicago Press.

Wilensky, H. L. (1965). The problems and prospects of the welfare state. In H. L. Wilensky and C. N. Lebeaux (eds.), *Industrial Society and Social Welfare*. Glencoe, Ill.: Free.

Zetterberg, H. (1979). Maturing of the Swedish welfare state. *Public Opinion*, 10/11, 42–47.

16

Switzerland

Peter Kunz

The various systems of social insurance in Switzerland reflect a federal structure of government protection against the risks of loss of income. The administrative, funding, and benefit features of the systems vary among the cantons (states), private insurance companies, and special organizations. The federal structure is important in understanding the historical and present conditions of the Swiss old-age pension scheme.

MAIN PROGRAM FEATURES OF OLD-AGE PENSIONS

The old-age pension system is based on three pillars. The first pillar, implemented in 1948, is the national Old-Age and Survivors Insurance program (AHV), which is designed to provide a subsistence income. The second pillar consists of occupational retirement schemes (pension funds and other employer-initiated programs) that are supposed to ensure that the aged, survivors, and disabled employees are able to maintain a standard of living comparable to preretirement levels. This feature has been operational as a mandatory provision only since 1985. The third pillar is that of private savings, which is intended to cover additional personal needs.

The three-level system was created in 1972 by a constitutional act. Up until that time, some 75 to 80 percent of all insurable employees were covered by company occupational schemes on a voluntary basis. With the constitutional amendment, the state resumed responsibility for encouraging the funding of the third pillar (especially through tax concessions). There are some differences between the systems of the first and second pillars, which are discussed below.

Coverage

AHV Program. Under the AHV program the entire population of Switzerland is insured, including manufacturers, employees, and nonworking persons whose legal domicile is in Switzerland.

The retirement age is fixed at 65 for men and 62 for women. The retirement age can be postponed up to five years, in which case the benefits are progressively increased by up to 50 percent.

Payroll contributions are made from the age of 20 up to the age of retirement. Contributions are normally related to salary and are paid without an upper limit. They are also paid by retired persons who are engaged in a salaried activity. Individuals may make a minimum contribution during nonactive periods of work in order to avoid a loss in years of contributions and coverage. Benefits from pension systems, which replace earnings, are also subject to contributions, including disability, unemployment, and military allocations.

Occupational Scheme. The legal retirement ages are the same as under the AHV system. The mandatory private pensions are managed by firms and companies. Their basic requirements are subject to law, but they are free to do more. Thus, they can have a lower retirement age if financing is assured. This option is more and more widespread. Payroll contributions begin at age 25 based on an insured salary that is equal to the AHV salary minus Sw Fr 19,200 (1990).

The system is based on insurance principles of capitalization; the size of the pension depends directly on the amount paid in. Persons who were over age 25 when the act came into force in 1985 are exempt unless they already had joined an insurance scheme. In order to build up the capital stock of these workers, private institutions are required, as far as funds permit, to establish special provisions that favor middle-aged and low-income persons.

Benefit Levels

Old-Age and Survivor Insurance. The general benefit rate is based on 80% of the minimum pension plus 20 percent of average revalued earnings. There is a minimum and a maximum amount of Sw Fr 800 and 4,800 a month (1990), respectively. A partial benefit rate is applied, if there are losses in years of contribution. Five to 6 percent of all old-age benefits are partial.

Several types of benefit rates are calculated, as shown in Table 16.1.

Benefits are adjusted to changes in salaries and prices. Normally this takes place every second year. Benefits may be adjusted earlier if prices increase more than 8 percent a year. Adjustment may be postponed if prices increase by less than 5 percent within two years

Occupational Pensions. Occupational pensions are defined-contribution plans, which provide a total capital of 500 percent of the insured salary at retirement age. This capital is converted to an annuity; the conversion rate is 7.2 percent, regardless of sex or marital status. It results in a pension of 36 percent of

Table 16.1
Monthly Basic Benefit Rates, 1990

Type	Percent	Minimum	Maximum
Single old-age pensioner	100	800	4,800
Couples man 65, wife 62	150	1,200	7,200
Couples man 65, wife 55-61	130	1,040	6,240
Widows until age 62*	80	640	3,840
Children of pensioners	40	320	1,920
Orphans	40	320	1,920

*Converts to single old-age pension at age 62.

coordinated salary, which is the amount of earnings between earnings covered by occupational pensions above a specified minimum and ceiling level.

In principle, there is no occupational benefit if earnings are below a specified minimum level. The second pillar starts only if earnings meet this minimum. If earnings do not meet the minimum, no contributional pension credit has to be paid and there is no capital stock and therefore no benefit. For persons with lower incomes, the AHV system provides a replacement rate of 60 percent or more without second-pillar benefits.

In the occupational pension scheme there is no credit for couples. There are survivor benefits, the amount of which is calculated according to the pension capital that the insured party would have accumulated if the person had remained active up to retirement age. The outstanding contributions are taken into account at the level of the last salary and accumulated with no interest. The conversion rate again is 7.2 percent. A widow pension is 60 percent and an orphan pension is 20 percent of such a calculated annuity. Contrary to the AHV system the widow pension is paid lifelong. Currently the law does not require the adjustment of occupational pensions to inflationary trends.

Administration

A personal identification number is given to every person to permit registration for the basic system at one of the 107 specialized pay offices. There are 26 offices managed by the cantons; the others are administered by professional organizations. The pay offices are connected to the central registering office, which collects contribution and benefit data for statistical use. The pay offices and employers are inspected twice a year. Old-age pension legislation is prepared by a standing committee in collaboration with the federal office of social security and acted upon by the parliament.

There is also a special executive board that manages the fund. All representatives in committees and boards are nominated by the Swiss authorities. The state has supervisory authority.

The occupational pension system is the obligation of employers, who must make insurance arrangements for employees. Employers have the following options:

1. They may set up their own personal scheme, which usually takes the form of a foundation. Mutual funds are also possible but less common. The important point is that the pension scheme has to be a legally independent entity and may not be part of the employer's company.
2. They may join an existing pension fund or an existing joint foundation set up by an insurance company or a bank.
3. They may joint a special state scheme, which accepts any employers having no other insurance provision.

The 1985 law introduced a decisive and fundamental shift in Swiss insurance practice by making a logical distinction between savings (old-age pension) and the risk components (disability and survivor benefits). This distinction means that employers' funds can:

• handle both parts itself (but to do this, it has to dispose of a well-balanced portfolio, which must be confirmed by a certified pension actuary)
• manage the savings itself and reinsure the risk component through group insurance
• reinsure both components through group insurance

The insurance is based on capitalization. By law, the financial mechanism has to be reviewed every three years by a certified actuary. The pension scheme is controlled by a fiduciary. The pension schemes are supervised by the cantons' authority and finally by Swiss federal authorities. There is no central registration in the pension system. It is planned that every five years statistical inquiries will be conducted to collect data.

It is important to note that in both the basic public AHV and the occupational systems there is a transfer guarantee when an employee changes jobs. In the basic system this is the responsibility of the central registration, while in the compulsory occupational system there are legal regulations whereby the pension capital is transferred from one fund to another, so that no loss is incurred by occupational changes.

SPECIAL PROVISIONS

Although the program features of the old-age-system pension follow insurance principles with contributions as well as benefits that are connected to a well-defined salary base, there are different specialties in the structure that favor groups of insured persons. As it is not possible to discuss all aspects inherent to the insurance systems, explanations are limited to the main points.

Couple Benefits

The basic AHV system incorporates the notion of couple benefits. The salaries of both partners are cumulated, so that the reference salary of couples may be higher than for a single person. Actually, the salary bases of couples are about 110 percent of single persons. Couples therefore reach the maximum level more readily than singles. By this mechanism the benefit of the surviving partner, which in 85 percent of the cases is the woman, is higher than if she had not been married.

Divorces

In the case of divorce, most women would receive a lower retirement benefit because they tend not to work for covered wages. As a contributory social insurance system, only the years of employment are considered in calculating benefit amounts and the years of marriage to a wage earner are not credited.

Security Fund

The pension system provides a security fund, which functions to subsidize pension funds, which have a particular ill-balanced age structure, and guarantee legal minimum benefits owed by occupational pension schemes that have become insolvent.

The average pension credit is approximately 12.5 percent. Subsidies will be obtained when total yearly pension is greater than 14 percent of the total relative coordinated salaries. The surplus is taken up by the fund.

The security fund is not expected to be used much, so it will utilize a very low contribution (on the order of less than one percent of coordinated salary.

Mortgages by Pension Credit

Pension credits can be used as mortgages to facilitate acquirements of residential homes. This was already possible before the second pillar became mandatory. Up to half of the total pension credit can be used as mortgages.

Special Measures

Although based clearly on capitalization, each pension fund is expected to provide special measures, especially adapting current pensions to increasing living costs.

Every fund is obligated to allocate a minimum of one percent of its total coordinated salary to this end in applying pay-as-you-go principles. These regulations are designed to stimulate the managements of funds not to accumulate contributions but to improve benefits in light of their own financial possibilities.

FINANCING

Old-Age and Survivor Insurance

The financing of AHV is based on payroll contributions, government subsidies, and interest. The level of wages and salary is subject to contributions for old-age pensions, which also serve as a base in other systems such as disability, accident, unemployment, and military allocation. This base has assumed an important economic meaning as GNP or national-income-volume.

The contribution rates are 8.4 percent for all employees and workers, paid equally by employer and employee, and 7.8 percent for self-employed professionals. There is a minimum contribution amount of Sw Fr 303 a year for nonworking persons (i.e., students). Housewives, widows, and unemployed persons are exempt from contributions. Contributions are paid without an upper earnings limit.

The state contributes 20 percent of annual expenditures. This participation serves to cover special social functions and other payments that are not strictly based on insurance principles, such as disability. Therefore, contributions on earnings have to cover about 80 percent of the yearly expenditures.

Occupational Pensions

As noted, benefits are actuarially calculated on the base of accumulated old-age capital. The contributions to the second-pillar system are a percentage of the insured salary composed of pension capital (12.5%), risk costs (2.5%), and the special measures and security fund (1.7%), for a total of 16.7 percent. The contributions to pension capital vary with age as shown in Table 16.2. As the coordinated salary is about 60 percent of earned income, the contribution to the mandatory second pillar is an average of 9.6 percent of earnings.

A total credit of 500 percent of accumulated capital is provided. The capital bears interest at a minimum interest rate set by the Federal Council. Currently the minimum is at 4 percent.

As every company manges its own system, it also has to take care of the fund. A 1984 decree on private funds sets a ceiling on the proportion of each type of investment in the funds portfolio as follows:

- 100 percent for liquid and short-term investments
- 100 percent for Swiss bonds
- 30 percent for Swiss franc-dominated foreign bonds

Table 16.2
Accumulated Old-Age Capital

Age Men	Women	Pension credit in % of coordinated salary
25-34	25-31	7
35-44	32-41	10
45-54	42-51	15
55-65	52-62	18

• 20 percent for foreign currency-dominated bonds

• 30 percent for Swiss shares

• 10 percent for foreign shares

The maximum authorized share exposure is 30 percent. Total claims on foreign debtors is also limited to 30 percent of total assets. The ceiling on foreign currency holdings is 20 percent.

POLICY ISSUES

Administrative Costs

Administrative costs in the old-age pension schemes are of minor importance. Functionaries in the AHV program are salaried by the state and not by the insurance system. Similarly, salaries for administering the occupational pension system are not separated from the budget of a company.

In the basic AHV program the costs of administration are 1.5 percent of total costs (the costs of occupational pension schemes are not yet available).

Coverage of Women

Under the AHV program a couple benefit provides 150 percent of a single pension. The couple benefit is payable even if the housewife has not contributed. The payment of a couple benefit can be split between both partners so that each receives a benefit in their own right. Widows are entitled to 80 percent of the spouse's pension, subject to a minimum and a maximum. As about 85 percent of all old-age survivors are women, the system is favorable to women.

Early Retirement

Early retirement is possible under the occupational pension system. A great number of pension funds offer such possibilities.

Early retirement is not possible under AHV, but a growing desire of the active population for more flexibility has led to increased discussion on the possibility. The leading idea is, that based on actuarial calculations the benefit could be reduced by 6.8 percent for one year of early retirement for up to three years. A main difficulty is that a reduced benefit at early retirement may defeat the objective of the first pillar to provide a subsistence income level.

CONCLUSION

The advantage of the Swiss system of federated government in terms of allocative efficiency must be weighed against certain drawbacks inherent in the decentralization of public activities. This incongruity is an important part of the historical development of social security in Switzerland. At its beginning health and income security systems were offered by private or professional organizations and it took time until fully compulsory systems came in force. Even today there is no compulsory health insurance system, although 97 percent of the population are insured against this risk by private contracts. The occupational accident system, being one of the oldest systems, reached a full compulsory level in 1984.

The side-by-side existence of centralization and decentralization is also illustrated by the three-pillar concept in old-age insurance. Such a combined system is rather complicated. Its main purpose is to provide adequate income protection in old age by diversifying the financing by supplementing the pay-as-you go system of the first pillar of a public pension with a funded system of the second pillar of occupational pensions. There is an assumption that this combination will be a good instrument to adjust to future developments.

It may be concluded that income distributional objectives have been attained to an acceptable extent. In general, the social security systems have been designed on the hypothesis that insured persons are employed full-time during their working life and the structure of contributions and benefits still corresponds to this thinking. The members of the Swiss social security schemes therefore directly fund a main portion of welfare expenditures via insurance contributions and insurance premiums, so that the contributors to, and the beneficiaries of, schemes are aware of the real costs of social security.

The ratio of total social security benefits to GNP is 21 percent. The subsidies of the Swiss state to all costs are about 15 percent. These are modest compared to other industrial countries, but one has to remember that legislation is predominately designed to set conditions for personal responsibility while assuring provisions for minimum benefits.

It is expected that the ratio of benefits to GNP will rise to 25 to 30 percent at the beginning of the next century because of an aging population. Discussions on this problem have commenced and will certainly influence future social security regulations.

BIBLIOGRAPHY

The following suggestions for further reading have been compiled by the editors.

Area Benefits Network. (1990). Social security provisions and occupational benefit plans in Switzerland. *AREA* (Brussels), 1–12.

Greber, P. Y. (1988). The Swiss basic pensions scheme is forty years' old: Criteria for its evaluation. *International Social Security Review* 41(2), 176–197.

Segalman, R. (1986). *The Swiss way of welfare: Lessons for the western world*. New York: Praeger.

Segalman, R., and Marsland, D. (1989). *Cradle to grave: Comparative perspectives on the state of welfare*. New York: St. Martin's Press.

Watts, G. (1989). Trends in funding employee benefit plans in Switzerland. *Benefits & Compensation International*, 18(8), 13–15.

17

Tanzania

Ayubu K. T. Nyanga and C. K. Omari

The United Republic of Tanzania is the administrative entity of two sovereign states that united in 1964. Before then the mainland was known as Tanganyika while the islands were known as Zanzibar and Pemba. The development of old-age pensions and social insurance in Tanzania has been largely influenced by the historic presence of three types of colonial administrative policies. There was the typically feudalistic Arab administrative structure, dating from about the fifteenth century until British rule assumed control of the coastal areas, Zanzibar, Pemba, and along the slave trade corridors. On the mainland German administrative policy dominated from 1888 to 1918, when the British took over the administration of the colony. The British policy was replaced in 1961 when Tanzania became independent.

Although Tanganyika was a trusteeship colony under British rule and Zanzibar was a protectorate, there were some similarities in policies related to social security. Most of the ordinances introduced during the colonial period reflected European influence and thinking.

In traditional societies, social security was a family matter. Old people, children, the sick, and the incapacitated were normally looked after by the family. With its extended family social structures, the family institution was ideal for social security programs and development. People took care of each other and mutual aids were developed (Nyerere, 1969; Kanywani, 1985). In general, no one was supposed to go hungry or be denied assistance because they were unable to provide for themselves (Nyerere, 1969).

Colonial power and Western civilization, accompanied by Christianity, weakened the African family institution and its social security function. The traditional power structure whereby the chief, kinship organization, and neighborhood communities worked as guarantors of security to both the individuals and community was greatly reduced. Yet, this kind of social security system still exists in many rural areas of Tanzania, and the government is trying to initiative programs through villagization in order to preserve various aspects of the traditional social security system.

The introduction of a capital economy and mode of production ushered in a new era for African social security. Wage labor created insecurity. Iliffe (1979) describes the unfavorable working conditions of laborers whose future was threatened without the security of their home and family. They needed some kind of social security protection other than that provided by the employer. Thus, the social networks that had constituted the fabric of economic and social security were impaired. Furthermore, peasants and rural dwellers were introduced to a cash crop production system that made them vulnerable to international markets and economic systems.

Since 1973, Tanzania's population has expanded at an average annual rate of 3.3 percent and is likely to reach 27 million by 1990 (Mallya and Mwankanye, 1987). The population growth is a result of government social policies to improve the health and well-being of the general population, reduce infant mortality, and allow more children to survive into old age. At independence an average Tanzanian could expect to live only 39 years. Life expectancy has been raised to 51 years for males and 52 years for females. The aim of the government is to reach 60 years life expectancy by the year 2000. In addition, few women use family planning services (5 to 11 percent of the eligible women), resulting in a high level of fertility (seven children in a family).

Tanzania is an agriculture-oriented country. Urbanization is quite modest. It is estimated that about 14 percent of Tanzanians live in urban areas. About half of the urban population live in Dar es Salaam (1.5 million), the business center of the country. The majority of urban people invest in real estate in rural areas to provide them with security in old age.

MAIN PROGRAM FEATURES OF THE NATIONAL PROVIDENT FUND AND PUBLIC PENSION SCHEME

The major legislation for old-age benefits initially included the Pensions Ordinance of 1932, which provided pensions for holders of high positions in public service, and the Provident Fund (Government Employees) Ordinance of 1942, which covered public servants in lower positions providing for payments in case of old age, invalidity, and other cases of premature termination of employment.

After independence in 1961 several pieces of legislation were enacted to supplement these provisions. These were the Severance Allowance Act of 1962, which provides indemnity to regularly employed workers upon leaving employment; the National Provident Fund Act of 1964, which provides lump-sum old-age disability, and survivor benefits; and the Parastatal Pensions Fund Act of 1978, which provides a pension annuity for certain categories of employees of parastatal organizations. It is thus a three-pronged social insurance system that

Table 17.1
NPF Membership, 1980–1984

Nature of the Membership	1980/81	1981/82	1982/83	1983/84
Active unpaid (current contributors)	460,607	522,501	573,137	615,975
Active Paid (some amount of Benefit)	95,902	92,214	109,647	129,345

Source: NPF, September, 1988.

involves a national provident fund, a pension scheme for public employees, and an employers' liability system.

These provisions, however, do not cover casual workers and self-employed persons within the agricultural and nonagricultural sectors. In the rural areas, *Ujamaa* villages have group insurance systems that cover various aspects of social security. Also the 1967 Arusha Declaration, the blueprint of the Tanzanian social goals, stipulates that organized villages (*Ujamaa*) should be able to care for the elderly, the disabled, and children. Generally, however, rural people utilize traditional social security protection while workers and civil servants rely on national social security legislation.

The National Provident Fund (NPF) is a parastatal institution operated by a tripartite board under the general supervision of the parent Ministry of Health and Social Welfare. Parastatal organizations are those established under the Public Corporations Act of 1968, by the president, under specific acts of parliament, or those incorporated under the provisions of the companies ordinance by other public corporations. As Table 17.1 shows, membership in NPF has increased from 460,607 in 1980 to 615,975 in 1984 (34%). The number of those who have been paid has grown steadily as well.

Under the provisions of NPF, membership is obligatory for all regularly employed persons in enterprises with one or more employees (changed from four or more employees in 1990) (International Social Security Association, 1990). This is mandatory where such enterprises are not covered by the public pension scheme or the parastatal pension scheme. NPF also provides for voluntary membership where the number of employees is less than four. Beginning in 1990, self-employed workers were also allowed to voluntarily contribute to the system.

The public pension scheme covers workers in public administration. Political leaders have their own scheme under the political leaders pension act.

Retirement Age

National Provident Fund. NPF does not have a uniform age limit. Under the parastatal pension, there is a voluntary age limit of 50 and an obligatory age limit of 55. It was proposed in 1988 that the obligatory retirement age be raised to 60 years. An employee may continue to work after the obligatory retirement year if the appropriate authority considers it to be in the public interest.

Public Pensions. The public pension scheme also allows voluntary retirement at age 50 and obligates retirement at age 55, except for certain categories of employment such as judges of the high court who are not subject to any age limit.

Qualifying Conditions

In both the parastatal and the public pension schemes, eligibility for old-age, disability, and survivor pensions is based on a qualifying period of at least 10 years (Mallya and Mwankanye, 1987). The provident fund can also be paid if the worker is unemployed or in uncovered employment for at least six months.

Benefit Levels

National Provident Fund. The whole accumulated credit balance is paid as a lump sum to the member of the NPF or to a legal heir in the event of the death of a member. An accrued interest is also included. A withdrawal benefit is payable in full to workers who retire and live in a cooperative village (USDHHS, 1990).

Parastatal Pension. Under the parastatal pension scheme, a full or reduced annuity is paid to retirees. A single lump-sum payment is granted in case of permanent disability. In the event of the death of an employee, a death benefit is paid. The death benefit is the amount of a quarter of the pension calculated at the time of death × 12.5 up to at least the amount of the full pensionable annual income that was being received by the deceased.

Where the deceased met the qualifying service period of 10 years, the act provides for the payment of a survivor pension for a maximum of three years. The rate payable is that of the reduced pension to which the deceased would have been entitled had he/she been retired at the time of death. The duration of the payment of the survivor pension is, however, decreased by the period of time over which the deceased had received old-age or disability pension.

Public Pension Scheme. Under the public pension, a public servant has choices like those of an employee of a parastatal organization upon reaching retirement age or being permanently disabled. The main difference is that benefit levels are considerably higher under the public pension. Workers have a choice between a full pension or a reduced pension plus a single lump sum.

In the event of the death of a public servant, a lump sum is paid amounting to a quarter of the full pension that the public servant would have received at the time of death × 12.5; the benefit must be at least equal to the amount of the last pensionable annual income.

A survivor pension is also provided. Where the death was not related to the deceased's duties, the benefit amount is that of the reduced pension that would have been awarded had employment ended on the day of death for reasons of disability. As in the case of the Parastatal Pension Act, the period of payment of such pension is limited to three years. If, however, the death was connected to the performance of the deceased's duties, a higher benefit amount is payable and is not limited to the period of three years.

Minimum and Maximum Benefits. The Parastatal Pension Act provides for a maximum pension equivalent to two-thirds of the highest pensionable income ever received. This also applies to the Pensions Ordinance. The latter also provides for a minimum pension, but it is restricted to pensioners of Tanzanian nationality and residents of Tanzania.

Financing

NPF is entirely financed by payroll contributions from employers and employees assessed at 10 percent each for salary and wages, respectively. Before July 1989 the contribution rate had been 5 percent each (Rys, 1990). Self-employed persons may voluntarily contribute to the NPF at an amount of their own choosing (International Social Security Association, 1990). The parastatal and public pension schemes are funded by the government. In the case of the government as an employer, it is bound by law to provide pensions for its workers through the state retirement benefits scheme.

War Service Pension Scheme

People who serve in the military forces have their own social security program. Under the Defense Forces (Service Pension and Gratuities) regulations, a range of noncontributory war service pensions and benefits are provided. Benefits are paid to insured individuals or to survivors. The amount paid may include costs that are related to funeral services.

Manual Workers and Workmen's Compensation

The National Provident Fund parastatal pension schemes do not provide benefits for manual laborers. Low-paid workers are covered by social security programs in one way or another, however. For example, manual workers and nonmanual employees earning about EA Sh 24,000 or less a year, and all apprentices (Mallya and Mwankanye, 1987), have been covered by workmen's compensation since 1983. Every employer is supposed to provide a range of work injury benefits through a compulsory insurance (varying according to the risks involved in the work) with insurance agencies or private carriers. The Ministry of Labor and Manpower Development administers the program and approves settlements and payments of benefits.

Labor laws also require that employers pay a severance indemnity. Generally, a lump sum of 54 months' earnings is paid in the event of total disability up to the maximum of EA Sh 108,000. A partially but permanently disabled person is paid according to the degree of disability. In the case of temporary disability, benefits are paid after a three-day waiting period for up to 76 months at the rate of half-pay. Medical benefits are also provided under this program (Mallya and Mwankanye, 1987).

Income-Tested Provisions

Persons who are not in the labor force are entitled to supplementary income schemes or other types of social protection systems that operate in the country. These may be at national or village levels.

Old Age

According to the ruling party document—the Arusha Declaration—care for the aged is the responsibility of the family, the village, and the state. At the family level most of the old people, especially in rural areas, still enjoy the support of their adult children (Omari, 1988). This traditional role of family care is threatened by youth labor migration into urban areas in search of employment. Culturally and economically, the old cannot follow the young into the urban areas. Culturally, many old people do not see the rationale of following their children. Economically, young people's salaries are not enough to take care of extra members in the family unit.

The traditional institution of care for the aged is further threatened by the prevailing economic situation facing the country. For example, a pensioner with a full benefit would not receive enough to supplement the income of children due to the devaluation of the Tshilling.

At the same time, if one took the pension fund received and moved into rural areas where the government wishes retirees to settle, it could hardly be sufficient to enter into a productive agricultural project. Thus, the breakdown of the traditional family structure and the prevailing economic situation make it difficult for the aged.

Ujamaa villages have been organized into meaningful economic productive units that can provide for the welfare of their people, the elderly will continue to suffer. An interim alternative is for old people and retirees to form an association to look after their affairs similar to groups for women and youth. The elders councils (Jopo la Wazee) initiated by the Ministry of Labour and Manpower Development may be an embryo of such an association. Until these programs are developed, the elderly will have to depend on their children and families and, in the case of former civil servants and political cadres, small funds from pensions.

CONCLUSIONS

The Tanzania social insurance programs for the elderly have been developed to cover the entire population—regardless of social, biological, or ideological differences. Existing programs, however, favor individual workers and civil servants. Casual laborers and agricultural workers, many of whom are women, have very little or no social insurance coverage. Thus, poor classes are left out. This state of affairs had led to the charge that social insurance is not yet established (Idd, 1985).

The social and economic environments are not conducive to the development of a modern social insurance system. Tanzania is one of the poorest countries of the world with one of the lowest GNPs. Thus, a modern social insurance system based on government financial support for all the people may never develop. The best alternative, especially for the elderly, the disabled, and other special groups, is to develop social security systems at the community level. The village development program of the 1970s established durable social structures that could be a base for such programs. The traditional family structures that are still viable in rural areas should be utilized fully, rather than resorting to modern social security systems based on Western models.

Programs for retired civil servants and workers need to be rethought. The current benefit amounts are very little given inflation rates and the loss of value of the Tshilling. The government needs to examine employer contribution rates to the National Provident Fund. A proposed compulsory retirement age of 60 and a compulsory age of 55 would help civil servants. This new retirement age, however, would be beneficial to retirees only if the level of contribution to the fund is increased, the inflation rates reduced, and the value of the Tshilling restored.

REFERENCES

Bradshaw, J., and Deacon, A. (1986). Social security. In P. Wilding (ed.), *In defence of the welfare state*, 81–97. Manchester, England: Manchester University Press.

Idd, M. R. (1985). *Pension schemes: Product development*. Dar es Salaam: Insurance Institute of Tanzania.

Iliffe, J. (1979). *A Modern history of Tanganyika*. Cambridge: Cambridge University Press.

International Labour Office. (1979). *Role of trade unions in social security: Report of regional seminar*. Bangkok.

International Social Security Association. (1990). *Tanzania: Annual survey on development in social security* (DT/20). Geneva: ISSA Document.

Kanywani, J. L. (1985). The effect of Ujamaa-socialism and nationalisation on insurance law and practice in Tanzania: A historical study in the political economy of insurance. Ph.D. thesis. Dar es Salaam: University of Dar es Salaam.

Kassim, S. (1982). A study of social security system in Tanzania, with special reference to the University of Dar es Salaam. LL.B diss. Dar es Salaam: University of Dar es Salaam, Faculty of Law.

———. (1988). Retirement on marriage and child birth: An option for female employees in Tanzania. Paper presented at Seminar Dar es Salaam, June 27.

Mallya, W. J., and Mwankanye, H. A. (1987). Tanzania. In J. Dixon (ed.), *Social welfare in Africa*, 218–246. London: Croom Helm.

Midgley, J. (1984). *Social security, inequality, and the Third World*. New York: John Wiley.

National Insurance Corporation. (1988). *Tanzania insurance year book 1985*. Dar es Salaam: Education Services Centre Ltd.

Nyerere, J. K. (1968). *Ujamaa: Essays on socialism*. Dar es Salaam: Oxford University Press.

———. (1969). *Freedom and socialism*. Dar es Salaam: Oxford University Press.

Omari, C. K. (1987). Special population groups: Children, youth and elderly. Paper presented to the Ministry of Finance, Economic Affairs and Planning, Dar es Salaam.

———. (ed.). (1988). *Persistent principles amidst crisis*. Paper presented at the VIth International Society on Family Law, April, Tokyo.

Forthcoming. *Persistent principles amidst crisis*. Nairobi: Uzima Press.

———. (ed.). Forthcoming. The Future of the elderly in the African family.

Rys, V. (1990). *Trends and developments in social security—worldwide*. Regional Training Course on Social Security Administration, Kuwait, Geneva: International Social Security Association.

U.S. Department of Health and Human Services. (1990). *Social security programs throughout the world—1989*. Social Security Administration. Office of Research and Statistics. Office of International Policy. Research Report No. 62. Washington D.C.: U.S. Government Printing Office.

Vaides, W. (1985). *Critical evaluation of pension schemes for workers in Tanzania*. Dar es Salaam: Insurance Institute of Tanzania.

World Bank. (1985). *World development report 1985*. New York: Oxford University Press.

18

Turkey

Marsel A. Heisel

Article 60 of the Turkish Constitution decrees that every citizen is entitled to social security and that the state shall take the necessary measures to establish the organizations that will achieve this right. Article 61 lists the groups requiring special social security protection such as widows and orphans of those killed in wars, the disabled and war veterans, children in need of protection, and the aged. The extent of these social and economic rights is circumscribed by Article 65, which specifies that the state shall fulfill these duties within the limits of its financial resources, taking into consideration the maintenance of economic stability (Flanz and Arsel, 1988).

There are three major social insurance institutions that have developed along parallel but independent lines, each with its own unique constituency, funding mechanisms, and benefit programs. The administration of these schemes is within the spheres of the Ministry of Labor and Social Security and the Ministry of Finance. The major responsibility for state-financed social assistance programs, which cover means-tested aid to children, families, the handicapped, and the aged, lies within the Ministry of Health and Social Assistance.

Since 1960, Turkey has been committed to a policy of planned development, and the five-year development plans have given progressively greater attention to social security, including both social insurance and social assistance. This chapter deals primarily with social insurance, by tracing the legislative history, describing current program features, benefits, and financing of the major schemes, and discussing some of the policy issues confronting the system.

During the last ten years, the Turkish social insurance system has undergone rather remarkable developments. Social insurance has been expanded to include the agricultural sector and, in all three major schemes, insured persons as well as their dependents and survivors are entitled to retirement and health benefits.

While the system is still far from attaining universal coverage, it offers a good example of progress achieved through significant legislative reforms.

BACKGROUND

A Middle Eastern country with a Western orientation, Turkey occupies nearly 80,000 square kilometers (301,000 square miles) at the junction of two continents, with 97 percent of its land in Asia and the remaining 3 percent in Europe. The Turkish Republic, established in 1923 following a war of independence that lasted for four years, is the descendant of the Ottoman Empire, which prevailed for six centuries (1299–1918) and at its height spread over significant parts of Europe, Asia, and Africa. The population is 98 percent Muslim and speaks Turkish.

From the first days of the Republic, radical reforms enacted under the leadership of Kemal Atatürk propelled the country into rapid modernization. The most fundamental reform was the replacement of the Shariah, the Islamic Law that constituted the legal framework of the Ottoman Empire, with a modified Swiss Code that secularized the state, put the country more in tune with the Western world, and gave women legal equality with men. Among major changes were the replacement of Arabic script with a phonetic alphabet based on Latin characters, and the adoption of Western-style clothing for both men and women.

The basic tenets of the ruling People's Republican party, which at the time was the only political party, were summed up under six principles: republicanism, nationalism, secularism, populism, reformism, and etatism. Etatism put the responsibility for the development and operation of modern industrial and manufacturing enterprises on the state rather than on private concerns, making the state a major employer. Social security, however, was not part of the agenda of the Atatürk reforms and the basic laws and programs of social insurance did not begin until 1945.

DEMOGRAPHIC AND SOCIAL FORCES

Turkey's population doubled twice since the beginning of the Republic, growing from 13.5 million in 1927 to 50.6 million in 1985 (State Institute of Statistics, 1986), and was estimated to be 56.5 million in 1990 (State Planning Organization, 1989). It is projected to reach 92 million by 2025 (United Nations, 1989a). The dramatic surge in the population growth rate started after 1950 and reached its peak by the end of the decade. There has been a marked decline in fertility in the last 20 years, with the crude birth rate dropping from 43 per 1,000 in 1960–1965 to 30 per 1,000 in 1980–1985, but its effect has been offset by a parallel prominent drop in deaths, with the death rate falling from 16 per 1,000 to 9 per 1,000 over the same periods (United Nations, 1989a).

The high fertility levels sustained over long periods of time have left Turkey with a young age structure. The mean age is 19, and the 1–14 age group constitutes 39 percent of the population, a proportion of children twice the size of that in economically developed countries. On the average, 300,000 new persons of working age have been entering the labor market every year (Kocaman and Özaltin, 1986). Thus, while the country needs to allocate a major portion of its resources to maternal and child health and to education, it must also develop policies that will create new jobs that enable the absorption of young people into the labor force.

Unemployment is a major problem that has been partially solved through emigration. Between 1961 and 1971 nearly 800,000 workers went abroad, mostly to Western European countries. In 1983, there were over half a million Turkish workers in the Federal Republic of Germany, and twice as many dependents. Of the one and a half million Turks who lived there, 42 percent were estimated to be below 45 years of age. When Europe stopped importing labor in 1974, the Turkish external migration of workers dropped from 60,000 to 15,000 to 20,000 a year, mostly to the Middle East and Africa (Kocaman and Özaltin, 1986).

While the high fertility rates have kept the proportion of older persons in the population consistently low, decreasing mortality has substantially increased their absolute numbers. Between 1950 and 1985 the proportion of those aged 65 and over rose from 3.3 percent to 4.2 percent of the population while their numbers more than tripled, growing from 685,000 to 2,136,000. This older segment of society is projected to grow to about 3.5 million by the turn of the century, and to 6 million by the year 2020 (United Nations, 1989a, 1989b).

The social security of older persons still rests primarily with the family, as few receive retirement benefits. Current social insurance legislation is designed to improve the financial status of future generations of elderly. Half the working population is covered by social insurance schemes with the deficiency being most pronounced in rural areas.

The precipitous increase of the population growth rate in the 1950s started the surge of rural to urban migration that accelerated in the 1960s and still prevails today (Table 18.1). Even the marginal labor available in urban areas was preferable to barely subsisting with a large family on a small plot of land or remaining unemployed. The State Planning Department estimates that rural-to-urban migration amounted to 1.6 million persons in 1965–1970 and 2.8 million in 1970–1975 (Kocaman and Özaltin, 1986). More than half the population lived in urban areas in 1985, and that share is expected to rise to 70 percent in 2025 (United Nations, 1989a).

Turkey is divided into 67 administrative provinces, with the metropolitan boundaries of the major cities corresponding to the province centers. While the overall annual growth rate of the provinces is 2.5 percent, the annual increase rate for major cities is 4.1 percent (State Institute of Statistics, 1986). Development in Istanbul illustrates the magnitude of population growth and urbanization experienced. In 1927, the total population of the province was about 800,000, 85 percent of whom resided in urban areas. In 1955, the population

Table 18.1
Population (in thousands) of Cities and Villages, 1935–1985

Year	Total Population	Population of Cities	Percent in Cities	Population in Villages	Percent in Villages
1935	16,158	38,033	23.5	12,355	76.5
1945	18,790	4,687	24.9	14,103	75.1
1955	24,065	6,927	28.8	17,138	71.2
1965	31,391	10,806	34.4	20,585	65.6
1975	40,348	16,869	41.8	23,479	58.2
1985	50,664	26,866	53.0	23,798	47.0

Source: State Institute of Statistics (1986).

reached 1.5 million, keeping approximately the same urban/rural proportion. The 1985 census, however, showed that the population of Istanbul was just short of 6 million persons, with 95 percent living in urban areas (State Institute of Statistics, 1988). This rapid urbanization, and the accompanying growth in industrialization, have spurred major developments in the social security and health programs of the country.

LEGISLATIVE HISTORY

Turkey has a long history of social security institutions. During the Ottoman Empire, a system of religious and philanthropic foundations created by endowed trust funds, called ''Vakif,'' provided health care and social welfare to those who were destitute. As early as the thirteenth century, guilds had special funds to help members who were unable to work because of illness, disability, or old age, and provided benefits to the families of poor tradesmen and artisans in case of births and deaths. These funds were accumulated on the basis of mutual assistance, and contributions to the fund were obligatory (Tunçomağ, 1988).

The first public policies on social insurance appeared during a period of reforms (the Tanzimat) about half a century prior to the collapse of the Ottoman Empire. These concerned preventive measures to protect miners from work-related accidents and illness and required mine operators to pay compensation for work-related accidents and death (*Yurt Ansiklopedisi*, 1985).

A parallel development was pension funds for civil servants and military personnel established in the late 1880s, which provided old-age, disability, and death benefits for officers and civil servants and their widows and orphans. The early 1900s saw the establishment of various other similar funds, such as those for railroad workers and naval employees, each one independent and financed by contributions from salaries and from the respective organizations (*Yurt Ansiklopedisi*, 1985).

Legal reforms in social insurance during the Republic have progressed along similar lines, with parallel but independent streams encompassing industrial workers and employees in commerce and agriculture, civil servants and army officers, self-employed and independent workers, and employees of private banks and insurance companies. The first three constitute the basis of the social security system and are administered by three independent government organizations.

The Social Insurance Organization

During the early years of the Republic, social insurance evolved in the form of workers' compensation. In 1921, mines were required to have a hospital and physicians, to treat workers for free, and to pay compensation to workers in case of accidents and to the family in case of death. More important for later developments was the establishment of a workers' union fund, financed primarily from obligatory and equal contributions paid by worker and employer (*Yurt Ansiklopedisi*, 1985). Among other important legal steps that led to social insurance for workers were the Law of Obligation of 1926, which established that workers who paid at least half of the necessary payroll taxes had exclusive rights to the accumulated insurance benefits, and the Health Law of 1930, which obliged some employers to provide health benefits (Tunçomağ, 1988).

The Work Law of 1936 aimed to regulate relations between employer and employees. It established the broad basis for compulsory social insurance, including paid maternity leaves and compensation for work-related disease, and the organizations to put those regulations into effect. The law remained on paper for ten years, until the end of World War II.

The basic laws and programs of social insurance did not start until 1945, and commitment to the systematic development of universal social insurance had to wait until 1965. These twenty years can be viewed as the period leading from work laws into social insurance laws. Among important developments was the law insuring workers for work-related accidents and disease and for maternity, which was put into practice in 1946. A law of old-age insurance went into effect in 1950, but was not enforced until 1957, when it was expanded to include disability and death benefits (*Yurt Ansiklopedisi*, 1985).

In 1964, the Social Insurance Act integrated the scattered fragments of social insurance regulations for wage earners into a single act, separating social insurance from the Work Law and enlarging its scope. Under this act, the Social Insurance Organization (SIO) provides long-term benefits of old-age, disability, and survivor pensions and short-term medical and maternity benefits, as well as employment-related accident and occupational disease benefits (Danişoğlu, 1987).

The new law encompassed almost all persons working for an employer, except agricultural workers, and provided specific health benefits for workers' spouses and children. The law initially was limited to establishments employing four or more workers in urban areas and eight or more persons outside of municipal boundaries of cities and towns (*Yurt Ansiklopedisi*, 1985). By April 1971, even establishments employing only one worker came under the jurisdiction of the social insurance law (Tunçomağ, 1988).

Following the 1982 Constitution, there have been five major pieces of legislation enacted in connection with the SIO. The first, passed in 1983, enables workers who have contributed to different insurance schemes to combine all of their insured service periods into a single unit in the calculation of retirement and survivor benefits (Ateş, 1988). The 1983 Law of Social Insurance for Agriculture Workers assures workers in agriculture protection similar to that provided under the Social Insurance Act of 1964. This law compulsorily applies to all agricultural workers who have reached the age of 18 years and are not insured by any insurance institution established by law ("Turkey," 1984).

A third law, enacted in 1985, but not scheduled to go fully into effect until 1990, eliminates the possibility of collecting monthly retirement benefits exclusively on the basis of years of insured service. The new law stipulates a minimum age of 60 for men and 55 for women in addition to years of insured service. For those in the labor force before 1990, the law specifies a series of gradually increasing minimum retirement ages, progressing from 46 to 60 for men and from 41 to 55 for women. The fourth law, enacted in 1986, deals with the issue of earned income while collecting pension benefits and allows the practice within certain limits.

The fifth law, enacted in 1987, is known as the Super-Retirement Law. Its purpose is to assist those earning the highest wages and salaries to also receive high pension benefits, and thus retain their living standard upon retirement. The law was to be in effect for only six months, during which time those who were already eligible for the highest bracket of pension benefits had the option to contract for a still higher level by opting to pay higher contributions for five years. This could also be paid in a lump sum, with the monthly retirement super-benefits starting when all contributory obligations have been fulfilled (Tunçomağ, 1988; Ateş, 1988).

The Government Employees Retirement Fund

Of the three social security institutions, the oldest is the "Emekli Sandiği," the Government Employees' Retirement Fund (GER Fund). Historically, this sector of the Turkish insurance system can be traced to establishing pension funds for career officers and their widows and orphans in 1866, followed by pension funds for civil servants in 1880. Both were financed from contributions paid by those enrolled and by their organizations. During the early years of the Republic, nine additional retirement funds were formed for different groups of civil servants working in central and local government and in various state-funded operations.

In 1949, retirement funds for all employees in the public sector were combined under a single social insurance umbrella, with only one retirement system known as the GER Fund. All previous funds were transferred into this new single account in order to standardize benefits and statutory requirements for all civil servants. Members consist of military and civil personnel as well as those working in various central government, state, or municipal organizations and state-owned enterprises.

The original purpose of the GER Fund was to provide long-range benefits of old-age, death, disability, and occupational diseases. A number of short-term health care benefits were added in 1973, and these are provided without charge in state institutions.

Until recently, retirement of civil servants was based entirely on years of service without any reference to age. This was changed under the 1983 legislation, which stipulated minimum pensionable retirement ages of 45 for women and 50 for men. In 1986, in harmony with the SIO, the retirement age was raised to 50 years for women and 55 for men, to be raised, respectively, to 55 and 60 for those entering the labor force in 1990 (Tunçomağ, 1988).

Bağ-Kur: Self-Employed and Independent Workers

Among the latest groups of people to be covered by social insurance are the self-employed, small farm owners, independent workers in agriculture, and housewives. The Social Security Institution for the Self-Employed and Independent Workers (Bağ-Kur) was put into effect in 1972 to include the self-employed, such as businessmen, artisans, and independently working professionals, in the social security system on a compulsory and contributory basis. Initially, in addition to being self-employed, the law required registered membership in an officially recognized profession or trade. (This requirement was removed in 1982 [*Yurt Ansiklopedisi*, 1985].) The law also excluded self-employed owners of small farms and those who worked in agricultural but remained outside of other insurance because they received no wages. Benefits were limited to old-age, disability, and death.

A law in 1973 that extended coverage to those permanently employed in agriculture with work contracts did not have much impact because most rural workers are either seasonal, temporary employees or independent owners of very small farms. Two laws, effective in 1983, addressed the needs of these two groups and are expected to have a major impact on rural coverage in the next decade. The Law of Social Insurance for Agriculture Workers stipulates that those employed under a work contract for an indefinite period will become members of the SIO. Temporary laborers working a maximum of 30 days a year could become members on request starting in 1984. The Law on the Social Insurance of Self-Employed Persons in Agriculture specifies that such persons will become members of Bağ-Kur. This requirement started in specific provinces and is expected to cover the whole country in 10 years (State Planning Organization, 1987).

Under the Health Insurance Act of 1985, Bağ-Kur members gained the right to request insurance against illness and work-related accidents. This was started in limited parts of the country and was in operation in 31 provinces, covering 2.8 million persons, in 1987 (State Planning Organization, 1988).

MAIN PROGRAM FEATURES

All three systems provide long-term benefits of old-age, disability, and survivor pensions, and short-term benefits of health care, maternity, employment-related accidents, and occupational diseases. They do not include provisions for family assistance and unemployment compensation. In spite of efforts to equalize the main program features of the three systems, there are still some important differences in benefits, financing, and the proportion covered by insurance in each of the targeted groups.

Coverage

As shown in Table 18.2, at the end of 1986 the number of dependents, widows, and orphans, together with those receiving retirement and disability benefits and their dependents, comprised 28,587,300 persons, which represented 56.4 percent of the population.

Since the Social Insurance Act of 1964, there has been a major attempt to provide universal coverage. The proportion of insured workers within the economically active population was less than 1 percent in 1955, 14 percent in 1970, 25 percent in 1980 (*Yurt Ansiklopedisi*, 1985), and 38.5 percent in 1986 (Danişoğlu, 1987). The annual growth rate in the number of those actively insured has gone from 1.8 in 1978, to an estimated 5.0 in 1989 (State Planning Organization, 1987a). Nevertheless, coverage is far from being universal.

As in the case in almost all developing countries, the uninsured are concentrated in the rural sector. While 47 percent of the Turkish population lives in rural areas, only 4.8 percent of those actively insured are in agricultural work. As noted, legislation in 1973, 1983, and 1985 attempted to improve on the persistently low coverage in the rural population. Excluding the agricultural sector, about 80 percent of the employed population has social insurance, a rather respectable proportion for a developing country.

As a result of extensive external migration, the social security coverage of workers abroad has been an important national and international concern. In accordance with reciprocal agreements, the wives and children of migrant workers residing in Turkey, amounting to about 2,550,000 dependents, are entitled to maternity and health benefits. A 1978 law specifies criteria to appraise the service of workers outside the country with reference to their right to social security and incorporate them into the Turkish system when they return home

Table 18.2
Number of Persons Covered by Social Insurance Programs, 1986

```
Social Insurance Organization
     Active Insured                     2,815,200
     Active Insured in Agriculture         20,000
     Pensioners (retired, disabled,
               widows & orphans)        1,156,600
                              Total....13,000,400

Government Employees Retirement Fund
     Active Insured                     1,450,000
     Pensioners (retired, disabled,
               widows & orphans)          720,100
     Dependents                        4,785,000
                              Total.....6,955,100

Social Security Institution for the Self-Employed
     Active Insured                     1,828,700
     Active Insured in Agriculture        291,900
     Pensioners (retired, disabled,
               widows & orphans)          361,200
     Dependents                        5,851,800
                              Total.....8,333,600

Private Funds (Banks and Insurance Companies)
     Active Insured                        82,200
     Pensioners (retired, disabled,
               widows & orphans)           18,900
     Dependents                          195,100
                              Total.......298,200

OVERALL SUMMARY OF POPULATION COVERED BY SOCIAL INSURANCE
     Active Insured                     6,176,100
     Active Insured in Agriculture        311,900
     Pensioner (retired, disabled,
               widows & orphans)        2,260,800
     Dependents                       19,838,500
                              GRAND TOTAL....28,587,500
```

Source: State Planning Organization (1988).

permanently. This is an optional condition and the criteria have not been popular and application of the law is not prevalent (*Yurt Ansiklopedisi*, 1985).

Qualifying Conditions

The basic conditions that entitle insured workers to receive old-age pension are:

• At least 50 (women) or 55 (men) years of age, and a minimum of 5,000 days of contributions

• At least 50 (women) or 55 (men) years of age, insured for 15 years, and a minimum of 3,600 days of contributions

- Below the ages of 50 and 55, insured for 20 (women) or 25 (men) years, and a minimum of 5,000 days of contributions.

Partial pensions are paid to those who have paid 15 years of contributions. Those who retire at age 50/55 without having met the minimum qualifying conditions receive a lump-sum payment. The pensionable age is reduced in certain extenuating conditions. For example, prematurely aged men and insured miners who have worked underground a minimum of 1,800 days are entitled to full pension at age 50. Some of these conditions, in particular the lowest possible retirement age, vary among the principal social insurance institutions.

Benefit Levels

Old-age pensions are calculated through a procedure that involves schedules of pensionable income levels, statutory coefficients, and social assistance supplements, all of which are periodically revised depending on inflation. The basic pension level is determined by averaging earnings for which contributions had been paid during the last five years and identifying the corresponding level on the schedule. This number is multiplied by a coefficient determined by the General Budget Law, and the monthly retirement benefits are 60 percent of this product, plus the social assistance supplement (Tunçomağ, 1988).

The ratio of 60 percent is increased by 1 percent for each year of insurance contributions paid beyond ages of 50 and 55 (for women and men, respectively) and for each year of coverage beyond 20 years, up to a maximum of 85 percent of average earnings times the statutory quotient. Full pensions are reduced by 1 percent for each year of insurance less than 20 years, but the minimum pension cannot be below 70 percent of the lowest average earning level specified in the schedule, times the statutory coefficients. Those who retire without being entitled to an old-age pension receive lump-sum payments equal to the total contribution paid by them and on their behalf.

Pensions are not automatically and constantly tied to inflation, which has been rather high. Adjustments are made every six months by means of revised schedules for average earning levels and statutory coefficients based on changes in prices and wages, and depending on financial conditions.

Survivor benefits are 50 percent of the pension the insured would have received, and is payable to the widow or to a dependent or invalid widower. Each orphan under age 18 are unmarried or invalid daughters receive 25 percent of the pension. The sum of survivor pensions cannot exceed 100 percent of the pension of the insured (USDHHS, 1990).

Health benefits include free diagnosis, treatment, general and specialist care, hospitalization, laboratory services, maternity care, and medication to the insured person, pensioner, and direct members of their families. Health care services are ordinarily provided through facilities of the SIO or of the Ministry of Health and Social Assistance. Cash sickness benefits last for a period of six months, but can be extended to 18 months. Dependents contribute 20 percent of the cost of medicine. Survivors and their dependents remain eligible for health benefits after the death of the insured worker or pensioner (Danişoğlu, 1987).

SPECIAL PROGRAMS

In addition to the three principal social insurance organizations, there are also special social security institutions that serve small constituencies. These fall into two groups: private retirement funds and organizations providing supplementary benefits to basic social insurance.

Some commercial organizations such as banks and insurance agencies have mutual social insurance funds to cover their own employees. The process of collecting contributions, investment, and disposition of funds is very much like private insurance. The law, however, requires coverage of all employees in the organization and provision of all benefits under the Social Insurance Act. In case of job change, the years during which workers paid contributions to a mutual fund would also count toward benefits from the insurance organization to which they currently belonged (*Yurt Ansiklopedisi*, 1985).

In 1986 there were 24 such funds, with 82,000 active insured employees, 18,900 pensioners, and 195,100 dependents (Table 18.2). Legal attempts to combine these funds with the SIO have failed. These organizations are seen by many as presenting problems, in that for some of them there is not much security or information on the funds. On the other hand, a considerable number of their subscribers are obtaining higher levels of health and retirement benefits and do not want to see the funds revert to the SIO.

Among organizations providing benefits supplementary to social insurance, the most important is the Armed Forces Mutual Benefit Fund, to which all officers and military civil servants must belong. Contributions are 10 percent of salary, and are returned to subscribers in the form of old-age, disability, and death benefits supplementary to the GER Fund, to which they also belong. The fund, which is heavily invested in industrial establishments and is half-owner of many, also provides housing mortgages for its members (*Yurt Ansiklopedisi*, 1985).

FINANCING

The social insurance system in Turkey is supposed to operate in compliance with the system of capitalization. According to the fifth five-year development plan for 1985–1989, however, "the State Pension Fund, the Social Insurance Institution and Bağ-Kur . . . have abstained from setting aside the legally compulsory mathematical counterparts (and) these organizations are expected to show a global deficit of about 400 billion TL [one Turkish lira equaled U.S. 0.06 cents in 1989] at 1983, at the end of the 5-Year Plan Period." Danişoğlu (1987) remarks that this growing deficit is the result of escalating costs and only on 80 percent level of collection of contributions. The system was originally conceived as a funded system, but appears to be evolving toward a pay-as-you-go system. The reserve funds still carry the major weight, maintaining the necessary amounts for old-age, disability, work-related illness and accidents, and death benefits.

Social insurance is financed from contributions paid by the employer and the employee and from the income generated by the investment of reserve funds, such as stocks, bonds, and real estate. The government does not contribute to the financing of social insurance. At the same time, social security does not contribute to the central government's revenue (World Bank, 1989). In 1981, 52.9 percent of the total income in social insurance came from contributions paid by employers, 33.7 percent from contributions paid by employees, and 13.4 percent from investments. This compared with a respective average in OECD countries, of which Turkey is a member, of 37.8 percent from employers, 17.2 percent from employees, and 6.4 percent from investments, with the remaining 38.4 percent of contributions coming from the central governments (*Yurt Ansiklopedisi*, 1985).

The relative cost of social insurance to employer and employee, and the allocation of contributions for various components of insurance, differ among the principal insurance institutions. Contributions over a minimum and up to a maximum wage are adjusted periodically. The maximum combined employer/employee contribution legally allowed is 39 percent of gross salary of wage, with the employer always providing a higher proportion of the share (Tunçomağ, 1988).

In 1985, the SIO received contributions between 35.5 and 39 percent of labor costs. For health alone, contributions corresponded to 11 percent of wages, 6 percent paid by the employer and 5 percent by the employee. Contributions for retirement amounted to 20 percent of total wages, 11 percent paid by employers and 9 percent by employees. Maternity contributions, at 1 percent, and contributions for occupational disease and accidents, at 1.5 to 7 percent, were paid totally by the employer. During the same period, contributions to the GER Fund were in the order of 10 percent of salaries for employees and 18 percent for the state as employer (Danişoğlu, 1987).

Bağ-Kur is financed by contributions collected from the insured, who choose a level of income at which they want to contribute. In 1985, the health insurance law gave Bağ-Kur members the right to obtain benefits in case of illness and work-related accidents, with contributions corresponding to 12 percent of an insurance step. In 1987, the number of steps in Bağ-Kur were raised to 24, and those in the highest steps were given the possibility of paying additional contributions and receiving super retirement benefits (Tunçomağ, 1988).

In general, the capitalization system of financing has provided much-needed funds for development. The percentage of investment funds appropriated to national bonds, financing of housing mortgages, and building business or industrial establishments, is limited by law. The portion appropriated to the public sector, however, is often invested in enterprises that are not profitable, and are even used in consumption expenditures and for payments (Tunçomağ, 1988).

The major social security institutions differ in the way in which their assets are distributed. In 1984, the SIO had 30 percent of its assets in bank deposits, 26 percent in bonds and securities, and 23 percent in buildings and land. The GER Fund had twice as much in bank deposits (59.5%), much less in bonds and securities (15.6%), 1.2 percent in real estate, and 20.7 percent in loans to members (Tunçomağ, 1988).

Because each of the social insurance institutions reports its own data, there are very few statistics to give a comprehensive view of the funding of pensions and of the relationship of the pensions to the national budget. The World Bank (1989) estimates the total expenditure for housing amenities, social security, and welfare as 3.5 percent of the central government expenditure in 1987, while Danişoğlu (1987), based on data from the State Planning Organization for 1985, estimates the share of pension expenditure as 2.4 percent of national income.

POLICY ISSUES

Among the major policy issues confronting the Turkish social security system are the low age of retirement and the entitlement to pension immediately upon retirement, conditions likely to create funding shortages in the near future. The mean retirement age has been declining in the last few years, reaching 47 for the SIO and 49 for the GER Fund in 1986 (Danişoğlu, 1988). In spite of shorter life expectancy, on the average Turkish workers collect more years of pension benefit than their counterparts in much richer nations. For 1980–1985, the average life expectancy in Turkey was 63 years and the period for which the average pensioner received retirement income was 20 years. By comparison, during the same period, life expectancy in Europe was 70 years or higher but the average period during which pensioners received monthly income was much lower: 9 years in Switzerland, 13 years in the Federal Republic of Germany, and 12 years in the United Kingdom (State Planning Organization, 1985). With life expectancy projected to increase to 65.3 years in 1985–1990, pensions will have to be paid for even longer periods in the future unless the system is modified.

In 1988, the State Planning Department called attention to conditions producing great financial problems for the social insurance institutions, citing widespread evasion in the payment of contributions, inability to invest social insurance funds in a way that will maximize profits, disparity between the numbers of active workers and pensioners (a state aggravated by early retirement), and an imbalance between the number of insured persons and dependents. The ratio of beneficiaries to contributors has been increasing significantly. Moreover, as noted, the social security institutions are able to collect only about 80 percent of contributions due, and already have rather large deficits. This deficit cannot well be reduced by increasing the cost of insurance either to the worker or the employer, as contribution rates have been steadily increasing over the years and are rather high. Contributions of the SIO have already reached 35 percent of gross salaries, a condition that deflates real salaries and wages and increases production costs.

The lack of standardization among the insurance institutions has created discrepancies in both costs and benefits to the insured. In general, the interests of civil servants are best served because they do not have to contribute for short-term insurance benefits and as a consequence pay a smaller percentage of their salaries toward contributions than do members of the SIO. In spite of recent attempts at making the benefit formulas more uniform, discrepancies still exist with regard to the age at which one can start receiving retirement benefits as well as in the calculation of monthly retirement incomes.

An issue of even greater significance is that of coverage. As of the end of 1986, only 39.1 percent of labor force participants were insured, leaving the majority of those economically active—close to 45 percent of the population—without any coverage. The uninsured in Turkey are concentrated in the agricultural sector, a situation that can be explained partially by the fact that the social security scheme for agricultural workers did not come into force until 1984. Another reason is the prevalence of small, independent farming. A national survey on the socioeconomic situation of households showed that only slightly half of households had incomes from wages and salaries. This low percentage of wage earners would suggest that unless Bağ-Kur becomes more prevalent, particularly in the rural sector, insurance coverage will remain low.

INCOME-TESTED PROVISIONS

Social welfare has traditionally been the duty of individuals and voluntary organizations. The responsibility for social assistance and noncontributory supplemental provisions, however, now officially lies with the state.

The government's social assistance programs are implemented by various ministries. In addition, municipalities and other local bodies furnish both policy and implementation of supplementary provisions. Priority is given to children, the disabled, and old people who are destitute. The major responsibility for social assistance lies with the overall administration and operation of social services.

One of the most important of the noncontributory and income-tested provisions is the Universal Old Age and Disability Pension Scheme, introduced in 1976. The law provides a flat-rate old-age (65 and over) or disability pension to needy individuals fulfilling certain criteria. The scheme is administered by the GER Fund, but is fully financed by the state. At the end of 1984, over 700,000 persons were receiving such pensions, and 80 percent of them were elderly (Danişoğlu, 1987). The monthly cash amount of LT 4,000, however, was too low to make much of a difference. A Special Committee on the Family convened by the State Planning Organization in 1987 reported that the basic purpose of the pension was to help poor families by assisting their old, frail, and destitute members, and thus reduce their burden, but that the miniscule amount provided left the pension as a strictly symbolic gesture (State Planning Organization, 1987b).

CONCLUSION

Social security in the Turkish Republic has developed in three parallel but independent lines, each with its own constituency, time frame, and benefit programs, making up three separate schemes: the Government Employees' Retirement Fund serving employees in the public sector, the Social Insurance Organization covering all persons working for an employer, including agricultural workers, and the Bağ-Kur providing coverage for the self-employed on a mandatory and contributory basis. All three systems are based on a system of social insurance with contributions from employer and employee, but not from the government.

Developments in the last 10 years have been significant. Social insurance has been extended to include the agricultural sector, and even to housewives if they wish to participate. All three systems now provide long-term benefits of old-age, disability, and survivor pensions as well as short-term benefits of health care, maternity, employment-related accidents, and occupational diseases. As of the end of 1986, 39.1 percent of the working population was actively insured. Adding pensioners and all the dependents, the total proportion of those protected by social insurance is 56.2 percent of the population.

The most pressing issues in the Turkish social security system are the early retirement age, which is already creating financial problems, and the fact that nearly half the population is still not covered by any retirement or health benefits. This deficiency is most pronounced in rural areas, where the proportion of insured persons in agriculture, whether self-employed or working for an employer, has remained disappointingly low. Excluding the agriculture sector, however, about 80 percent of the employed population has social insurance, and the system has the potential of extending social security and the accompanying health benefits to the whole population—a rather remarkable achievement for a developing country.

REFERENCES

Ateş, A. (1988). *Sosyal Sigortalar Yasasi* [The Social Insurance Act]. Ankara: Yorum Matbaacilik.
Danişoğlu, E. (1987). *Social security and health programmes in Turkey.* Ankara: State Planning Organization.
———. (1988). *Nüfus gruplari. A. Yasli nüfus* [Population groups. A. The older population]. Ankara: State Planning Organization.
Flanz, G. H., and Arsel, I. (1988). Turkey. In A. P. Blaustein and G. H. Flanz (eds.), *Constitutions of the countries of the world.* Dobbs Ferry, N.Y.: Oceana.
Kocaman, T., and Özaltin, I. (1986). *Türkiyede nüfus yapisindaki gelişmeler ve uluslararsi karşilaştirmalar* [Developments in the Turkish population structure and international comparisons]. Ankara: State Planning Organization.
State Institute of Statistics. (1986). *Census of population by administrative division 20.10.1985.* Ankara: Author.

————. (1988). *Census of population 20.10.85. Social and economic characteristics of population. Province 34: Istanbul*. Ankara: Author.

State Planning Organization. (1985). *Bes yillik kalkinma plani döneminde sektörel gelişmeler* [Sectional developments during the five-year plan period]. Ankara: Author.

————. (1987a). *Five year development plan: 1985–1989*. Ankara: Author.

————. (1987b). *Türk aile yapisi özel ihtisas komisyonu saǧlik, sosyal refah ve sosyal güvenlik alt komisyon raporu* [The structure of the Turkish family. Report of the special commission for health, social welfare and social security]. Ankara: Author.

————. (1988). *Beşinci beş villik kalkinma plani, 1985–1989: 1988 yili programi* [Fifth five-year development plan, 1985–1989: Program for 1988]. Ankara: Author.

————. (1989). *Altinci bes yillik kalkinma plani: nüfus tahminleri* [Sixth five-year development: Population projections]. Ankara: Author.

Tunçomaǧ, K. (1988). *Sosyal sigortalar* [Social insurance]. Istanbul: Beta Basim Yayim Daǧitim A.Ş.

Turkey: Extension of social security to self-employed farmers. (1984). *International Social Security Review*, 37(2), 212–213.

U.S. Department of Health and Human Services (1990). *Social security programs throughout the world–1989*. Social Security Administration. Office of International Policy. Research Report No. 62. Washington, D.C.: U.S. Government Printing Office.

United Nations. (1989a). *World population prospects: 1988* (ST/ESA/SER.A/106). New York: Author.

————. (1989b). *Global estimates and projections of population by sex and age: 1988 revision* (ST/ESA/SER.R/93). New York: Author.

World Bank. (1989). *World development report 1989*. New York: Oxford University Press.

Yurt Ansiklopedisi [National Encyclopedia]. Vol. 11. (1985). Ankara: Author.

19

United Kingdom

Dorothy Wilson

The origins of state social security in the United Kingdom lie in the Elizabethan Poor Relief Act of 1601, which, in response to the growth in population, the increase in the numbers of poor, and the possible threat to law and order if destitution were not relieved, laid upon parishes the duty to appoint officers to provide relief for the poor and to raise a tax on property for that purpose. Local resources came under mounting pressure over the next two centuries with the continuing increase in population, rapid industrialization, the emergence of urban poverty, and the need to supplement low wages in times of high food prices.

Following the new Poor Law Act of 1834 outdoor relief in cash was discouraged in favor of the very unpopular indoor relief in workhouses, where adequate care would be provided for the old, the sick and orphans, and work and minimal care for the able-bodied poor in conditions "less eligible" than those of the lowest class of laborer. Conditions varied widely from workhouse to workhouse, scandals were not infrequent, and the central government had to exercise increasing control. Meanwhile growing numbers of the poor were receiving assistance from a wide array of charities, and, of great significance for future developments, workers with the means to do so were providing for their own security through mutual aid associations of different kinds. These provided help during short periods of sickness or unemployment but their funds could not cope with the heavy unemployment of the nineteenth century nor with the increasing numbers of people surviving into old age. Poverty was particularly prevalent among the old and demands were growing for a state pension.

In 1905 a new Liberal government came into office, anxious to secure the votes of newly enfranchised workers and with a commitment to reduce dependence on the stigmatizing Poor Law. It moved quickly to extend the Workmen's Compensation legislation of 1897 and to legislate in 1908 for modest, means-tested pensions for poor people of "good character" over the age of seventy. Converted to the principle of contributory insurance by the success of Bismarck's social insurance schemes in Prussia, and by the cost to the general budget of noncontributory old-age pensions, in 1911 the government introduced compulsory contributory health and unemployment insurance. The United Kingdom was in fact the first country to provide contributory benefits for the unemployed.

The 1920s were difficult years. Unemployment was high, the means tests for pensions were highly unpopular, and the pensions were costly. In 1925 contributory pensions were finally legislated for the elderly, widows, and orphans. After various unsuccessful attempts to help the long-term unemployed by extended insurance benefits or local public relief, means-tested assistance for the unemployed was eventually put on a national basis in 1934. By the outbreak of war in 1939 social insurance was providing coverage for old age, widowhood, sickness, and short-term unemployment but with wide variations in levels of benefits for different risks and a complex and costly administrative structure. Means-tested assistance, on a national or local basis, provided help with varying degrees of generosity for needy persons without insurance coverage.

The war years saw the publication of Sir William Beveridge's widely acclaimed plan for the postwar reform of social insurance as "the way to freedom from want" ("Social Insurance and Allied Services," 1942). The plan was to be comprehensive in the population and risks covered, to provide flat-rate subsistence benefits in return for flat-rate contributions in one unified scheme at times when earnings from employment were interrupted by sickness or unemployment or ended by old age. For the limited and decreasing number of cases of need not covered by social insurance, national means-tested assistance would provide a safety net. The necessary conditions of success for social insurance were, in Beveridge's view, family allowances, a free national health service, and full employment policies. Beveridge's recommendations formed the basis, but with some important divergences, for the national insurance and national assistance legislation introduced by the postwar Labour governments in 1946 and 1948, respectively. Family allowances had already been introduced in 1944 and a free national health service in 1946.

The history of British social security over the next four decades was largely concerned with adjusting these arrangements to social, economic, and demographic changes and dealing with problems inherited from the postwar legislation, in particular the increase, rather than the anticipated decrease, in dependence on means-tested assistance, largely to meet the housing costs of insurance beneficiaries. For a quarter of a century improvements in the benefit system were facilitated by the prevailing high rates of economic growth and full employment. Benefit levels were raised from time to time to take account of rising prices or increases in earnings. Adjustments were made in the system of benefits to meet newly recognized needs such as those of the increasing numbers of single-parent families and low-wage working families, and new benefits were introduced for large numbers of disabled people whose lifespans had been greatly extended by advances in medical science.

After the oil crisis of the mid–1970s, the state of the economy was such as to make further adjustments difficult. Attention focused instead on the rising costs of the increasingly complex structure of social insurance, noncontributory payments, and means-tested benefits that had emerged, and in particular on the potential future cost of the unfunded State Earnings-Related Pension Scheme (SERPS), which had been legislated for in 1975. The intentions of the new Conservative government elected in 1979 were to restrain the growth of social expenditure, to simplify the system, and to concentrate help on the most needy. With these ends in view a broad zero-cost review of the system was put in hand in 1983. The resulting government proposals for reform were put forward in 1985, in *Reform of Social Security: A Programme for Action* (1985), which formed the basis for the Social Security Act of 1986, operative from 1988. The new arrangements left large areas of the benefit structure untouched; apart from important modifications in SERPS, the changes were confined to the means-tested programs.

MAIN FEATURES FROM 1988

As noted, the benefits provided by the social security programs are of three kinds: contributory insurance payments, noncontributory allowances payable without a test of means, and means-tested benefits of various types. The same conditions of eligibility, rates of contribution (where appropriate), and levels of benefits apply nationally. The administration and payment of benefits are centralized in the Department of Health and Social Security (DHSS) acting through its national, regional, and local offices, with the exception of housing benefits, which are administered by local authority housing departments but following national guidelines and financed out of general tax revenues. The uniformity of benefits and centralization of administration are distinguishing features of the British system.

National Insurance Benefits

The national insurance benefits are the central feature of the system. One compulsory, contributory scheme covers the whole employed and self-employed population for all risks, on the lines recommended by Beveridge. The basic standard benefits are flat-rate but paid at lower rates for short-term risks (such as unemployment and sickness) and at higher rates for long-term contingencies (such as retirement, invalidity, and widowhood) (see Table 19.1). All benefits in payment are indexed annually in line with movements in the Retail Price Index. The flat-rate, long-term pensions are supplemented by earnings-related

Table 19.1
Standard Flat-Rate National Insurance Benefits, 1989 (in British pounds sterling)

	Personal allowance	Adult dependent	Child dependent
Retirement & Invalidity Pension	43.60	26.20	8.95
Widows benefits:			
1. Lump sum	1000		
2. Widowed mother's allowance	43.60	–	8.95
3. Widow's pension (full rate)	43.60	–	–
Unemployment benefits	34.70	21.40	–
Sickness & maternity benefit	33.20	20.55	–

Statutory Sickness and Maternity Pay

	Personal allowance	Adult dependent	Child dependent
If weekly earnings between 43.00 & 84.00	36.25	–	–
If weekly earnings over 84.00	52.10	–	–

Source: Department of Health and Social Security.

additions, which may be provided by the state or through occupational or personal pension plans.

All benefits, flat-rate and earnings-related, are covered by one earnings-related contribution paid jointly, but not in equal shares, by employee and employer and at higher rates if the insured person is contributing toward the SERPS (i.e., contracted-in) for the second part of the pension (Table 19.2). In the case of the employee, no contributions are paid if earnings are below a certain (very low) minimum (roughly one-fifth of average male earnings), although the worker will still be eligible for the basic benefits. In this way it is hoped not to discourage people from taking up part-time or very low-paying full-time employment. Nor does the worker pay contributions on earnings above a certain maximum (roughly one and a half times average earnings). In the case of the employer, contributions are payable on *all* earnings without minimum or maximum limits and at rates that increase with the level of earnings (as Table 19.2 shows). Self-employed workers pay a flat-rate contribution, plus a supplement related to income or profits, which entitles them to a more limited range of benefits.

Certain conditions have to be met for entitlement to the standard flat-rate benefits. In the case of retirement pensions, contributions have to have been

Table 19.2

National Insurance Contributions for Employees and Employers, October 1989 (in percentage of gross income)

Earnings per week	Not Contracted Out of SERPS		Contracted Out of SERPS	
	Employee	Employer	Employee	Employer
Up to 43 pounds	-	5%	-	5%
43 - 74.99				
up to 43	2	5	2	5
43 - 74.99	9		7	
75 - 114.99				
up to 43	2	7	2	7
43 - 114.99	9		7	
115 - 164.99				
up to 43	2	9	2	9
43 - 164.99	9		7	
165 - 325				
up to 43	2	10.45	2	10.45
165 - 325	9		7	
over 325	no increase	10.45[1]	no increase	10.45[1]

[1] On all earnings without ceiling.

Source: Department of Health and Social Security.

paid for 90 percent of working life for a full pension, which is payable at age 65 in the case of men and age 60 in the case of women who have contributed and earned a pension in their own right. Pensions may be proportionately reduced if the contribution record is shorter than this and increments to pension may be earned for years during which a pensioner works beyond the age of 65/60 up to age 70. Full invalidity pensions are payable irrespective of the length of contribution record if the insured person is unable to work after 28 weeks of sickness. In the case of retirement and invalidity pensions, allowances are paid for adult dependents and dependent children (provided, in the case of the adult, their personal earnings do not exceed certain limits). All widows of insured persons receive a lump-sum payment on the death of their husbands. If the widow has dependent children, she will receive an allowance for herself and each child; in other cases, both eligibility for pension and its size depend on her age at the death of her husband. If she is under age 45 she is entitled to no pension; if she is over 55 she receives a full Pension. If she is between 45 and 55 a partial pension is payable.

Unemployment benefits are dependent on contribution record and availability for work and are payable for one year, after which the insured person has to work for 13 weeks before a new benefit period starts. Sickness and maternity benefits are payable to those workers, decreasing in numbers, who are not entitled to receive Statutory Sick or Maternity Pay (SSMP) from their employers (this is paid at one of two rates according to earnings). Both sickness benefit and SSMP are payable after four days of sickness and continue for 28 weeks. The employer recovers the cost of SSMP payments from the Inland Revenue authorities.

The government shifted the administrative responsibility for these benefits in the mid–1980s onto employers as part of a more general policy to cut the public role in social programs and to save on administrative costs. Sickness pay was an obvious choice. Employers had in the majority of cases already been providing sick pay in addition to the state benefits and it appeared logical in such cases to devolve complete administrative responsibility. Not all employers, however, seem entirely happy with the extra work entailed.

Major changes were introduced in 1988 in the State Earnings-Related Pension Scheme, again to reduce government involvement but, of much greater importance, to cut the projected cost to the contributors in the twenty-first century of an overgenerous, pay-as-you-go, unfunded scheme. SERPS itself was heavily pruned and incentives were introduced to encourage the growth of occupational pension schemes and of personal pension plans as alternatives to reliance on the state scheme. Workers were thus given greater freedom of choice in providing for their retirement. It is too soon to say how successful the government will be in its attempt to shift more of the responsibility onto the private sector; one in two workers are still contracted-in to SERPS.

If SERPS is already in payment or will be drawn before 1998, a full pension, paid in addition to the flat-rate state pension, will be 25 percent of earnings between certain lower and upper limits in the 20 best earnings years. In the transitional period from 1998–2008 both factors in the formula will be revised annually until by the year 2008 SERPS for a newly retired person will be 20 percent of average lifetime earnings, thus giving a total pension that is substantially lower than the original SERPS. Widows, and in some cases widowers, inherit in the first period 100 percent of their late spouse's SERPS but their entitlement will be reduced to 50 percent over the period 1998–2008. SERPS benefits, like the flat-rate pension, are indexed annually in line with the movements in the Retail Price Index.

It is difficult to say anything in detail about the wide diversity of occupational and personal pensions that retired persons are actually drawing or to which the present generation of workers are building up rights. The occupational schemes are required, as a condition of being recognized as alternatives to SERPS, to offer a guaranteed minimum pension (GMP). Most occupational schemes, however, have been more generous than this, paying benefits based on some fraction, typically half although as much as two-thirds is permitted, of final year earnings. Part of this, a sum the equivalent of up to one and a half times final year earnings, may be commuted into a tax-free lump sum. The schemes are required to index the GMP for price rises up to 3 percent annum, the state being responsible for meeting the cost of price inflation above this level. Since 1986, the choice to prospective pensioners and employers has been extended to cover individual personal pension plans. In such cases the employee and employer will continue to pay full rate national insurance contributions but the DHSS will pay the difference between the full contracted-in and the lower contracted-out contributions into the chosen personal plan, which may be provided by an approved insurance company, bank, building society, or other financial institution. Workers and employers may choose to make additional contributions (tax-free within limits) to assure higher pensions. On retirement the rights built up under the personal plan, which will depend not only on the initial contributions but on the investment performance of the plan, will be used to provide a regular income for the pensioner. This will be indexed by the plan for inflation up to 3 percent and by the DHSS for inflation above that rate. It is hoped that this type of defined contribution pension arrangement will prove more attractive to employers than the open-ended commitment of an occupational pension based on final salary, and so encourage the spread of private provisions.

The state pension arrangements provide special protection for the pension rights of married women, single parents, the disabled, and those not in employment because of caring for a disabled person. For years spent out of the workforce they receive "home responsibility" allowances or contribution credits and the minimum number of years of contributions required to qualify for a full pension is reduced from the normal 40 to 20. In some respects women have received preferential treatment since 1940 when their pension age was reduced from 65 to 60, in spite of their greater longevity. Insofar as women have been at a disadvantage, the reasons have lain mainly in lower female earnings, more part-time employment, intermittent contribution records, and the fact that fewer women in the past have been in employment offering occupational pension rights.

Women, or men, who are bringing up children on their own as single parents receive various preferential concessions, such as additional child benefit for their first child and special treatment under income support, family credit, and housing benefit schemes. There are different views as to whether sufficient assistance is being given to one-parent families, whether complete families, who are helping to finance these concessions through the tax system, are being put at a disadvantage, and whether single parents are being discouraged by the benefit system from seeking employment.

Noncontributory Benefits

The most important of the noncontributory benefits without a test of means is the universal child benefit, payable at a uniform rate to every child up to age 16 (up to 18 if unemployed or 19 if disabled or in full-time, nonuniversity education) (Table 19.3). Indexation of this benefit, unlike other benefits, is not

Table 19.3
Noncontributory Benefit Amounts, Weekly Rates (in British pounds sterling)

	Personal	Adult Dependent	Child Dependent
Child benefit	-		7.25
One-Parent benefit	-	-	4.90
Retirement pension	24.75	14.80	8.40
Benefits for the Disabled			
Severe disablement	24.75	14.80	8.40
Invalid care allowance	24.75	14.80	8.40
Attendance allowance			
Day and night rate	32.95		
Day or night rate	22.00		
Mobility allowance	23.05 (tax-free)		

a statutory requirement but at the discretion of the government. The benefit has increased in real terms by only some two-thirds since the 1940s and has been falling in value since 1983. The other noncontributory benefits, introduced in the 1970s in response to increases in the disabled population, are directed to meeting their income needs or the additional living costs that disability may entail. Eligibility for most of these benefits depends on an independent medical assessment.

Income-Related Benefits

The most important of the income-related benefits is income support (formerly national assistance and later supplementary benefit), which provides an income for people without other means of support or whose other resources are below the income support level. It is not payable to people in full-time employment, and claimants under age 60 must sign on at an unemployment office as available for work unless they are sick or caring for a child or other dependent relative. The benefits payable vary with age and marital status, and the number and age of children in the family. In addition to the personal subsistence allowances, special premiums are payable to certain groups such as families, the elderly, and the disabled to cover other needs (see Table 19.4).

The special premiums can add very substantially to the basic benefits, especially for the very elderly, the severely disabled, and single parents. It is of interest to note that virtually the only groups not eligible for any premium are

Table 19.4
Principal Income-Related Benefits (in British pounds sterling)

	Income Support
Personal allowance:	
Single person:	
age 18-24	27.40
age 25 or over	34.90[1]
Couple:	
both under 18	41.60
at least one age 18 or over	54.80
Dependent children:	
under age 11	11.75
age 11-15	17.35
Premiums:	
family	6.50
pensioner[2] single	11.20
couple	17.05
disability[3] single	13.70
couple	19.50
disabled child	6.50

	Family Credit (maximum rates)
Adult	33.60
Child under age 11	7.30
age 11-15	12.90
age 16-17	16.35

[1] A lone parent will receive this higher rate if age 18 or over and will also receive an additional premium of 3.90 as well as the normal family premium.

[2] There are additional premiums for pensioners aged 75-79 and over 80 and for disabled pensioners of 60 and over.

[3] There are higher premiums for the severely disabled.

Source: Department of Health and Social Security

married couples and single people without children and not disabled. Applicants may have certain (small) amounts of earnings or income from other sources without affecting their entitlement to benefits. The Social Fund will provide grants for maternity expenses or funeral expenses to low-income families, community care grants to enable elderly and disabled people to be looked after in their own home, and interest-free, repayable loans to cover exceptional expenditure such as renewal of clothing or furniture, awarded at the discretion of local DHSS officials. Receipt of income support gives exemption from NHS charges for prescriptions, dental, and optical treatment.

People on income support are also eligible for housing benefits from their local authorities. This covers their rent in full, help with mortgage interest in the case of owner-occupiers, and an 80 percent rebate of the community charge (the replacement for property tax that helps meet the cost of providing local services such as education, roads, public libraries, etc.). Other people with low income from work, social insurance benefits, or other sources may also receive assistance with housing costs in whole or in part subject to a means test.

The third important income-related benefit is family credit, which is designed to help families with children who have low income from full-time work (24 hours per week). The amount payable depends upon the number of children in the family, their ages, and the income and capital resources of the family. In determining eligibility, benefits such as child benefit, single-parent benefit, attendance and mobility allowances, and housing benefit are not counted as income. Maximum credits are payable when net income from work is at about income support level (Table 19.4); if earnings are above this level the payment is reduced by 70 percent for each extra pound earned (net of income tax and national insurance contributions). Family credit replaced family income support (FIS), originally introduced by a Conservative government as a more economical way of helping poor working families than an increase in the universal family allowances. FIS suffered from problems of low take-up. The more generous family credit benefits and a simplified application process were designed to reach a wider range of low-income families.

The widespread use of means-tested benefits of various kinds and the complexity of the system, even with periodic modifications, have in the past deterred people from applying for all the benefits to which they are entitled. Whether the new arrangements operative from 1988, which for the first time employ a common income and capital test for all the selective benefits, will result in improved rates of take-up, remains to be seen.

FINANCING SOCIAL SECURITY

The United Kingdom is unusual in the extent to which social security benefits are financed out of general tax revenues. This stems from the large part played by noncontributory and income-related benefits, which account for over two-fifths of total expenditures. The social insurance benefits are also unusual in that completely earnings-related contributions finance both the flat-rate benefits and the earnings-related pensions. Current benefits are paid for on a pay-as-you-go basis out of current contributions and no funds (except for a small contingency reserve) are accumulated to meet future obligations. This implies an intergenerational contract, implicit if not explicit, that if the present generation of workers pay for the benefits of the present generation of beneficiaries some future generation of workers will be willing to pay for the benefits of current workers when they fall sick, lose their jobs, or retire. The modifications in SERPS introduced in 1988 were designed to reduce the contribution burden that the original system was building up for workers from the second decade of the next century onwards, a burden that they might not be willing, or able, to shoulder.

Figure 19.1
Social Security Transfers as Percentage of GNP at Market Prices, 1951–1986

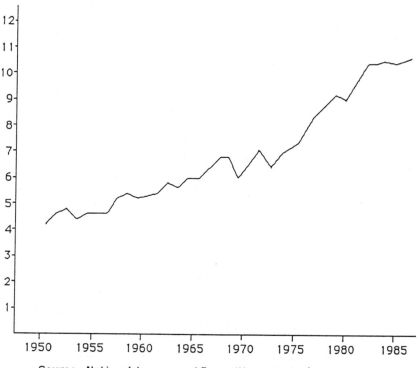

Source: <u>National Income and Expenditure</u>, HMSO (various years).

POLICY ISSUES

Rising Costs

In most industrially developed countries expenditures on cash transfers have been rising for many years faster than their Gross National Products. In the United Kingdom it rose from approximately 4 percent of GNP in 1951 to a peak of nearly 12 percent in 1986 at which it has leveled off (see Figure 19.1). The main causes were the rise in the real value of benefits (which roughly doubled in the case of short-term benefits while long-term benefits rose 2.5 times), the growth in beneficiary numbers, and the introduction of new benefits. The rate of increase was marked in the early 1980s when rates of unemployment were high. The leveling-off since the mid–1980s has been largely due to rises in the GNP itself and the fall in unemployment subsequent to 1986. The final severance of the link between benefits and earnings in the early 1980s also helped to restrain the rate of growth of social expenditure, as rises in earnings have consistently outpaced price inflation. It may be difficult, however, for government to resist indefinitely pressure for some discretionary increase in the real value of benefits if economic growth should be sustained.

Demographic Change

The main impetus for future growth in expenditure is likely to come from demographic change. Retirement pensions already account for about three-quarters of expenditure on social insurance and to this has to be added the cost of income support and housing benefits for low-income pensioners. The growth in the population of those aged 65 and over will be slow until after the turn of the century—from 8.8 million in 1987 to 9.2 million by 2001—but thereafter numbers will grow more rapidly to 11.3 million by 2025. The numbers of people in the higher age brackets—over 75 and over 85, in particular—are projected to grow more rapidly than the elderly as a whole and this will involve heavy expenditure out of government revenues for health and welfare services.

The Roles of the Public and Private Sectors

Rising costs are one aspect of the growing debate about the respective roles of the public and private sectors in the provision of welfare, including health care, education, housing, and social security. This debate largely follows party political lines. The objective of the Conservative government, on both financial and ideological grounds, has been to cut the role of government and restrain the rate of growth of public expenditure, of which social security benefits are the single largest component and account for about a third of the total. Private provision was to be encouraged wherever possible and state assistance was to be more directly targeted to those in greatest need, in particular low-income families with children. Evidence of this economy drive has already been seen in the modifications introduced in SERPS, the encouragement given to occupational and personal pensions, the severance of the link between benefits and earnings, the freeze in child benefits, and the changes in the means-tested programs.

These policies have come under strong criticism from the political Left, which argues for a larger government role, increased expenditure on higher benefits, and greater redistribution of incomes through the social security and tax systems. In particular, there have been strong reservations on the Left about the continued widescale use of means tests; these they see as an invasion of the claimant's privacy and an affront to personal pride, which taken together with the complexity of the application procedures, they claim have deterrent effects on the take-up of benefits. The consensus about the welfare state that appeared to have been achieved in the 1950s, 1960s, and early 1970s, has come under increasing threat, although the evidence does not support the claim sometimes made that the Conservative government is out to dismantle the welfare state.

Figure 19.2
Percentage of Total Spending by Benefit Type, 1949/50–1984/85*

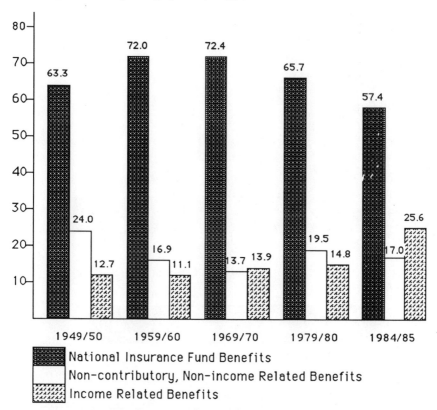

National Insurance Fund Benefits
Non-contributory, Non-income Related Benefits
Income Related Benefits

*Not all benefits have remained in the same category since 1949/50.
Source: <u>Reform of Social Security: Background Papers</u>, v.3 Cmnd
      9519.

Social Insurance and the Role of Means-Tested Benefits

In spite of the twofold increase in the real value of social insurance benefits since the late 1940s, the numbers applying for means-tested supplements to these benefits have grown steadily. Figure 19.2 demonstrates how income-related benefits have doubled as a proportion of total expenditure on cash transfers to a quarter of the total while insurance payments, after rising to nearly three-quarters of the total by the end of the 1960s, had declined to less than three-fifths by the mid–1980s.

The persistent dependency on means-tested benefits is a central issue in the social policy debate and accounts to a large extent for the British preoccupation

Figure 19.3
Number of Supplementary Benefit Claimants by Client Group

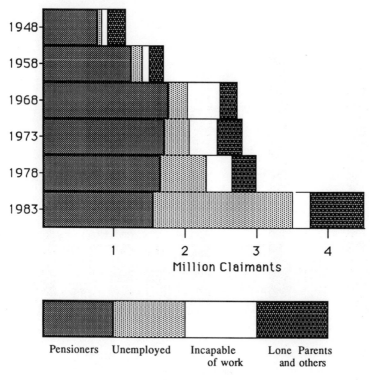

Source: <u>Reform of Social Security</u>, v.2 Cmnd 9518, HMSO 1985.

with "poverty," with which means tests are frequently associated (see Figure 19.3).

Much of the responsibility here rests with the social insurance system itself. Most important, levels of benefit are low if measured, as is a common convention, by their relationship to average earnings from work (see Table 19.5). Large numbers of the unemployed have exhausted their insurance rights; many disabled people have never been able to work and pay contributions. Even an insurance scheme as comprehensive as that of the British has never devised a contributory benefit for divorced, separated, or unmarried parents. In 1987 the unemployment benefit was the equivalent of only a fifth of adult male earnings (net of tax and insurance contributions) for a single man and less than a third if he had a dependent wife. The ratios are also higher if comparisons are made with lower male manual earnings (see Table 19.5).

For retirement and invalidity pensions the comparable figures were somewhat

Table 19.5

Benefits as Percentage of Average Male and Male Manual Earnings Plus Child Benefit, 1987

	All Adult Male Earnings		Adult Male Manual Earnings	
	Gross	Net	Gross	Net
Retirement pension				
Single person	17.7	25.5	21.1	29.9
Married couple	28.4	39.0	33.8	45.4
Standard rate unemployment benefit plus child benefit, where appropriate				
Single person	14.1	20.3	16.8	23.8
Married couple	22.9	31.4	27.2	36.5
Man, wife + 2 children	27.8	37.0	32.4	42.5
Man, wife + 3 children	29.7	39.5	34.8	45.1
Supplementary benefit scale rates with housing benefit				
Single householder	22.6	32.4	26.9	38.0
Married couple	32.9	45.1	39.1	52.5
Man, wife + 2 children[1]	40.5	54.4	47.7	62.5
Man, wife + 3 children[2]	45.7	60.8	53.5	74.1

[1] One child under 5, one aged 5-10.
[2] One child under 5, one aged 5-10, one aged 11-12.

Source: Department of Health and Social Security.

higher at more than a quarter and two-fifths, respectively. Both sets of figures· are, of course, raised substantially if account is taken of the means-tested assistance with housing costs, for which insurance beneficiaries are eligible in many cases. Housing costs in fact account in considerable measure for the dependence of so many insurance beneficiaries on income-related benefits. About one in five pensioners have their state pensions supplemented largely for this reason, although the number has been declining, and will continue to decline, as more and more people retire with a second earnings-related pension in addition to their flat-rate basic pensions. It is estimated that total per-capita incomes of the elderly population are already 70 percent of those of the nonpensioner population, or 75 percent if the free health services of which they make many times average use, are included (Fiegehen, 1986). Figure 19.4 demonstrates the importance of state benefits for the elderly.

Other groups of beneficiaries, however, have much lower incomes. For example, in 1987 three out of five unemployed males were totally dependent on means-tested benefits having exhausted their insurance rights or, in the case of

Figure 19.4
Main Components of Pensioners' Total Incomes, 1951–1986

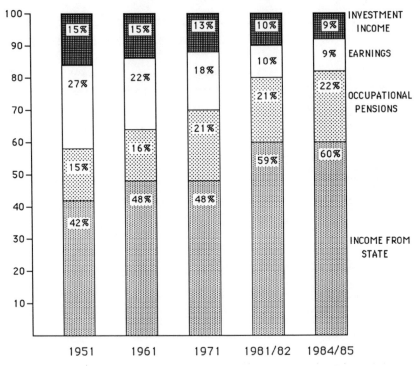

Note: The percentage for 1951 and 1961 do not total 100 due to rounding.
Source: E.C. Fiegehen, "Income in Retirement," Social Trends, 16, HMSO 1986.

many young unemployed, not having worked long enough to build up an adequate contribution record. Many others were drawing both unemployment benefits and means-tested benefits. Large numbers of divorced, separated, or unmarried mothers who choose to remain at home to look after their children or are unable to find employment, are entirely dependent on means-tested benefits, and many disabled people who are unable to work have their noncontributory benefits supplemented by income support.

CONCLUSION

The social insurance arrangements in the United Kingdom are comprehensive in population and risk coverage by international standards and unitary in administration. Benefit levels, however, are low and the use of means-tested benefits as an economic means of substituting for or supplementary insurance benefits or other low incomes has given rise to a complexity of benefits and administrative procedures. Earnings-related pensions have been grafted onto the long-term flat-rate insurance benefits and further erode the seeming simplicity of the unitary national insurance system, originally based on Beveridge's recommendations. The arrangements underwent considerable changes in the late 1980s as a part of the Conservative government's efforts to control the growth of public expenditure, to simplify the system, to extend private provision and enhance freedom of choice, and to target assistance on groups in particular need, especially families with children. The welfare consensus of the postwar decades may have gone but there appears little prospect of massive changes in the objectives or methods of welfare provision, although social security payments, and health, education, and housing benefits too, are in process of more radical restructuring than at any time since Beveridge. Future developments in social security policy will be largely determined by external constraints—the state of the economy and levels of unemployment, demographic trends, and institutional factors. Within these parameters, any further changes will obviously reflect the politics of the government in power.

REFERENCES

Creedy, J., and Disney, R. (1985). *Social insurance in transition: An economic analysis.* Oxford: Oxford University Press.

Dilnot, A., Kay, J., and Morris, C. (1984). *The reform of social security.* Oxford: Oxford University Press.

Fiegehen, G. C. (1986). Income after retirement. *Social Trends*, 16. London: HMSO.

Fraser, D. (1973). *The evolution of the welfare state.* London: Macmillan.

Gilbert, B. B. (1966). *The origins of national insurance.* London: Michael Joseph.

Johnson, P., Conrad, C., and Thomson, D. (eds.). (1989). *Workers versus pensioners: Intergenerational justice in an ageing world.* Manchester: Manchester University Press.

Klein, R., and O'Higgins, M. (eds.). (1985). *The future of welfare.* Oxford: Blackwell.

Reform of social security: A programme for action. (1985). Cmnd 6691. London: HMSO.

Social insurance and allied services (Beveridge Report). (1942). Cmd 6404 HMSO, London: HMSO.

Thane, P. (1982). *The foundations of the welfare state.* London: Longman.

Wilson, T., and Wilson, D. J. (1982). *The political economy of the welfare state.* London: Allen and Unwin.

20

United States

Robert J. Myers

This chapter describes the development, present status, and policy issues of the national pension system of the United States. The proper name of this system is "old-age, disability, and survivors insurance" (OASDI). As it happens, the term "Social Security" is often used to describe this program, but it has different meanings to different people in different countries. At times, included within the meaning of "Social Security" are medical-cost benefits of the Medicare program, unemployment insurance, and work-connected injury benefits, but they will not be considered here, nor will the extensive network of private pensions that has been built up to supplement the government national plan.

COVERAGE

The original 1935 act applied only to workers in commerce and industry, representing about 60 percent of the total workforce. The groups excluded were those for which there appeared to be great administrative problems or questions of constitutionality, or who already had pension plans such as federal civilian and military employees. For example, coverage of agricultural and domestic workers and of the self-employed seemed to pose great administrative problems at the start. Employment by state and local governments was thought not to be possible if on a compulsory basis, because of constitutional considerations. Likewise, coverage of employees of nonprofit organizations of a charitable, educational, or religious nature was not done, because of the traditional tax-exempt nature of these organizations.

Legislation in the early 1950s extended coverage to most of the previously excluded groups. The operations of the program had indicated that the administrative problems of covering farm and domestic workers and self-employed persons could be handled. The problems as to coverage for employees of state and local governments and of nonprofit organizations were solved by permitting coverage on an elective basis; at present, about 70 percent of state and local employees are covered. (In 1984, coverage of nonprofit employees was made mandatory.) Members of the armed forces were covered in 1957 (and retained in full their previous existing pension plan). Permanent federal civilian employees who have their own pension systems were not covered in the legislation of the 1950s; beginning in 1984, however, all newly hired employees are under compulsory coverage (with a modified, supplemental pension plan).

The principal groups not now covered are federal civilian employees with their own independent retirement systems who were hired before 1984, some state and local employees, and relatively low-paid and short-service workers in farm and domestic employment.

Geographical coverage has always applied throughout the present 50 states and the District of Columbia. Coverage has been extended to all other geographical parts of the United States, such as Puerto Rico and Guam. In addition, persons working on American ships and airplanes are covered, as are citizens and resident aliens going abroad to work for American employers (or, on an elective basis, for subsidiaries of American employers).

ELIGIBILITY REQUIREMENTS

In order to be eligible for the various types of benefits, the worker must be "insured" by having the required number of "quarters of coverage." Before 1978, a QC was obtained by having been paid wages of $50 or more in a calendar quarter; covered self-employed persons (who were covered only if they had at least $400 of earnings) were credited with four QC each year. In 1978, the basis for QC was changed, so as to be based on annual earnings—one for each $X of earnings (up to a maximum of four); for 1991, each $540 of earnings produced a QC.

There are three types of insured status. Fully insured status produces eligibility for all types of retirement and survivor benefits and is one of the requirements for disability benefits; it is obtained by having one QC for every year that elapses after age 21 and before age 62 (or if earlier, disability or death). Currently insured status produces eligibility only for young-survivor benefits (monthly benefits to children and their surviving parent and lump-sum death payments); it is obtained by having 6 QC in the 13 calendar quarters preceding death. Disability insured status, along with fully insured status, produces eligibility for disability benefits; it is obtained by having 20 QC in the 40 calendar quarters preceding disablement (a less stringent alternative is available for those disabled before age 31).

BENEFICIARY CATEGORIES

The original 1935 act provided monthly benefits only for retired workers aged 65 and over. In addition, lump-sum refund benefits were available, "guaranteeing" each covered individual that total payments would be at least equal to the employee contributions, plus some allowances for interest. In 1956 for women, and in 1961 for men, actuarially reduced benefits were made available at ages 62 to 64. Currently, benefits are reduced by 20 percent for retirement at age 62.

Auxiliary benefits for retired workers were provided in 1939. At the same time, survivor benefits were provided for widows aged 65 and over, and for children under age 18 and their mothers, regardless of age.

A lump-sum death payment has always been available. Currently, it is a uniform $255 and is payable at the death of a worker or retiree only if there is an eligible spouse or child present.

The benefit rates for auxiliary beneficiaries (spouses and children) and for survivors have always been expressed as percentages of the primary insurance amount (the benefit received by a retiree at the normal retirement age, currently 65). Currently, these rates (prior to the effect of the maximum family benefit provision) are as follows:

- Fifty percent for auxiliary beneficiaries, except with reduced amounts for spouses without an eligible child (under age 16, or disabled before age 22) who claim benefits between age 62 and the normal retirement age—a 25 percent reduction being currently applicable when benefit is claimed at age 62. Children are eligible if under age 18 or if age 18 and in elementary or secondary school, or if disabled before age 22.

- One hundred percent for widow(er)s who are at the normal retirement age or older at the time of the claim, with reduced amounts for claims at earlier ages—between 60 and the normal retirement age if nondisabled and between 50 and the normal retirement age if disabled—with the reduction being 28.5 percent for claim at age 60 or before.

- Seventy-five percent for surviving children (eligible on the same basis as stated in item 1 and their widowed parent with an eligible child in care (under age 16, or disabled before age 22).

In 1983, the first change in the normal retirement age for workers, spouses, and widow(er)s was made. Such age will increase gradually from 65 to 67, beginning in 2003 and reaching the ultimate level in 2027. The early retirement age will not change but the reductions for early retirement will be larger percentages for retired workers and spouses. Thus when the normal retirement age is 67, workers retiring at age 62 will have a 30 percent reduction, and spouses first claiming benefits at age 62 will have a 35 percent reduction. Such change was made to recognize increased longevity and thereby assist in alleviating the long-range financial problem that had been present.

220 *International Handbook on Old-Age Insurance*

Benefits are increased for persons who defer retirement beyond the normal retirement age. For those attaining such age before 1990, the increase is 3 percent per year per delay. Beginning for those who reach such age in 1990, the increase will become larger, eventually 8 percent (for those attaining age 66 in 2009).

In the past unequal treatment occurred with regard to auxiliary and survivor benefits. For example, during some periods, men could receive such benefits on proof of dependence, whereas dependency was always presumed for women. During such periods, child-survivor protection was not available for female workers on as broad a basis as for male workers. Over the years, both due to legislative changes and court decisions, this unequal treatment has been eliminated.

An "antiduplication" provision has been present. Under this, persons receive only the largest of the several benefits for which they may be eligible in a particular month. For example, if a person is eligible for benefit as a retired worker on her or his earnings record and also for a survivor benefit on a deceased spouse's earnings record, then only the larger of the two amounts is payable.

This procedure is followed on the grounds of social adequacy. This principle dictates that only one benefit should be payable for a given month, in order to satisfy the social responsibility aspect of the program, rather than paying all the benefits for which the person is eligible. The latter approach, if followed, would be justified solely on individual-equity grounds.

It should be recognized that, even if a person does not receive benefits on her or his own earnings record because another available one is larger, this does not mean that the individual has received nothing for the contribution paid. Actually, such an individual has already received valuable disability and survivor protection in the past. Further, such an individual may have received a retirement benefit based on her or his own earnings before the spouse had retired and claimed a benefit (at which time the auxiliary benefit was not available).

Disability benefits were added in 1956, with the amount being the same as for a retiree at age 65. At first, these were payable only to disabled workers aged 50 to 64. Later, auxiliary benefits for spouses and children, comparable to those available for retired workers, were added. Still later, the age 50 limitation was removed, so that disabled workers could qualify for disability benefits at ages below the normal retirement age.

LEVEL OF BENEFITS

The level of OASDI benefits has always been influenced by several general principles. The benefit structure has always provided "weighted" amounts, so that those with lower earnings receive relatively higher benefits than those with higher earnings.

Furthermore, the floor-of-protection concept has always been present. Specifically, there has been the underlying principle that the benefits under OASDI should not provide complete retirement income for all persons, by having them at a level closely approximating previous after-tax earnings. Rather, it is viewed that the vast majority of workers can be expected to supplement their OASDI benefits with other forms of income, such as a private pension, individual savings, and home ownership (which produces significant imputed income). Considerable differences of opinion occur, however, as to the relative height of the floor of protection to be provided by OASDI benefits. Some persons would have it set at a relatively high level.

In any event, in considering the level of the OASDI benefits over the years, one should always keep in mind that the important consideration is their relative level in comparison with earnings, and not the absolute dollar amounts. The latter are affected by changes in economic conditions over the years, and thus the standard of comparison should be a relative one, not an absolute one.

The original 1935 act provided benefit amounts that were larger for those with high earnings than for those with low earnings, although by no means proportionately so. A maximum limit was imposed on the amount of earnings per year that is creditable toward the computation of benefits. This amount has been increased over the years. Similarly, larger benefits were provided for those with long periods of coverage than for those who would retire in the early years of operation, but again not proportionately so. In other words, the benefit structure was not based entirely on individual equity, but rather considerable elements of social adequacy were present.

In the 1939 act, adopted before monthly benefits were first payable, the design of the benefit structure was changed significantly, not only by adding auxiliary benefits for spouses and children, but also as to the basic design. Specifically, less emphasis was given to increasing the benefit amounts to recognize length of coverage, while at the same time the principle of relatively higher benefits for low-paid persons than for high-paid ones was continued. The 1950 act moved farther in this direction by eliminating any recognition of length of coverage in computing benefit amounts (for persons with steady, continuous employment histories); this was done in the benefit computations by removing the provision for a one percent increment for each year of coverage (for periods after 1950).

The formula for the basic benefit (or primary insurance amount) under the 1950 act and under subsequent legislation is of the following general form: a percent of the first $X of average lifetime covered earnings, plus B percent of the next $Y of average earnings, plus C percent of the next $Z of average earnings, and so on (where A, B, C, etc. are termed "benefit percentages" and $X, $Y, $Z, etc. are termed "bend points"). Under present law, there are three bend points (which are adjusted each year according to changes in nationwide average wages—the revised formula being applicable to persons first eligible for benefits that year—while the benefit percentages are 90, 32, and 15). The basic benefit formula applicable to 1989 eligibles (i.e., those attaining age 62 in 1989, or becoming disabled or dying before age 62 in 1989) is 90 percent of the first $339 of average indexed monthly earnings, plus 32 percent of the next $1,705 of such average earnings, plus 15 percent of such average earnings in excess of

$2,044. The average earnings are computed over the total potential working lifetime in which the person could have been covered and are indexed, but with provision for eliminating a few years of low earnings.

Following the 1950 act, a number of ad hoc benefit increases were made. The changes in 1954 represented some real increase in the benefit level, but the changes in other years up through the 1965 act, on the whole, merely kept the benefit level up to date with the changes in prices, as measured by the Consumer Price Index (CPI). The benefit increase under the 1967 act and the three legislative enactments in 1969–1972 made significant real increases in the benefit level. For example the increase in 1969–1972 represented, in the aggregate, a "real" rise of about 23 percent.

The 1972 act, besides increasing benefits currently by 20 percent, inaugurated automatic indexing of the benefit level, based on increases in the CPI being applied to the benefits in current-payment status and to the benefit percentages in the benefit formula, beginning in 1975. Incidentally, the indexing procedure adopted in computing the initial amounts, which was actually the same as had been done on an ad hoc basis during the 1950s and 1960s (when it had worked well), turned out to be faulty under the changed economic conditions of the 1970s and what would appear likely to occur for subsequent periods.

Some of the overexpansion of the benefit level resulting from the faulty indexing procedure in the 1972 act, and also some of the "real" increases in the benefit level resulting from the legislation in 1969–1972, was eliminated later. This was the result of: (1) the ad hoc benefit increases enacted in 1974 being less than what they would have been if they had been based on the actual CPI rises; and (2) the benefit formula under the 1977 act (first effective in 1979) being designed to produce levels about 6 percent lower than would have resulted under the previous law for persons becoming newly eligible in 1979 and later.

At the same time, the 1977 act provided that, in the computation of average earnings for the benefit calculation, the earnings record is to be indexed. The earnings of each past year is updated to two years before the time of eligibility so as to reflect changes in general earning levels over the years. Also, in connection with the basic benefit formula, a new formula was adopted. In the future, the benefit percentages therein will not increase by the rises in the CPI (as formerly), but instead the bend point will be increased by the rises in the average wage. The result of the new benefit computation procedure, as can be mathematically demonstrated, is to produce stability of replacement rates. For persons retiring at the normal retirement age (currently 65), or retiring on account of disability, the benefit rate for a steadily employed worker with average earnings at all times will be about 41 percent of final earnings (regardless of the year of retirement). The corresponding figure for a worker with earnings at about half of the average will be about 55 percent, while for a worker with the maximum covered earnings (about 2.3 times the average earnings), it will be about 28 percent.

The 1983 act introduced a financial stabilizing device, to be applicable when the OASDI trust funds are at a relatively low level. The indexing of benefits in a current payment status will then be based on the lower of the CPI increases or the rise in the general wage level. If the trust funds later build up to a moderately high level, any decrease in the indexing due to using wage increases would be restored prospectively.

RESTRICTIONS ON BENEFITS

Several restrictions on the benefits payable are applicable. The antiduplication provision, mentioned previously, results in individuals receiving only the largest of the benefits for which they are eligible each month. Specifically, if a person is eligible for both a benefit based on own earnings record and a benefit based on the spouse's earnings record, the amount payable is equal to the larger of the two.

An overall limit is placed on the benefits available to the family members of a retired, disabled, or deceased worker. In general, full benefits at the percentage rates mentioned previously are payable only when there are no more than two beneficiaries in the family (such as retired worker and a spouse, or a widow and one child) for retirement and survivor cases. In essence, a partial benefit is payable to the third family member if there are three beneficiaries in the family (e.g., a widow and two children), but no benefit recognition is given for family members in excess of three. For disability beneficiaries, the maximum is lower— generally, not providing any additional benefits when more than two beneficiaries are present.

Another restriction on OASDI benefits is the so-called retirement test, which is more accurately described as the earnings test, because it applies not only to retirees, but also to other types of beneficiaries, other than the disabled (who, if they have substantial earnings, are no longer considered disabled). The test does not apply to beneficiaries aged 70 or over. Such a test has always been present in the program, being based on the philosophy that the benefits are supposed to be available only when there is not substantial earnings from employment.

The general basis of the earnings test is that a certain amount of earnings is allowed without any reduction in the OASDI benefit payable, but that for earnings in excess of such an amount, $1 of benefits is withheld for such $2 of "excess" earnings. In 1989, these annual exemptions were $8,880 (or about 43 percent of the nationwide average wage) for beneficiaries aged 65 and over and $6,480 for other beneficiaries, with such amounts being adjusted upward in future years on the basis of changes in the general wage level. (Currently [1991], the exemptions are $9,720 and $7,080, respectively.) Since 1990, the basis for withholding of benefits in excess of the annual exempt amount is on a $1 for $3 basis for persons at and about the normal retirement age.

There is a limitation on the benefit paid to disabled workers if they are in receipt of disability pension payable under other government plans. The limitation is that the total of the disability payments received should not exceed 80 percent of the recent average earnings prior to disablement. If this would be the case, the OASDI benefit is reduced accordingly, but the total payable will be no less than the OASDI benefit would be in the absence of the provision.

Benefits payable to spouses of insured workers (whether as a wife, husband, widow, or widower) are reduced if the spouse is receiving a pension under a government-employee retirement system under which the members were not also covered under OASDI on the last day of service of such spouse. Under such circumstances, any OASDI benefit payable to the individual from the earnings record of the spouse is reduced (or even eliminated) by two-thirds of the amount of the government-employee pension.

TAXATION OF BENEFITS

Until the 1983 act, OASDI benefits were not subject to federal, state, or local income taxes. Now, up to 50 percent of these benefits will be considered as taxable income for federal income taxes for high-income persons. The income limits are $25,000 per year for single persons and $32,000 for married couples, with only 50 percent of OASDI benefits being counted as "income" for this purpose (but with tax-exempt interest being counted for this purpose as income). Unlike many elements of the OASDI program, these threshold amounts are not indexed in the future. Thus, over time, an increasing proportion of beneficiaries will be affected (only about 10 percent currently). In general, state and local income taxes do not apply to OASDI benefits.

FINANCING

The payroll taxes (and other sources of income, such as the transfer of the income taxes on benefits from the General Treasury, and the interest on investments) are placed in trust funds—one for the old-age and survivor benefits and the other for disability benefits. Similarly, the benefits and the administrative expenses are paid out of these trust funds.

Over the years, the OASDI system has generally been supported entirely from the scheduled payroll taxes. The only exceptions are certain closed groups for which benefits are financed from general revenues (e.g., persons who became age 72 before the early 1970s were not "insured"). For a period during the 1940s, the law provided the possibility of general revenues being injected into the OASDI program (introduced because the tax rate was frozen during the 1940s), but this was eliminated by the 1950 act. The 1983 act, however, introduced some general revenues financing in indirect manners. By far the major method is to return the federal income taxes on OASDI benefits to the OASDI trust funds.

When the program was initiated in 1935, the funding basis was what might be called a modified-reserve one, under which a rather sizable fund would be developed. The interest thereon would finance a substantial part of the ultimate cost of the program. Over the years, the emphasis on building up a relatively large fund has lessened. Now, it may be said that, for all practical purposes, the OASDI system has been financed on a pay-as-you-go (or current cost) basis in recent years. This procedure has not been completely followed at all times and will not be followed in the future if present law is not changed. For example, beginning in the early 1990s, the trust funds will build up rather substantial balances over several decades, but these will then decline and become exhausted by about 2050, according to the intermediate-cost estimate.

Another basic principle in the financing of the OASDI program is that a schedule of increasing tax rates has always been incorporated into the law, extending into the long range. This procedure gives the public an indication of likely future cost trends, which is especially important for programs financed on a pay-as-you-go basis.

The payroll tax rates with regard to employees has always been divided equally between the employer and the employee (with the exception of 1984, when there was a small difference). This has not been dictated by actuarial or economic reasons, but rather on what might be called aesthetic logic—namely, that each of the parties directly involved should share the cost equally. The combined employer-employee tax rate began at 2 percent in 1937 and continued at this level until 1950. Since then, it has gradually increased. The current (1991) combined rate is 15.3 percent (7.65 percent each) an earnings up to $53,400 (with an additional combined 2.9 percent on earnings from $53,400 to $125,000 for Medicare).

When the self-employed were first covered by the 1950 act, there was considerable difference of opinion as to the appropriate tax rate to charge them. Some argued that the basis should be the combined employer-employee rate, on the grounds that the system should receive the same amount of income regardless of whether the covered worker is an employee or self-employed person. Others argued that the self-employed should pay only the employee rate, on the grounds that both would receive the same benefit amount for a given earnings record. Under the political compromise actually reached, the self-employed paid only one and one-half times the employee rate. The 1983 act, in order to raise additional revenues, provided the ''logical'' basis of the self-employed paying the combined employer-employee rate, but with a credit to reflect the fact that employers can count such taxes as business expenses for income tax purposes; the trust funds are credited with the entire employer-employee tax, with the difference coming from the general treasury.

The payroll tax has always been applied up to a certain amount of annual earnings, which is termed the ''earnings base'' (and benefits are determined only from such amounts). Initially, the earnings base was established at $3,000, which covered about 92 percent of all earnings in covered employment. Beginning in

1951, the earnings base was increased periodically by ad hoc legislation, and until 1972 it covered about 80 percent (or, in some years, somewhat less) of the total earnings in covered employment.

The 1972 act (and subsequent legislation) provided for several significant increases in the earnings base, with the automatic adjustment thereof being applicable for 1975 and thereafter. This would have stabilized the proportion of the total covered earnings that would be taxable at about 85 percent. The 1977 act provided for ad hoc increases in the earnings base for 1979–1981 that raised it more than the automatic adjustment would have done. The automatic adjustments apply after 1981, and the proportion of total earnings taxable is about 90 percent, with the base in 1989 at $48,000 ($53,400 for 1991).

Legislation in 1981 provided for interfund borrowing (repayable with the appropriate interest) among the OASI, DI, and Hospital Insurance Trust Funds. The purpose of such borrowing was to make additional financing resources available to the OASI Trust Fund, whose balance had been declining steadily since 1975, and was expected to decrease in the future until it would be unable to meet benefit payments in late 1982. Such borrowing was permitted only during 1982, and could not exceed an amount sufficient to pay benefits during the first six months of 1983. The 1983 act extended this provision through 1987, with repayment of any loans being required before 1990. (Actually, all of the loans made in 1982 were repaid by 1986.)

The investments of the trust funds have always been required to be in obligations of the federal government. These obligations can be obtained in any of three ways: purchase on the open market, purchase of obligations available to the public when they are first offered for sale, and special issues.

The vast majority of the investments have been in special issues, which are available only to the trust funds and are a part of the national debt. The law prescribes the interest rates on the special issues; namely, the average market rate on all federal obligations having four or more years to go until maturity. As a result, all newly invested monies that are placed in special issues carry an interest rate that is very close to that available if purchase had been in the open market in medium- and long-range securities. The special issues are redeemable at par when funds are needed to meet benefit payments. The law does not prescribe the duration until maturity of the special issues, but the procedure has been to issue, initially, short-term certificates maturing on the next June 30. At that time, long-term securities are issues, with the aim of having the investment portfolio of special issues being, as nearly as possible, in 15 equal blocks maturing over the next 15 years.

POTENTIAL PROBLEMS

In the early 1980s, the OASDI system was confronted by significant financing problems, both over the short run and the long range. The balance in the OASI Trust Fund was falling rapidly and would soon have become exhausted if legislative action had not been taken. At the same time, it was estimated that the outgo in the next seventy-five years (the valuation period) would be significantly higher than the income.

Accordingly, with bipartisan support, legislation was enacted in 1983 to restore the financial integrity of the program, according to the best available actuarial cost estimates. In fact, as to the short run (the remainder of the 1980s), the financing was based on the assumption that the economic conditions would be quite unfavorable. The actual experience to date has been much better than this.

The 1983 legislation involved many changes, so that all groups, present and future beneficiaries, workers, employers, and the general taxpayer, bore some part of the burden of providing additional financing resources. Among the many changes made were the following: (1) permanent delay by six months each year for the cost-of-living adjustments; (2) increasing the payroll tax rates for 1984 and 1988–1989; (3) increasing the tax rates for the self-employed to the combined employer-employee rate; (4) making up to half of the benefits taxable for high-income beneficiaries; (5) compulsory coverage of newly hired employees of the federal government and all employees of nonprofit organizations; (6) appropriating monies from the General Fund for payment of the costs arising with respect to certain military-service benefit credits; and (7) increasing the normal retirement age (when unreduced benefits are first available) from 65 to 67, beginning in 2003 and phased in over the next 24 years.

Although some persons believe that the system may have another financing crisis in the near future, this seems very unlikely. It would take a very severe, long depression in the next year or two with high unemployment and with prices rising as rapidly as wages (or more so) to cause such a crisis.

Further, the demographic situation in the 1990s and the early 2000s will be relatively favorable. The number of persons reaching retirement age each year will level off (or even decrease somewhat), because the annual number of births in 1925–1939 were smaller than in the preceding and succeeding years. Significant financial pressures will appear gradually after 2010, when the post-World War II baby boomers enter the retirement age group. It is believed that this financial strain will be handled by the higher contribution rates that will be in effect after 1989 and by the increase in the normal retirement age from 65 to 67 over the period 2003–2027. As a "safety valve," there is always the possibility of solving any financial problems due to unfavorable demographic conditions through the demographic means of raising the normal retirement age even more.

BIBLIOGRAPHY

The following suggestions for further reading have been compiled by the editors.

Bernstein, M. C., and Bernstein, J. B. (1988). *Social security: The system that works.* New York: Basic.

Burtless, G. (1987). *Work, health, and income among the elderly.* Washington, D.C.: Brookings Institution.

Gist, J. R. (ed.). (1988). *Social security and economic well-being across generations.* Washington, D.C.: American Association of Retired Persons, Public Policy Institute.

Hardy, D. (1988). Financing of retirement pensions in the United States of America. *International Social Security Review,* 41(1), 68–75.

Levine, M. L. (1988). *Age discrimination and the mandatory retirement controversy.* Baltimore: Johns Hopkins University Press.

Lovejoy, L. M. (1988). The comparative value of pensions in the public and private sectors. *Monthly Labor Review,* 111(12), 18–26.

Mitchell, O. S., and Luzadis, R. A. (1988). Changes in pension incentives through time. *Industrial and Labor Relations Review,* 42(1), 100–108.

Packard, M. D., and Reno, V. P. (1989). A look at very early retirees. *Social Security Bulletin,* 52(3), 16–29.

Ross, J. L. (1987). Changing the retirement age in the United States: A case study on research and social security policy-making. *International Social Security Review,* 40(3), 231–247.

Schulz, J. H. (1985). *The economics of aging.* 3d ed. Belmont, Calif.: Wadsworth.

Suggested Readings

Anderson, G. R., Esterman, A. J., Braunack-Mayaer, A. J., and Rungie, C. M. (1986). *Aging in the Western Pacific: A four-country study*. Manila: World Health Organization, Regional Office of the Western Pacific.

Ascoli, U. (1987). The Italian welfare state: Between incrementalism and rationalism. In R. R. Friedmann, N. Gilbert, and R. Sherer (eds.), *Modern welfare states: A comparative view of trends and prospects*, 110–150. Brighton: Wheatsheaf.

Ashford, D. E. (1987). *The emergence of the welfare states*. New York: Basil Blackwell.

Ashford, D. E., and Kelley, E. W. (eds.). (1986). *Nationalizing social security in Europe and America*. Greenwich, Conn.: JAI.

Atchley, R. C. (1985). Social security-type retirement policies: A cross-national study. In Z. S. Blau (ed.), *Current perspectives on aging and the life cycle. Vol. 1: Work, retirement and social policy*, 275–293. London: JAI.

Ballantyne, H. C. (1989). Social security financing in North America. *Social Security Bulletin*, 52(4), 2–13.

Benda-Beckmann, F. von, Benda-Beckmann, K. von, Casino, E., Hirtz, F., Woodman, G. R., and Zacher, H. F. (eds.). (1988). *Between kinship and the state: Social security and the law in developing countries*. Providence, R.I.: Foris.

Binstock, R. H., Chow, W. S., and Schulz, J. H. (1982). *International perspectives on aging: Population and policy challenges*. New York: United Nations Fund for Population Activities.

Bolderson, H. (1989). Comparing social policies: Some problems of method and the case of social security benefits in Australia, Britain and the USA. *Journal of Social Policy*, 17(3).

Brocas, A. M. (1988). Equal treatment of men and women in social security: An overview. *International Social Security Review*, 41(3), 231–249.

Brocas, A. M., Cailloux, A. M., and Oget, V. (1990). Women and social security: An overview. *International Social Security Review*, 41(3), 231–249.

Brown, C. K. (1988). Aging in Swaziland: Accentuating the positive. *Social Development Issues*, 12(1), 56–69.

Butcher, P., and Erdos, J. (1988). International social security agreements: The US experience. *Social Security Bulletin*, 51(9), 4–12.

Carney, T., and Hanks, P. (1986). *Australian social security law, policy and administration*. Melbourne: Oxford University Press.

Casino, E. S. (1988). Person-centered and state-centered social security in Southeast Asia. In F. von Benda-Beckmann (eds.), *Between kinship and the state: Social security and the law in developing countries*, 53–67. Providence, R.I.: Foris.

Castro-Gutierrez, A. (1989). Pension schemes in Latin America: Some financial problems. *International Social Security Review*, 42(1), 35–61.

Chow, N. W. S. (1988). *The administration and financing of social security in China*. Hong Kong: University of Hong Kong.

Cnaan, R. A. (1987). The evolution of Israel's welfare state. In R. R. Friedmann, N. Gilbert, and R. Sherer (eds.), *Modern welfare states: A comparative view of trends and prospects*, 174–207. Brighton: Wheatsheaf.

Council of Europe. (1989). *The flexibility of retirement age*. Strasbourg: Author.

Cowgill, D. O. (1986). *Aging around the world*. Belmont: Wadsworth.

Danişoğlu, E. (1987). Turkey. In J. Dixon (ed.), *Social welfare in the Middle East*, 130–162. London: Croom Helm.

Deaton, R. L. (1989). *The political economy of pensions: Power, politics and social change in Canada, Britain and the United States*. Vancouver: University of British Columbia Press.

Deleeck, H., De Lathouwer, L., and Van den Bosch, K. (eds.). (1988). *Social indicators of social security: A comparative analysis of five countries*. Antwerp: Centre for Social Policy.

Delsen, L. (1990). Part-time early retirement in Europe. *The Geneva Papers on Risk and Insurance* 15(55), 139–157.

Diessenbacher, H. (1989). The generation contract, pension schemes, birth control and economic growth: A European model for the Third World. *Journal of Cross-Cultural Gerontology*, 4, 357–375.

Dixon, J. (1986). *Social security traditions and their global applications*. Canberra: International Fellowship for Social and Economic Development.

———. (ed.). (1987). *Social welfare in Africa*. London: Croom Helm.

———. (1987). *Social welfare in the Middle East*. London: Croom Helm.

Dixon, J., and Kim, H. S. (1985). *Social welfare in Asia*. London: Croom Helm.

Dixon, J., and Scheurell, R. P. (eds.) (1989). *Social welfare in developed market countries*. New York: Routledge.

Dulcey-Ruiz, E., and Ardila, R. (1988). *Work and retirement in Latin America*. Tampa, Fla.: International Exchange Center on Gerontology.

Evans, J. (1988). *Old age security in Indonesia and its implications*. International Population Dynamics Program, Research Note No. 85. Canberra: Department of Demography, Australian National University.

Falkingham, J. (1989). Dependency and ageing in Britain: A re-examination of the evidence. *Journal of Social Policy*, 18(2), 211–233.

Flora, P. (ed.). (1987). *Growth to limits: The Western European welfare states since World War II*. Berlin: De Gruyter.

Friedmann, R. R., Gilbert, N., and Sherer, M. (eds.). (1987). *Modern welfare states: A comparative view of trends and prospects*. Brighton: Wheatsheaf.

Fuchs, M. (1988). Social security in Third World countries. In F. von Benda-Beckmann et al. (eds.), *Between kinship and the state: Social security and the law in developing countries*, 39–51. Providence, R.I.: Foris.

Gordon, M. S. (1988). *Social security policies in industrial countries: A comparative analysis*. New York: Cambridge University Press.

Greber, P. Y. (1988). The Swiss basic pensions schemes is forty years' old: Criteria for its evaluation. *International Social Security Review*, 41(2), 176–197.

Gupta, N. H. (1986). *Social security legislation for labour in India*. New Delhi: Deep and Deep.

———. (1988). Rural social security in India: A holistic view. *Indian Labour Journal*, 21(3), 333–344.

Haanes-Olsen, L. (1989). Worldwide trends and developments in social security, 1985–1987. *Social Security Bulletin*, 52(2), 14–26.

———. (1990). Investment of social security reserves in three countries. *Social Security Bulletin*, 53(2), 2–9.

Hardy, D. (1988). Financing of retirement pensions in the United States of America. *International Social Security Review*, 41(1), 68–75.

Hatland, A. (1986). *The future of Norwegian social insurance*. Oslo: Institute of Applied Research.

Heisel, M. A. (1987). Women and widows in Turkey: Support systems. In H. Z. Lopata (ed.), *Widows: The Middle East, Asia, and the Pacific*, 79–105. Durham: Duke University Press.

———. (1989). Older women in developing countries. In L. Grau (ed.), *Women in the later years*, 253–272. New York: Haworth.

Holmans, S. (1987). *Social security systems in selected countries and their integration with tax systems*. London: HM Treasury.

Horlick, M. (1987). The relationship between public and private schemes: An overview. *Social Security Bulletin*, 50(7), 15–24.

International Labour Office. (1984). *Into the twenty-first century: The development of social security*. 2d ed. Geneva: Author.

———. (1987). *Demographic development and social security*. Report II. Geneva: Author.

———. (1988). *The cost of social security: Twelfth international inquiry, 1981–83*. Geneva: Author.

———. (1989). *Social security protection in old-age*. Report III (Part 4 B). Geneva: Author.

———. (1989). *From pyramid to pillar: Population change and social security in Europe*. Geneva: Author.

———. (1989). *Introduction to social security*. 2d ed. Geneva: Author.

International Social Security Association. (1983). *Social security and family policy*. Geneva: Author.

———. (1985). *Social security documentation: Eighth African regional conference*. Geneva: Author.

———. (1985). *Social security, unemployment and premature retirement*. Studies and Research No. 22. Geneva: Author.

———. (1987). *Social security protection for the rural population*. Report of the Asian regional round table meeting, Jakarta. Social Security Documentation Asian Series, No. 11. New Delhi: ISSA Regional Office for Asia and the Pacific.

———. (1988). *Economic and social aspects of social security financing. Social Security Documentation.* European Series No. 14. Geneva: author.

———. (1988). *Women and equal treatment under social security.* Studies and Research No. 27. Geneva: Author.

———. (1989). Developments and trends in social security 1987–1989. *International Social Security Review*, 42(3), 247–349.

———. (1990). *Evolution of family policy in the light of demographic development.* Social Security Documentation. European Series No. 16. Geneva: Author.

———. (1990). *World bibliography of social security.* Geneva: Author.

Ismael, J. S. (1987). *Canadian social welfare policy: Federal and provincial dimensions.* Montreal: McGill-Queen's University Press.

Japan Social Insurance Agency. (1988). *Outline of social insurance in Japan 1987.* Tokyo: Author.

Jimenez-Castro, W. (1985). Economic implications of the aging of the population in Latin America and the Caribbean. In *Toward the well-being of the elderly*, 87–93. Scientific publication No. 492. Washington, D.C.: Pan American Health Organization.

Johnson, P., and Falkingham, J. (1988). Intergenerational transfers and public expenditure on the elderly in modern Britain. *Ageing and Society*, 8(2), 129–146.

Judge, K. (1987). The British welfare state in transition. In R. R. Friedmann, N. Gilbert, and R. Sherer (eds.), *Modern welfare states: A comparative view of trends and prospects*, 1–43. Brighton: Wheatsheaf.

Kamerman, S. B., and Kahn, A. J. (eds.). (1989). *Privatization and the welfare state.* Princeton: Princeton University Press.

Kessler, D. (1988). The four pillars of retirement. *The Geneva Papers on Risk and Insurance*, 13(49), 342–349.

Kjonstad, A. (1987). *Norwegian social law.* Oslo: Norwegian University Press.

Kludze, A. K. P. (1986, June). *Formal and informal social security in Ghana.* Paper presented at the Symposium on Formal and Informal Social Security, Tutzing, Germany.

Knudsen, P. (1988). The Norwegian national insurance scheme: The pension system in an equal status perspective. In *Equal treatment in social security*, 107–118. Studies and Research No. 27. Geneva: International Social Security Association.

Kohler, P. A., and Walker, H. F. (eds.). (1982). *The evolution of social insurance 1881–1981: Studies of Germany, France, Great Britain, Austria and Switzerland.* New York: St. Martin's.

Kohli, M., Rein, M., Guillemard, A. M., and Van Gunsteren, H. (In press). *Time for retirement.* Cambridge: Cambridge University Press.

Kolb, R. (1989). One hundred years of German pensions insurance legislation. *International Social Security Review*, 42(2), 195–202.

Kozlov, K., and Minev, D. (1989). The pensions system in the USSR and social justice. *International Social Security Review*, 42(1), 62–69.

Laczko, F. (1988). Partial retirement: An alternative to early retirement? A comparison of phased retirement schemes in the United Kingdom, France and Scandinavia. *International Social Security Review*, 41(2), 149–169.

Lee, K. (1987). The Japanese welfare state in transition. In R. R. Friedmann, N. Gilbert, and R. Sherer (eds.), *Modern welfare states: A comparative view of trends and prospects*, 243–263. Brighton: Wheatsheaf.

Liu, L. (1984). Social security problems in Western European countries. *Social Security Bulletin*, 47(2), 17–22.

Macarov, D. (1987). Israel. In J. Dixon (ed.), *Social welfare in the Middle East*, 32–70. London: Croom Helm.

Martin, L. G. (1988). The aging of Asia. *Journal of Gerontology: Social Sciences*, 43(4), S99–S113.

———. (1990). The status of south Asia's growing elderly population. *Journal of Cross-Cultural Gerontology*, 5, 93–117.

Mesa-Lago, C. (ed.). (1985). *The crisis of social security and health care: Latin American experiences and lessons*. Pittsburgh, Pa.: Center for Latin American Studies.

———. (1986). Comparative study of the development of social security in Latin America. *International Social Security Review*, 39(2), 127–152.

Midgley, J. (1984). *Social security, inequality, and the Third World*. New York: John Wiley.

Mouton, P. (1975). *Social security in Africa: Trends, problems and prospects*. Geneva: International Labour Office.

Mouton, P., and Gruat, J. V. (1988). The extension of social security to self-employed persons in Africa. *International Social Security Review*, 41(1), 40–54.

Munz, R., and Wintersberger, H. (1987). The making of the Austrian welfare state: Social policy and social security in the twentieth century. In R. R. Friedmann, N. Gilbert, and R. Sherer (eds.), *Modern welfare states: A comparative view of trends and prospects*, 186–215. Brighton: Wheatsheaf.

Naifu, C. (1988). Reflections on a social security system with Chinese characteristics. *International Social Security Review*. 41(2), 170–175.

Novelo, G. (1985). Actions of the Inter-American conference on social security with regard to the promotion of social protection to rural populations. In *Proceedings of the round table on the protection to marginal groups in rural zones*, 85–117. Mexico City: Institute Mexicano del Seguro Social.

Nusberg, C., and Osako, M. M. (eds.). (1981). *The situation of the Asian/Pacific elderly*. Washington, D.C.: International Federation on Aging.

Olsson, S. (1987). Towards a transformation of the Swedish welfare state? In R. R. Friedmann, N. Gilbert, and R. Sherer (eds.), *Modern welfare states: A comparative view of trends and prospects*, 44–82. Brighton: Wheatsheaf.

Organisation for Economic Co-operation and Development. (1988). *Ageing populations: The social policy implications*. Paris: OECD.

———. (1988). *Reforming public pensions 1988*. Paris: OECD.

Palmer, J., Smeeding, T., and Torrey, B. (eds.). (1988). *The vulnerable*. Washington, D.C.: Urban Institute Press.

Pampel, F. C., and Williamson, J. B. (1985). Age structure, politics, and cross-national patterns of public pension expenditures. *American Sociological Review*, 50(6), 787–798.

Pampel, F. C., and Stryker, R. (1990). Age structure, the state and social welfare spending: A reanalysis. *British Journal of Sociology*, 14(3), 16–24.

Pelletier, A. D. (1989). Pension planning in Italy: The challenge. *Benefits & Compensation International*, 18(12), 15–21.

Perrin, G. (1984). A hundred years of social insurance. Part One. *Labour and Society*, 9(2), 179–191.

———. (1984). A hundred years of social insurance. Part Two. *Labour and Society*, 9(3), 297–308.

———. (1984). A hundred years of social insurance. Part Three. *Labour and Society*, 9(4), 399–410.

Peterka, J. (1988). Equality of treatment of men and women in the pension insurance scheme in Austria. In *Equal treatment in social security*, 61–68. Studies and Research No. 27. Geneva: International Social Security Association.

Pusic, E. (1987). The development of the welfare state in Yugoslavia. In R. R. Friedmann, N. Gilbert, and R. Sherer (eds.), *Modern welfare states: A comparative view of trends and prospects*, 151–173. Brighton: Wheatsheaf.

Reday-Mulvey, G. (1990). Work and retirement: Future prospects for the baby-boom generation. *The Geneva Papers on Risk and Insurance*, 15(56), 100–113.

Rix, S., and Fisher, P. (1985). *Retirement-age policy: An international perspective*. New York: Pergamon.

Ron, A., Abel-Smith, R., and Tamburi, G. (1990). *Health insurance in developing countries: The social security approach*. Geneva: International Labour Office.

Ross, J. L., and Upp, M. M. (1988). The treatment of women in the United States social security system, 1970–1988. In *Equal treatment in social security*, 69–92. Studies and Research No. 27. Geneva: International Social Security Association.

Rowhani, I. (1988). Social security for women in Austria: The issues. In *Equal treatment in social security*, 179–194. Studies and Research No. 27. Geneva: International Social Security Association.

Schmahl, W. (1988). Economic and social aspects of social security financing. In *Economic and social aspects of social security financing*, 13–70. Geneva: International Social Security Association.

Schott, R. (1988). Traditional systems of social security and their present-day crisis in West Africa. In F. von Benda-Beckmann et al. (eds.), *Between kinship and the state: Social security and the law in developing countries*, 89–107. Providence, R.I.: Foris.

Schulz, J. H. (1985). *Pensions and retirement policy: The unemployment factor*. Waltham, Mass.: Policy Center on Aging.

Schulz, J. H., and Davis-Friedmann, D. (eds.). (1987). *Aging China: Families, economics, and government policies in transition*. Washington, D.C.: Gerontological Society of America.

Sicron, M. (1989). Recent trends in social services in Israel. In R. Morris (ed.), *Testing the limits of social welfare: International perspectives on policy changes in nine countries*, 215–240. Hanover, N.H.: University Press of New England.

Social Insurance Institution (Turkey). (1986). *The national experience of Turkey in the field of social security protection for the rural population*. Asian Regional Round Table Meeting on Social Security Protection for the Rural Population, Jakarta. Geneva: International Social Security Association.

Sotirova, M., and Duhomir, N. (1988). Social security: Functions of regulations in the treatment of women and men. In *Equal treatment in social security*, 171–177. Studies and Research No. 27. Geneva: International Social Security Association.

Steinmeyer, H. D. (1986). Social security reform: Its consequences for women in industrialized and developing countries. *Benefits & Compensation International*, 3, 413–416.

Swaan, de A. (1988). *In care of the state: Health care, education and welfare in Europe and the USA in the modern era*. Cambridge: Polity.

Swabey, J. (1990). Social security in the German Democratic Republic. *Benefits & Compensation International*, 19(2), 13–17.

Tamburi. G. (1985). Social security in Latin America: Trends and outlook. In C. Mesa-Lago (ed.), *The crisis of social security and health care: Latin American experiences and lessons*, 59–84. Pittsburgh: Center for Latin American Studies.

Tibaudin, R. J. (1985). Social security for self-employed workers in Latin America. *International Social Security Review*, 38(4), 396–417.

Tomandl, T., and Fuerboech, K. (1986). *Social partnership: The Austrian system of industrial relations and social insurance*. Ithaca, N.Y.: Cornell University Press.

Torczyner, J. (1987). The Canadian welfare state: Retrenchment and change. In R. R. Friedmann, N. Gilbert, and R. Sherer (eds.), *Modern welfare states: A comparative view of trends and prospects*, 264–281. Brighton: Wheatsheaf.

Tracy, M. B. (1987). Women's old-age pension replacement rates in ten industrial countries. *Journal of International and Comparative Social Welfare*, 3, 37–43.

Tracy, M. B., and Adams, P. (1989). Age of first pension award: Patterns in ten industrial countries, 1960–1986. *International Social Security Review*, 42(4).

Tracy, M. B., and Ward, R. L. (1986). Trends in old-age pensions for women: Benefit levels in ten nations, 1960–1980. *The Gerontologist*, 26(3), 286–291.

U.S. Department of Health and Human Services. (1990). *Social security programs throughout the world–1989*. Social Security Administration, Office of International Policy. Research Report No. 62. Washington, D.C.: U.S. Government Printing Office.

Woodman, G. R. (1988). The decline of folk-law social security in common-law Africa. In F. von Benda-Beckmann et al. (eds.), *Between kinship and the state: Social security and the law in developing countries*, 69–88. Providence, R.I.: Foris.

Index

About the Editors and Contributors

LEAH ACHDUT is the director of the Bureau of Basic Research Methods and Surveys in the Research and Planning Administration of the National Insurance Institute, Jerusalem. Her research is on the economics of old age and income distribution.

PAUL ADAMS, Ph.D., is a professor at the School of Social Work, the University of Iowa. His interests are in the political economy of the welfare state and comparative family policy.

FLORENCE AMATTEY is an official with the Statistics and Research Department of the Ghana Social Security and National Insurance Trust. She specializes in population studies.

ALLAN BOROWSKI, Ph.D., is a senior lecturer in the Department of Social Work, La Trobe University, Bundoora, Victoria, Australia. His research has focused on the economics of aging.

JEAN-LOUIS CAYATTE is a professor at the University of Paris and has also taught at the University of Lille. He specializes in social and labor economics.

RICHARD M. COUGHLIN, Ph.D., is professor and chair of the Department of Sociology at the University of New Mexico in Albuquerque. His research interests include comparative social policy and social change in advanced industrial societies.

FRED GROSKIND, Ph.D., is an assistant professor in the School of Social Work at Boston College. He is currently working on public attitudes toward social welfare and families in poverty.

JACK HABIB, Ph.D., is an economist who is director of the JDC-Brookdale Institute of Gerontology and Adult Human Development in Israel. He also holds joint appointments in the Department of Economics and the School of Social Work at the Hebrew University.

MARSEL A. HEISEL, Ed.D., is an associate professor in the School of Social Work at Rutgers University. She is a native of Turkey. Her research interests include aging in developing countries, older women, and methods of social research.

SENTANOE KERTONEGORO is the director of the Social Insurance System ASTEK in Indonesia.

BRIGITTE KITCHEN, Ph.D., is on the faculty in the Department of Social Work in Atkinson College, York University, Toronto. Her research interests are tax and income policies for families.

PROSPER KOFFI KOUASSI is the president-director general of social security in the Ivory Coast.

PETER KUNZ, Ph.D., is an actuary who heads the Mathematical Division of the Swiss Federal Office of Social Security. He is also chair of the Permanent Committee of Actuaries and Statisticians of the International Social Security Association.

LILLIAN LIU, Ph.D., is a research analyst with the Office of International Policy, U.S. Social Security Administration. She specializes in social security policies in the Soviet Union, Japan, and the People's Republic of China.

GUIDO MIRANDA-GUTIÉRREZ, M.D., is a physician who is the executive president of the Costa Rica Social Security Institute.

ERNESTO MIRANDA-RADIC, Ph.D., is a professor in the PIAS, Programa Interfacultades en Administracion de Salud at the University of Chile in Santiago.

ROBERT J. MYERS held various actuarial positions with the United States Social Security Administration and its predecessors in 1934–1970, being chief actuary during the last twenty-three years. In 1981–1982, he was deputy commissioner of Social Security and in 1982–1983, executive director of the National

Commission on Social Security Reform. He is professor emeritus at Temple University.

AYUBU K. T. NYANGA is a tutorial assistant at the National Social Welfare Training Institute in Dar es Salaam. He has also written on child labor issues in Tanzania.

C. K. OMARI, Ph.D., is an associate professor in the Department of Sociology at the University of Dar es Salaam. His research focus is on family, rural sociology, and population issues.

FRED C. PAMPEL, Ph.D., is a professor of sociology and senior research associate at the Population Program at the University of Colorado, Boulder. His research interest is in sociological aspects of class, age, and politics in welfare program development in a cross-national context.

EMILIO RABASA-GAMBOA is the secretary general of the IMSS in Mexico.

JOSEPH L. SCARPACI, Ph.D., is an assistant professor in the Department of Urban Affairs and Planning, Virginia Polytechnic Institute and State University, Blacksburg, Virginia. His research interest is in health care issues in Chile.

HEINZ-DIETRICH STEINMEYER, Ph.D., is a professor at the University of Augsburg Law School, Augsburg, Federal Republic of Germany. He specializes in labor and social security law.

RICHARD F. TOMASSON, Ph.D., is a sociologist and writer who has taught at the University of Illinois and the University of New Mexico.

MARTIN B. TRACY, Ph.D., is an associate professor in the School of Social Work at the University of Iowa, Iowa City, Iowa. His research interest is in comparative analysis of pension policies and income issues concerning older women.

JOHN B. WILLIAMSON, Ph.D., is a professor of sociology at Boston College. He specializes in cross-national studies of age, class, and politics in welfare development.

DOROTHY WILSON, is a lecturer in social administration at the University of Glasgow and a former civil servant. She has written on the political economy of the welfare state and on comparative social administration.